Cities in Crisis

Cities in Crisis

The Political Economy of Urban Development in Post-War Britain

Gareth Rees

Department of Sociology, University College,
Cardiff and Department of Town Planning, UWIST
and

John Lambert

Department of Social Administration, University
College, Cardiff

Edward Arnold

© Gareth Rees and John Lambert 1985

First published in Great Britain 1985 by
Edward Arnold (Publishers) Ltd, 41 Bedford Square, London WC1B 3DQ

Edward Arnold (Australia) Pty Ltd, 80 Waverley Road, Caulfield East,
Victoria 3145, Australia

Edward Arnold, 3 East Read Street, Baltimore, Maryland 21202, USA

British Library Cataloguing in Publication Data

Rees, Gareth, *1949–*
    Cities in crisis: the political economy of urban
    development in post-war Britain.
    1.Cities and towns——Great Britain——History
    ——20th century
    I.Title   II.Lambert, John, *1940–*
    307'.14'0941   HT133

    ISBN 0-7131-6456-5

Text set in 10/11pt Times Compugraphic
by Colset Private Ltd, Singapore
Printed in Great Britain by
Richard Clay (The Chaucer Press) Ltd,
Bungay, Suffolk

Contents

Preface

Our initial intention in writing this book was to present an analysis which would engage critically with the state's current inner-city initiatives from a perspective which was informed by the 'new urban sociology' and which would make a modest contribution to the development of alternative, socialist policies for the cities. It soon became apparent, however, that *in order to achieve this*, it would be necessary to undertake a much wider examination of the origins of the urban crisis and of the history of state policy with respect to urban and regional change generally. This has led us to attempt a reinterpretation of post-war urban development, which emphasizes its distance from the dominant accounts within what we have termed the 'Whig' tradition. The latter is significant not only because it is the norm of academic discourse, but also because it has important consequences for the formulation and evaluation of state policy. This is why the exposure of its flaws and weaknesses is a necessary precondition of fulfilling our original objective.

In its initial conception, this book was a wholly cooperative effort; John Lambert and I worked together to define the scope and aims of the project, and in the preliminary stages of drafting. However, subsequently, additional teaching and administrative duties – part of the hidden costs of the cuts in university financing – prevented John Lambert's full participation. Accordingly, the responsibility for developing the book and writing it in its present form is mine; although John Lambert has continued to comment generously and has made numerous drafting suggestions. (Incidentally, we remain the best of friends!)

Many debts are incurred in the writing of any book; as this one has taken an inordinately long time to finish, the debts are especially numerous. University College, Cardiff and UWIST granted periods of study-leave at critical times. Thanks are also due to the following for a variety of contributions: Mick Bruton, Camilla Lambert, Ray Pahl, Victoria Winckler and, in particular, Phil Cooke and Kevin Morgan. Michael Harloe, Doreen Massey and an anonymous reader read the whole manuscript in draft and are responsible for

substantial changes which they will hopefully regard as improve-
ments; we are grateful anyway. My publishers, Edward Arnold,
have been a model of patience, encouragement and occasionally
pointed exhortation. Finally, Teri Rees has not only commented on
various drafts of the book professionally, but also has borne far
more than her fair share of domestic responsibilities during its
writing. In more ways than she is aware, it could not have been completed without her.

Gareth Rees
Llandudoch
August 1984.

1

The state, urban policy and the inner-city crisis

'The most frightening civil disorder ever seen in England' was how a *Guardian* leader summarized the violent events in Toxteth in inner Liverpool during the first few days of July 1981. It is, of course, easy to exaggerate the significance of such events; and undoubtedly the media fell willing prey to the temptation to sensationalize and distort. Nevertheless, even writing some years afterwards, it is impossible to ignore what took place. For the urban riots of 1981 were the most acute expressions of deep-seated shifts in the structure and organization of British society; shifts, moreover, in which the British state has been profoundly implicated and to which it is still trying to respond adequately. They provide, then, an essential starting-point in uncovering the *long-term* trajectory of Britain's inner-city crisis.

It was not as if there had not been warnings. The July riots in Toxteth took place whilst an official inquiry, presided over by an eminent judge, Lord Scarman, sought out the causes of a weekend of violence in Brixton, in south London, in April 1981. A year earlier, rioting had erupted in St Paul's in inner Bristol. And for those with a memory and an interest in these things, violent clashes involving for the most part younger residents and the police had been a commonplace in many urban communities up and down the country over the years. But there is no denying the scale and intensity of what happened in 1981. Not only Toxteth and Brixton, but also in Southall in west London, Moss Side in Manchester and a host of other urban areas witnessed violent outbursts of varying degrees of intensity (Kettle and Hodges, 1982).

The immediate response to these events was unsurprising; at least since the nineteenth century, Britain's cities have been a focus both of social unrest and state attempts to control it. In 1981 as previously, the most pressing need for the government and the police was to regain control. The sanctity of the rule of law was publicly affirmed: the inexcusability of violence – in the face of whatever provocation – was stressed: 'ringleaders' were sought out for court appearances: and police forces were given new weaponry and training (much of it tried and tested in the less immediate periphery of Northern Ireland) to provide an improved anti-riot capability (Joshua and Wallace, 1983).

There are strong resonances here of the American experience of urban riots following 'the long hot summers' of the late 1960s. Then, there had been a marked development of 'could it happen in Britain?' anxieties, which had been influential in sparking off a decade of urban policy-making which drew explicitly on American practice. It is ironic, therefore, that in the United States in 1968, the famous Kerner Commission had warned about the limitations of a 'law and order' response; had identified white racism as a fundamental cause of the riots; and had posed the challenge that it was in the extension of justice and equality of opportunity that solutions lay.

Nevertheless, the violence in Britain did subside. Yet, as Kerner had suggested, the response could not simply be in terms of riot police, arrests and court appearances. The immediate shock of the riots elicited from the state measures of directly *repressive* social control; longer-term developments required responses of a different kind. Hence, just a few days before the scenes of devastation in Toxteth filled the newspapers and television news programmes, the former Conservative Prime Minister, Mr Edward Heath, was given widespread media coverage for his trenchant criticisms of the government's economic policies and their consequences in burgeoning unemployment, especially amongst young people. 'Of course,' Mr Heath was reported as saying 'if you have a million young people hanging around the streets all day, you will have a major increase in juvenile crime. It is inevitable.' Indeed, it was a widespread judgement, subsequently backed by the influential Scarman Report (Cmnd. 8427, 1981), that the underlying causes of the riots were social and economic.

What was crucial, then, was the *interaction* of mounting unemployment and persistent deprivation with a sustained experience of racialist attacks, street violence and conflicts with the police. Inner-city areas of the kind which experienced rioting in 1981 had been the victims of particularly acute and severe problems arising from entirely *general* trends in British society: the catastrophic decline in Britain's domestic economic base, especially in manufacturing industry; change in the distribution and character of the urban population as a result of international and internal migration; the operation of a land market which had produced larges areas of dereliction and desolate physical environments; the failure of the Welfare State to yield adequate housing provision or education or health care for its citizens: the list is long, but even so could be extended. Moreover, it is clear that the conditions which stemmed from such general trends were as significant in determining the day-to-day experiences of inner-city residents as the more obvious harassments by racists or sections of the police.

Accordingly, the political impact of the riots derived from much more than the dimension of racial conflict which was present. Rex (1982), in one of the first academic analyses of the events of 1981, has made the same point:

> [W]hat was happening was not specifically or only a revolt against racial oppression and mistreatment. Unemployment was mounting to unprecedented levels and, with the police and the government no longer enjoying universal support, rioting, arson, looting and the use of petrol bombs appeared as possible effective means of changing the power balance, of protesting at government policies and bringing about a change in police behaviour. The riots, in short, had assumed a national political significance, wider in its implications than that of race relations, even though racial conflict had been at the heart of the first events. (1982: 106)

This is not to suggest (as the media reports of left-wing agitators did) that the riots may be interpreted as *conventional, directed* political statements. Nevertheless, in ways that parallel Victorian experience to a remarkable extent (Stedman Jones, 1971), they *did* reflect in a particular form the profound political effects in Britain's cities of the broad social and economic trends to which we have referred.

It was therefore inevitable that the most senior government minister with responsibility for urban affairs, the Secretary of State for the Environment, Mr Michael Heseltine, was dispatched to Liverpool in the immediate aftermath of the riots, for three weeks of consultation and study. There was, of course, an irony in this also. For Mr Heseltine's study-visit came at the end of more than a decade of the most sustained analysis of urban problems and policy experiments ever witnessed in Britain. Indeed, it was somewhere in Liverpool's inner districts that the first ever Secretary of State for the Environment, Mr Peter Walker, was converted to the need for a concerted 'total approach' by government to the solution of Britain's urban ills. Mr Walker launched a number of initiatives of research and action, but did not remain long enough at the Department of the Environment to follow them through. However, alone amongst high-ranking Conservatives he is on record as arguing for massive public expenditure programmes for inner-city areas.

The post-1979 Conservative administration was, of course, committed to very different strategies: to massive *reductions* in public expenditure and to the limitation of the powers of inner-city local authorities to spend heavily to alleviate their special needs. Nevertheless, the student of urban policy would know that Mr Heseltine was going to Liverpool in 1981 not to launch an essentially new initiative, but as chairman of a Partnership Committee, which since 1978 had brought together central and local government, representatives of local industry, and community and voluntary organizations in an attempt to devise programmes of action to tackle inner-city problems. Moreover, these Partnerships were directly related to the plethora of policy initiatives which had preceded them, through a major review of urban policy, which had led to the 1977 White Paper, *Policy for the Inner Cities* (Cmnd. 6845), and to the Inner Urban Areas Act of 1978 (Higgins *et al.*, 1983).

These policy initiatives will be analysed in some detail in Chapter 5. The point to be made here is that if 1981 ushered in a new and frightening phase of urban crisis, it occurred after 15 years of truly phenomenal research and policy innovation, directed at the eradication of urban problems. Moreover, the whole of the post-war period in Britain may be characterized as one in which, more than ever before, there had been a sustained attempt by the state to improve the urban condition. So, in a real sense, the urban crisis which manifested itself so dramatically in the riots was a crisis too for the state, whose claim was to be able to understand and manage urban change by means of the whole battery of new powers and policies which had been devised throughout the post-war period.

Indeed, some commentators would pose the issue even more acutely. For example, Waller (1981–2) reflects on the Toxteth riots in these terms:

> A sense of devastation pervaded the city *before* the rioting wreaked new havoc. It was as if the Luftwaffe had returned nightly, incessantly, for 40 years from its first blitz in 1940. A generation and more has been raised in an environment of official vandalism and dereliction. As the novelist Beryl Bainbridge, one-time resident of Toxteth, observed, the rioters only gutted the Rialto, the Racquets Club, part of a hospital and most of Lodge Lane; people should ask, 'who knocked down the rest of it?' (1981–82: 349)

Hence, it is argued, it is not simply that the claims of urban policy also went up in flames in 1981, but rather that these policies themselves fuelled the fire.

The urban riots of 1981 raise, then, in a particularly acute form, the issues which will concern us in this book: the relationships between the urban condition and more general shifts in Britain's economic and social structure; the nature and effectiveness of the state's urban policies; and the mediation of these two by a *politics* of urban change. In the remainder of this chapter, we spell out our theoretical perspectives on these matters.

The inner city in context

Given the enormous outpouring of analysis and writing on Britain's inner-city problems in recent years, it may seem that there is very little left to say. Indeed, the review of research recently produced under the auspices of the (then) Social Science Research Council's Inner Cities Working Party (published in summary form as Hall, 1981), whilst acknowledging the needs for future work, is much more impressive in its indication of the breadth of material which is already available. Hall (1981) spells out the agenda which is covered:

> We need to take the central objective of our project to see *the inner city in context*. This means that we must first consider the inner city in the *spatial* context of the rapidly changing economic and social geography of contemporary Britain. . . . Then, we turn to the inner city in the context of the continuing debate about *poverty and deprivation* in Britain. . . .
>
> Then, after a brief diversion to look at the parallel American experience, we use that story to provide an introduction to the study of the inner city in its *political* or *governmental* context. . . . Following that, we turn to look at the inner city in its *historical* context. . . . And at greater length we develop possible scenarios for the inner city in the medium-term future, assuming a dominant set of social and economic trends to which policy makers may respond in different ways.
>
> Lastly, and springing directly from that analysis, we turn to the future, and look at the inner city in a *total research* context. We argue for a new kind of approach to the problem, and use the insights from different social sciences in a combined attempt to understand the nature of the forces that shape the fate of the inner cities, now and in the future. (Hall, 1981: 4–5)

In spite of the impressive range covered, however, this official research review is as instructive in what it *omits*, as in what it includes. And in this reflects a much wider conventional wisdom with respect to Britain's inner-city problems.

What is provided is an admirably succinct and coherent *description* of some of the major trends which have affected the character of Britain's inner cities.[1] The decline of population and the collapse of manufacturing employment are carefully demonstrated from the available research; the nature and incidence of poverty and deprivation are conscientiously defined and documented. However, despite protestations to the contrary, little attempt is made to explore the roots of such phenomena in the basic features of the organization of British society. Indeed, the reader is left with the impression that it is possible to understand what has happened in the inner cities almost without reference to the *social relationships* which shape them.

[1]The following arguments coincide substantially with those made by Duncan (1982).

Hence, for instance, the sharp drop in manufacturing jobs in inner-urban areas is correctly related to shifts in the spatial organization of British industry, to Britain's economic performance more widely and to the immediate effects of the current recession. Yet the *causes* of these latter are not traced through coherently; they remain, as it were, independent, unexplained variables in the explanatory equation. Accordingly, the day-to-day realities of industrial reorganization and change never make an appearance in the account which is offered. There is no place for conflicts between workers and management over plant closures or the reorganization of the production process; for the controversies which frequently surround the activities of multinational companies, both at home and abroad; for the clashes of interest between industrialists and 'the City' over state economic policy; and so forth. And certainly, there is never any suggestion that there may be *systematic* relationships between these everyday realities and the fate of the inner cities.

Similarly, whilst poverty is carefully defined in *relative* terms and the incidence of deprivation in the inner-urban areas is shown to be one manifestation of quite *general* distributions, there is no thoroughgoing examination of the *inequalities* which characterize the British social structure as a whole. The persistent disadvantages experienced by some of Britain's citizens – many of them residents of the inner cities – are not specified in relation to their necessary corollary: the advantages and privileges enjoyed by others – most of whom, of course, do *not* live in the inner areas. And, again, the conflicts of social interest which are thereby implied, and which are frequently manifest in political activity, go wholly unacknowledged: urban riots, for example, are not accountable within the framework offered.

This failure to investigate the wider origins and context of Britain's inner-city problems goes hand-in-hand with an absence of serious attention to the historically conditioned *processes* which have given rise to them. It is true that Hall's (1981) summary does include a brief passage on 'The Inner City in History'; but this is merely a prelude to a profoundly *un*historical exercise in the writing of 'future scenarios'. Equally, it is clear that *chronology* – in the sense of sequences of events – is not entirely absent. However, the conceptualization of historical development which is embodied in the analysis remains largely implicit and uninterrogated. In consequence, the social *changes* which give rise to the present condition of the inner cities cannot be comprehended adequately.

In particular, the complex determination of patterns of social development out of the structured actions of individuals, groups or institutions is largely unexamined. Hence, as we have seen, there is only the most partial sense of the ways in which the trends (of population, employment, poverty or whatever) which are so meticulously documented are related to conflicts between real human agents: workers and managers; rich and poor; and so on. It is this, in turn, which results in the absence of any consideration of the wider politics of urban development. To the extent that patterns of inner-city change have been bound up with conflicting social interests, they imply political *struggles* in pursuit of those conflicting interests. And, of course, our brief discussion of the 1981 urban riots confirmed precisely this.

Many of these issues reappear when attention shifts from research on the nature of inner-city problems to the analysis of state policies. In spite of the wide-ranging review of trends in economic structure, population distribution, land-use patterns and so forth in the former discussion, examination of state intervention scarcely touches on the policies directly related to these matters. Rather, the reader is directed toward a purported *progression* of policy initiatives whose purpose was the development of the means to combat urban poverty and deprivation: beginning with the Educational Priority Areas, the Community Development Project and the Urban Programme, each started in the later 1960s; continuing with the Inner Area Studies, experiments with area management and the Comprehensive Community Programmes of the earlier 1970s; and culminating, in effect, with the announcement of the Inner Areas policy of 1977–78.

What is being argued here, it should be emphasized , is not simply a succession of policy initiatives, but also a process whereby each new stage of policy development contributes to a better understanding of the nature of the urban question, eventually producing the kinds of definitions offered in the 1977 White Paper. Indeed, this document is itself explicit in acknowledging the importance of the findings of the previous 15 years of state-sponsored analysis of the inner city and its inhabitants.

That the state should present its own policies in these terms is not, of course, surprising. What *is* more note-worthy is that this account should have been adopted uncritically into academic (and therefore independent?) analysis. In part, this consistency of approach derives from the wholly desirable intention of Hall (1981) and his colleagues to exert an influence over the direction of future state policy. Hence, common understandings of what has happened in the past are necessary to shared definitions of what is possible and reasonable for the future.

More fundamentally, however, the treatment of state intervention reflects a poverty of theoretical analysis which directly parallels that which, as we saw earlier, characterizes the approach to the genesis of inner-city problems. Accordingly, the relationships between, initially, social research, social problems (however defined) and the formulation of state policies are simply not examined explicity. And certainly, there is no attempt to formulate the wider role of the state in British society. Ironically, then, the development of *policy* is presented without serious reference to *politics*. The analysis ignores the complex determinations of state intervention out of conflicts of interest between social groupings with varying political power and access to the policy-making process. It is this, in turn, which leads directly not simply to the distortion of those policy initiatives which *are* considered, but also to the exclusion of major elements of relevant state activity from consideration: to the acceptance of the state's own account of developments as uncontested and unproblematic.

Now, the significance of these arguments goes beyond their immediate origin in the work of the Inner Cities Working Party (Hall, 1981). For, in reviewing the research, the Working Party was, in effect, giving expression to very widely held views on the inner cities and on urban development more widely. Moreover, as we shall show, the proper understanding of these views and, more specifically, the nature of their constituency and influence is integral to the analysis of the current state of inner-city policies.

The historiography of urban change and the state

The study which we have been discussing, then, is but one example of a much wider current in the analysis of change in British cities and the attempts by the state to mould that change. Moreover, the form of this analysis is broadly akin to what in general historical writing has come to be known as the 'Whig interpretation'.

Butterfield (1931), from a perspective which in most respects is very different from our own, has described this interpretation as '. . . a tendency in many historians to write on the side of Protestants and Whigs, to praise revolutions provided they have been successful, to emphasize certain principles of progress in the past and to produce a story which is the ratification if not the glorification of the present.' (1931: 2) Hence, historical change, on this view, is preconceived as 'progress', and *accounted for* as a movement closer toward the present. The institutions of earlier periods are treated as partially completed versions of our own: earlier beliefs as partial representations of what is now wholly understood; earlier innovations as steps toward the more 'advanced' forms found now. Hence, '[t]hrough [a] system of immediate reference to the present day, historical personages can easily and irresistably be classed into the men [sic] who furthered progress and the men [sic] who tried to hinder it . . .' (Butterfield, 1931: 11).

Such history – in the more specific context of urban studies – traces a continuous process of 'onward and upward' policy development and improvement from the origins of reform in the chaos of Victorian urbanization, through successive stages of legislative innovation, to the present-day system. And the question 'How did urban policy and planning arise?' becomes, by a subtle organization of the Whig historians' sympathies, 'To whom should we be grateful for our urban policy?': the analytical task is to identify, retrospectively, those individuals and their glorious victories.

Hence, the very origins of urban policy are traced to the conditions generated in the rapid urbanization which was one of the outstanding features of British society from the late eighteenth century onwards. As Anthony Sutcliffe (1981), one of the most distinguished of current urban historians, has argued recently, whilst much urban development during this period was deemed to be essentially satisfactory, the failure to ensure adequate facilities for public health and to provide acceptable housing for the urban working class constituted an enduring focus of reformers' agitation, which was one of the preconditions of the development of legislative innovation during the nineteenth century, culminating in the 1875 Artisans' and Labourers' Dwellings Improvement Act and its subsequent amendments. However, it was the failure of such legislation to eradicate these problems, manifested in the housing crisis and the 'rediscovery of poverty' during the 1880s, which led to a renewed and intensified interest in the well-established (since at least the 1840s) idea of *decentralizing* the population of the inner-urban areas. And it is here, it is argued, that we may locate the origins of those classical antecedents of subsequent urban planning: the 'garden city', encapsulated in the writings and propaganda of Ebenezer Howard and his disciples (Fishman, 1977); and town-extension planning on the German model, which became embodied in the 1909 Housing and Town Planning Act and ensuing legislation.

In similar fashion, it is suggested that it was the response to the acute housing crisis experienced in the immediate aftermath of the Great War which set the context for one of the earliest implementations of these 'decentralizing' ideas, in the 'Homes Fit for Heroes' public housing campaign made possible by Addison's Housing Act of 1919 (Murie *et al.*, 1976). For a brief period at least (until 1921), housing was provided by the state at rents which made very high-quality homes genuinely accessible and thereby prefigured a solution to the problem of houses for the working class, which was to re-emerge in a more fully worked-out form after the Second World War.

Moreover, the rapid collapse of the 'Homes Fit for Heroes' campaign should be viewed against the background of the emergence of new, even more far-reaching crisis conditions, as the national economy foundered and unemployment – at least in the older industrial regions – began to soar in the build-up to the cataclysm of the 1930s. Even here, it has been argued, there were the due policy responses. Indeed, for some commentators (for example, Cherry, 1974), the appointment of the Royal Commission on the Distribution of the Industrial Population under the chairmanship of Sir Montague Barlow in 1937 to investigate the real nature of the massive urban and regional problems which were endemic to the inter-war years, was one of the most significant steps forward in the development of modern urban policy. Taken together with the work of the Special Commissioners for the distressed regions and the first, faltering attempts at devising regional policy, the Barlow Commission's recommendations are often held up as a cornerstone in the emergence of a post-1945 system of state policy, which, at least to some extent, recognized the interdependencies of economic development at the regional level and land-use and other urban changes (Hall *et al.*, 1973).

These examples, of course, are no more than suggestive; and we shall return to them later. Nevertheless, they do serve to illustrate the *general* form which the Whig theory of history takes in the field of urban studies. Hence, what are taken to be the manifest problems thrown up in a – relatively unexamined – unfolding of urban development are presented as *themselves* sufficient to evoke progressive responses from reformers and, later, the state itself: the promotion of particular forms of (especially suburban) residential growth; the provision of state housing; the encouragement of a more even spatial distribution of population and economic activity; and so forth. And all these (and other) initiatives are depicted as leading inexorably toward their culmination in the creation of a comprehensive *system* of urban policy and planning in the years after 1945.

We have already begun to indicate the analytical inadequacies of this form of account in our criticisms of conventional treatments of inner-city problems and policies in the previous section. However, the predominance of this interpretation has more than a narrowly scholastic significance: it is an historical perspective which has enriched and enlarged a particular *practical* orientation in urban policy.

Jon Gower Davies (1972), for example, has characterized the urban planner as 'The Evangelistic Bureaucrat': a label which rather aptly sums up key elements in the ideology of planning as it developed in post-war Britain. The 'evangelism' derived from its Victorian origins – to eradicate physical and social malaise by primarily spatial and architectural means; the bureaucratic element reflects the adoption of planning and planners by central and local government, as one of the key means of administering interventionist and welfare-orientated policies. Hence the advent in the years immediately following the Second World War of something that could be termed a system of urban and regional planning; its survival, albeit in attenuated form, through two post-war decades;

the remarkably rapid making of a new system of planning through the 1968 Town and Country Planning Act and other reforms of the period; the 1970s reform of local government, which greatly expanded the number and status of planners in the new local authorities: these were all consistent with the way in which planning was supposed to have developed and were confirmatory signals reinforcing the sense of an historically progressive mission. In addition, by the 1960s, the ambitions of urban policy and planning were coming to be matched by the increasing availability of the technical and scientific means to ensure the rational fulfilment of those ambitions.[2] In short, then, urban planners came to the 1960s with a sense gained from a conventionally abridged account of their history, that the wisdom of the pioneering seers, endorsed by the liberal reforms enshrined in legislation, had created the conditions in which the processes of urban development could be orchestrated to achieve a satisfactory and humane environment.

In this, they exemplified a much wider optimism which characterized all those professional groups which had come to prominence as the Welfare State expanded in post-war Britain (for example, Dunleavy, 1980); those whom, at the level of the individual town or city, Pahl (1975) has called the 'urban managers'. As Donnison (1981) has put it, the commonly held view was that '. . . many of the nation's problems could in time be solved by redistributing a growing volume of resources between rich and poor cities and regions without any major group, interest or area suffering a real decline in living standards . . .' and that to do this required '. . . programmes which promised to redistribute resources more equally and manage a growing economy more fairly and efficiently. To do that the country would need more government, recruiting more planners, social workers, administrators, lawyers and so on from a steadily expanding system of education.' (1981: 4)

Such views were, of course, significantly shaped by the Whig interpretation of history. At the more specific level, each of the professional groups involved was able to base a claim as to its future contribution to the alleviation of social problems on a Whig account of its past development, in ways which parallel our example of urban planners. However, the Whig theory exerted a much more pervasive ideological influence too. Hence, it provided an important resource for the state itself in its task of ideological construction. It offered a theoretical foundation by means of which changes both in the form of the state and in the policies it administered could be presented as

---

[2]It is thus no coincidence that Hall *et al*. (1973) reproduce Ebenezer Howard's famous diagrammatic representation of the forces shaping urban development – 'The Three Magnets' – as '. . . the definitive statement of the objectives in English planning philosophy', limited only by the inevitable *technical* shortcomings of the period.

rational and legitimate: for *history showed* that what was required to achieve proper social improvement was the development of more responsive and technically efficient forms of government.

Viewed from the vantage point of the 1980s, it is clear that the certainties of such analysis (and, indeed, the actual policies which they supported) were crucially dependent upon the peculiar material conditions of the post-war decades. The long economic boom of the 1950s and 1960s and the relative affluence which it generated, created a basis for a form of broadly social democratic politics – often abbreviated into the oversimplified shorthand of 'Butskellism' – which provided a context highly conducive to the influence of the Whig interpretation (Gamble, 1981). Correspondingly, the radically deteriorating economic conditions of the 1970s and the austerities to which they gave rise have exposed the fragility of this view of the role of the state's development; a fragility which has been even more emphatically confirmed by the eruption of the 'New Right' into British politics, especially since the election of Mrs Thatcher's administration in 1979 (Hall and Jacques, 1983). It is just no longer possible to subscribe to a view of a progression of state-instigated reforms in response to social problems. Indeed, current experience is of major cut-backs in state expenditures and personnel in key areas of social policy in the face of a growing incidence of problems and hardships.

It is the implications of these changes, however, which have not been worked through properly. They clearly create an immediate practical crisis for those professions whose *raison d'être* is the implementation of social policy. They are no longer in a situation where their own conception of their past and future roles broadly coincides with that of the state which employs them. It is this disjuncture which, on the one hand, at least in part accounts for the growth of trade union militancy amongst many such groups; but, on the other, gives rise to the uncertainties which beset them as to what their functions *should* be.

The essential point here is that the theoretical basis of their traditional self-conception has itself been undermined by the changes in the nature of state intervention to which we have referred. As we have seen, the Whig interpretation of the development of state activity, which secured the position of these professional groupings by means of the analysis which it offered, is simply insufficient to explain the situation in which they now find themselves. Hence, it can no longer provide an adequate and uncontested basis for the prescription of appropriate future roles.

Much more generally, however, it is clear that a Whig account of the past development of state intervention cannot provide a foundation for the specification of what future policies should be. To the extent that such analysis fails to explain adequately how the present situation has come about, then it does not offer a framework from which to show how this situation may be changed. Ironically, then, accounts of the current inner-city crisis such as that presented by Hall (1981), in spite of their adoption of an avowedly 'practical' mode of analysis with the explicit intention of influencing real events, are in no position actually to do so, precisely because of the inadequacies of this analysis.

We believe, therefore, that a re-evaluation is an urgent *practical*, as well as analytical or academic necessity. It is a precondition not only of good history, of a proper understanding of past development: but also of effective future practice and policy. And, as we have already begun to demonstrate, this re-evaluation requires a radical rejection of the Whig theory of urban development and its substitution by an approach which takes as its major focus the essentially conflictual nature of the processes of social development and change.

Urban crises and the development of state urban policy[3]

A beginning may be made in this task of re-evaluation by returning to the origins of British urban policy in the conditions of nineteenth-century urbanization. In outline, the nature of these conditions is not in dispute. Hence, Hall *et al.* (1973) describe a period up until the 1860s which saw a rapid rise in the overall proportion of the total population of England and Wales living in urban areas and the emergence of a characteristic pattern of densely populated cities. At the beginning of the century, although some 17 per cent of the English and Welsh population lived in urban areas of 20,000 people or more and it was the most urbanized in the world, cities remained few and relatively small: only London, with its 1,000,000 inhabitants, had a population greater than 100,000. By 1850, however, London's population had grown to 2,500,000; Liverpool's and Manchester's exceeded 300,000; Birmingham's had reached 235,000; whilst Bradford, Leeds and Sheffield all topped 100,000.

This spectacular growth of the large, predominantly industrial cities entailed, of course, a rapid depopulation of many agricultural areas: the basic social process of the Industrial Revolution. Engels's 1845 account of *The Condition of the Working Class in England* (1973) remains one of the most graphic accounts of this process, whereby an impoverished and propertyless mass, uprooted from the rural hinterlands, flocked to the new centres of employment in the factories, mills and mines, which were the core of the new settlements. Whilst some improvement on what they had previously

[3]Earlier drafts of our arguments in this section have been substantially improved by our reading of Ball (1983), especially Chapter 7.

experienced, these migrants endured the extremities of poverty and squalor in their new urban environments. Rapid and unregulated urbanization had created the severest problems of public health (inadequate provision of sewerage facilities and clean water), pollution (conflicting and noxious land-uses), housing (over-crowding and substandard building) and traffic congestion. These bore especially hard on the poorest town-dwellers. However, some problems – and in particular the widespread incidence of diseases such as cholera – affected the more wealthy as well; in spite of the growing separation of middle-class from working-class residential districts (Wohl, 1977).

What is more controversial, however, is the explanation of these developments and the responses which were made to them. The essential point here is that there was no impetus by which a *different* set of conditions in the new urban centres could have been achieved. Hence, contemporary economic development was entirely compatible with the pattern of urbanization which we have outlined. Indeed, Scott (1982) has argued that we can characterize nineteenth-century urban development in terms of the locational activities of two types of industrial enterprise. Firstly, there were those indus-tries – such as textiles and iron and steel – which were able to make use of the revolutionary new technologies which were becoming available and which were locationally constrained to proximity to central rail and water transport terminals because of their dependence on the input of heavy and bulky commodities to their production process. Secondly, there was a group of indus-tries – clothing, footwear and so forth – which were *labour-tensive* and which consequently sought out central locations (especially in major population centres such as, say, London and Birmingham) so as to be maximally accessible to their potential workforce. In both these ways, then, the emergent core of the nineteenth-century city appeared, and around it there sprang up dense residential districts housing the main workforce.

If these characteristic patterns of economic development created the essential material conditions for the urbanization of this period, political changes were equally significant. The extension of the franchise by the Municipal Reform Act of 1835 ensured the domi-nance of most towns and cities by their local bourgeoisies – the entrepreneurs and businessmen who were rapidly accumulating substantial fortunes out of the economic growth which we have described. This dominance implied the powerful resistance to attempts to establish central government control over urban development and the strict limitation of public spending (Fraser, 1979). Indeed, public intervention was for the most part restricted to the creation of an apparatus of social control – a police force, jails and so forth; to the building of conspicuous public buildings, such as the great town halls; and to the limited improvement of sewage and water systems (Briggs, 1968). Accordingly, the main elements of urban development occurred in an essentially *ad hoc* fashion and were geared almost exclusively to the interests of the private capital which instigated them: a pattern which is perhaps most acutely exemplified by the enormous disruption caused to established land-uses by the activities of the railway companies (Kellett, 1969).

Moreover, those attempts at reform and other philanthropic activities which *were* made should be understood in their contemporary context, rather than from the retrospect of the present. Of major significance here is Stedman Jones's (1971) account of the nature of urban poverty and the attempts to deal with it in Victorian London: a London which, whilst certainly not typical of nineteenth-century cities, was the wholly dominant focus of social reform until after the First World War. What he demonstrates is that the relationships between urban problems and reforms were essentially ones of class and other social conflicts. Hence, the existence in the inner areas of London of a large working class and, critically, of a mass of casual labourers, was perceived by the dominant middle and upper classes as posing a threat to the stability of the social order; and this perception, of course, fed upon the frequent reality of civil disturbance in Victorian London. Accordingly, housing reforms and more general philanthropic activities were aimed at re-establishing the social control over the lower classes, which it was believed had broken down, in large part as a result of the growing physical separation of the social classes into distinct residential districts and the consequent removal of direct supervision. And it is in this light that the strong moral codes enforced in the model dwellings schemes and the housing management system devised by Octavia Hill, as well as the remarkably uncharitable (to twentieth-century observers) attempts of the Charity Organization Society to reverse the 'demoralization' of the urban poor by 'indiscriminate alms-giving' should be interpreted.

It was only as general circumstances began to change during the later decades of the nineteenth century that new and more substantial efforts in the direction of effective state intervention in urban development emerged. Hence, Hall *et al.* (1973) describe a second stage of urbanization, underway by the 1870s and continuing through the early decades of the twentieth century, which saw the repopulation of the rural rings by those urban residents who were able to take advantage of the various forms of transportation which developed during this period. This was the phase during which the boundaries of the Victorian city expanded in a cumulative process of suburbanization. Initially, this expansion occurred along the railway lines which were established between the urban centres and the smaller outlying settlements; subsequently, with the development of the electric railway, trams, buses and so forth, it assumed a freer, more circular form. However, it is the *scale* of this spread of the urban areas which was most remarkable; indeed, the overall proportion of the total population living in urban areas has remained more or less constant since the turn of the century.

This relative suburbanization of the residential population was accompanied by the clear diffferentiation of central business districts and some suburbanization of factories. In short, then, this second stage of urban development saw the beginnings of the separation of residence from place of employment. Moreover, this separation had very different impacts upon different types of urban dweller.

The last quarter of the nineteenth century was marked by the imposition of stricter standards for new housing through the implementation of by-laws, which were intended to prevent the re-creation of the health hazards of the earlier part of the century. Speculative builders responded to such restrictions by the development of profit-maximizing spatial forms, principally the long rows of terraced and semi-detached houses on the grid pattern, which remain so much an aspect of the inner areas of British cities. These implied lower densities and higher costs which, in turn, worsened the degree of overcrowding for those working-class families unable to pay the higher rents needed to finance this improved housing, and the travel costs incurred. Given the fact that urban rents had followed an irregular, but nevertheless continuously upward trajectory throughout the century, this latter category included a substantial proportion of the urban working class. It was thus only the higher-paid workers who could take advantage of this new housing provision and join more affluent middle-class families in suburban locations (although, of course, not the same ones). Moreover, as had been the case throughout, the *principal* beneficiaries of this urban growth were the land-owners, house-builders and financiers who were, in effect, able to control the pattern which this growth took.

To understand the fuller implications of these shifts at the urban level, however, it is necessary to locate them in the much wider context of the development of the British economy as a whole from the 1870s onwards. The emergence of the United States and Germany during this period as substantial industrial powers ended Britain's unparalleled ascendancy in the world economy. Moreover, whilst these economies concentrated on their *internal* markets and nurtured their new industries behind tariff barriers, Britain, having led the world into an Industrial Revolution which depended on world-wide trade, doggedly pursued a strategy of free trade (Hobsbawm, 1968). This strategy was viable only because of Britain's advantaged position at the centre of a world empire; the significance of which, ironically enough, was most fully recognized by the tariff reformers, who advocated the creation of an even more closely integrated imperial system, insulated from foreign (i.e., non-Empire) competition (Gamble, 1981).

What is crucial, however, is to recognize the nature of Britain's imperial domination. The chief economic significance of the Empire was that it provided a relatively safe and exclusive arena for *investment*, for the export of *capital*; indeed, the proportion of British overseas *trade* that went to the colonies was stationary or declining during the years up until 1900 (Pollard, 1962). More widely, it was financial capital, rather than industrial capital, which was emerging as the pre-eminent sector within the British economy. Hence, Britain was rapidly becoming established as the financial and commercial centre of the world economy: the international monetary system was based upon sterling and a complex of shipping, insurance and banking services came to be provided for the international economy from London. And clearly, any attempt to subvert the free flow of trade and capital would have undermined the basis of this growing prosperity, irrespective of the potential benefits which may have accrued to British industry.

Nevertheless, increasing international competition *did* force British industry into a substantial restructuring during the later decades of the nineteenth century. Industrial production came to be concentrated around the leading sectors of coal, steel, chemicals and electricity; whilst production methods increasingly involved the intensive utilization of labour through scientific management and, later, the production line (both of which, significantly enough, were developed initially in the United States). Large factories, increasingly owned by large, complex companies, came to dominate through their capacity to produce mass outputs (Pollard, 1962).

To begin with at least, these changes had relatively little impact upon the spatial distribution of industrial activity. Hence, the transportation requirements of these leading industries generally continued to restrict them to the traditional urban centres; although, as we have seen, the increasing scale of production did begin to encourage some suburbanization of factories. Moreover, the continued significance of coal as a source of fuel tended to intensify ᴇ *regional* differentiation which had been apparent from earlier in the nineteenth century. Hence, there grew up what may be termed an 'imperial spatial division of labour', broadly characterized in terms of an 'Outer Britain', focused upon the coalfields of the North and West, and an 'Inner Britain' of the South East and Midlands. It was, of course, the former which continued to be the centre of Britain's industrial activity, at least until the dramatic shifts which occurred during the years between the world wars.

What *did* change, however, were requirements for labour. The large, new factories required big workforces, much of which had to be skilled. Moreover, the new methods of production required workers who were both physically capable of sustained periods of work and appropriately trained. This, in turn, created general pressures for the improvement of the conditions in which at least a section of the working class lived, raised children, physically sustained itself and so forth. And ultimately, it was the state which was to assume the large part of the responsibility for ensuring this improvement in the conditions for reproducing labour-power.

However, it is clearly important to go beyond the general economic context to understand how such state intervention actually came about. Hence, for example, the intense housing crisis which was engendered out of these developments was not readily amenable to a *political* solution. On the one hand, the essentially unregulated housing provision which had characterized the earlier decades of the nineteenth century was incapable of yielding a housing stock adapted to the new conditions. This was recognized by the working-class organizations which were emerging during this period; and housing rents became a major element in the growing struggles between capital and labour over the living standards of the latter. On the other hand, those political groupings which remained dominant even after the extensions of the franchise in 1867 and 1884, continued to champion the virtues of private landlordism and sound public finance; and thereby, of course, precluded the most obvious solution to the problem of housing provision through the exchequer subsidy of working-class houses to rent.

It was only in these circumstances (largely unexplored in the 'Whig interpretation') that those reforming groups which had previously been agitating for the adoption of urban planning policies came to exert a more powerful influence. Hence, for example, town-extension planning appeared to offer the possibility of providing new, improved residential areas, by means of careful architectural design and municipal regulation of standards, without incurring major public expenditure or challenging the effective operation of the private market in housing and land. This possibility exerted a clear appeal to the Liberals, who were continuously in power between 1906 and the First World War. Their 1909 Housing and Town Planning Act, in facilitating town-extension schemes, reflected their opposition to the political power of the traditional landed interests (and corresponding support for financial and industrial interests), whilst sustaining the operation of a private land market and private housing landlords (McDougall, 1979).

Similarly, within the Unionist (Conservative) Party, the increasing influence of Joseph Chamberlain and the Social Imperialists was mirrored in a growing willingness to inter-vene – albeit in a strictly limited fashion – in urban development.

Thus, the Social Imperialists' programme of stemming Britain's relative economic decline by the creation of a racially exclusive, Anglo-Saxon economic bloc, based upon those parts of the Empire which had been colonized by British settlers, appeared to be threatened by the supposed 'degeneration' of the home population (Gamble, 1981). This 'degeneration', in turn, was explained in terms of the effects of a degraded urban environment, especially upon the 'deserving' sections of the working class (Stedman Jones, 1971). What was required, then, was carefully controlled state intervention, sufficient to secure the improvement of urban conditions, but again without subverting the workings of the free market: a form of intervention which was well exemplified by the programme of town-extension schemes and inner-area redevelopment undertaken in Birmingham under John Nettlefold's leadership (Sutcliffe, 1981).

More generally, it is also important to understand that the conceptualization of the urban problems at which these proposed planning solutions were directed remained one of the threats posed by the concentration of a mass working class (especially in the East End of London) to the orderly functioning of society. As Stedman Jones (1971) again demonstrates conclusively, the development of both the new Liberalism and Social Imperialism was conditioned by the major social unrest in London during the mid-1880s and the consequent need to separate the 'deserving' and 'respectable' working class (those who would, of course, be most needed in the new factories) from the 'casual residuum'. And it was precisely this separation which contemporary urban planning appeared to guarantee.

This point is well illustrated by even the most radical of planning proposals of the period: Ebenezer Howard's 'garden cities'. It is thus significant that his book, *Garden Cities of Tomorrow* (1902), in which he summarized the key elements of his scheme, was originally published (in 1898) as *Tomorrow: a peaceful path to real reform*. As befitted someone who was imbued with the ideas of the radical Liberalism of the day, he rejected both the state and the organized working class as vehicles by which such 'real reform' might be achieved. Accordingly, his 'garden cities' were to attain the desired combination of city and country by means of a judicious mixture of rather conventional architectural principles (the separation of different land-uses; the provision of plentiful open spaces; good quality housing design; etc.) and a *cooperative* programme of industrial organization and, crucially, land acquisiton (Fishman, 1977). The latter elements, of course, reflected radical opposition to the power of the landed interests and the belief in the potential for the improvement of society through the greater participation and democratic involvement of the '*respectable*' working class.

The actual difficulties of such a programme – and, indeed, the other attempts to solve the problems of the urban condition of the working class, whilst maintaining an essentially private market in housing and land – are clearly demonstrated by the subsequent history of the 'garden cities' idea. Hence the enormous problems encountered in raising the financial backing for the development of Letchworth (given the significance attached to a relatively quick return on investment), in effect, implied the perversion of even the limited radicalism expressed in Howard's original ideals. Fishman (1977) makes the point well in his description of the Garden Cities Conference held at Bourneville in 1901:

> The scene at the conference was richly symbolic of the future direction of the movement. The 'little men' to whom Howard had originally addressed the Garden City were nowhere to be found. At his side were millionaires, and in front of him government officials. Neither group wanted to hear of the cooperative commonwealth or radical social change. They looked to the Garden City as a plausible and thrifty means to relieve urban overcrowding. (1977: 61)

It is clearly possible to argue that things would have been different if there had been more concerted working-class agitation over housing and other urban issues during the years before 1914. At the national level, the Workmen's National Housing Council and, after its formation in the early 1900s, the Labour Party did press for the extension of direct exchequer grants for municipal housing. Similarly, local housing organizations and trades councils campaigned during these years over the improvement of workers' living conditions. In reality, however, they were simply not powerful enough to exert very much influence. Hence, for example, the unprecedented working-class agitation over housing provision during and immediatley after the First World War did contribute significantly to the passage of the 1919 Housing Act, which, by its provision for almost unlimited subsidies to council housing, provided the basis for the 'Homes Fit for Heroes' campaign to which we referred earlier. But it must be remembered that this campaign was abandoned after only 18 months in the interests of reducing state capital expenditure. Moreover, as Swenarton (1981) has argued, '[i]deology provided the *raison d'être* of the housing campaign and it was through design that the ideological function was to be performed: as MPs said – repeatedly – the design of houses was to prove to people that revolution was unnecessary.' (1981: 195) Presumably, by 1921, this proof was deemed to have been provided.

Contrary, then, to the conventions of the 'Whig interpretation', the emergence of urban planning policies during the Edwardian period reflected the attempt to resolve the immanent crisis of

Britain's towns and cities on terms which reflected the interests and ideologies of those upper- and middle-class groups which were *politically* dominant. The ideas and initiatives of the 'great men' (such as Howard) who feature so prominently in the 'Whig' accounts, were of any significance only within this framework. Moreover, the consequent failure to challenge the workings of the private market in anything but the most specific and partial ways constituted the severest of constraints on the real effectiveness of what could be done.

This failure to resolve the contradictions of urban development became even more acute in the dramatically changed economic circumstances of the two decades between the World Wars. The eruption of mass unemployment and economic deprivation in the traditional industrial regions of 'Outer Britain', set alongside the growth of new types of industries in the heartland of 'Inner Britain' in the South East and the Midlands, exposed ever more starkly the frailties of the free market. And hence the need for state intervention and the form which it should take became an issue of urgent debate, reflected (amongst other things) in the creation of the Barlow Commission, to which we referred earlier. It was out of this context that the substantial changes in the form and actions of the state which occurred during the Second World War emerged. These, in turn, set the scene for the development of the post-1945 system of urban policy. Accordingly, we shall defer any further discussion of these matters until our detailed examination of the latter in Chapter 3.

For the moment, however, we shall conclude this section by setting out the *general* argument which emerges from this re-evaluation of the origins of British urban policy. In sharp contrast to the 'Whig interpretation' which we examined earlier, our analysis has emphasized not only the pervasiveness and persistence of the disorderliness and crisis in the urban condition, but also the roots of this crisis in class relationships, themselves structured by the development of the British economy. Moreover, whatever the specific features of particular urban reforms, they should be interpreted as emanating from the politics of class and other social conflicts and their nature and consequences are constrained by them. It is the implications of this mode of understanding for the contemporary urban crisis in Britain which will concern us in the remainder of this book. Before proceeding with this analysis, however, we shall attempt to specify this general argument in somewhat greater detail.

The political economy of urban development: an overview

Our objective, then, is to offer a re-analysis of the processes of urban change and policy development in Britain, such that we shall be better equipped to understand the contemporary crisis (in both the senses in which we have used the term here) and, perhaps more optimistically, to offer some suggestions as to appropriate future policy directions. In attempting this, it will be clear that we have been strongly influenced by the growth in recent years of new approaches to urban and regional studies – sometimes referred to as the 'new urban sociology' or 'urban political economy' – which explicitly derive their theoretical inspiration from those traditions of social analysis originating in the writings of Max Weber and, more particularly, Marx (Lebas, 1982). Whilst we think that it is unprofitable to enter into any prolonged discourse on the merits or otherwise of the diversity of theoretical perspectives subsumed under this kind of label; given this diversity, it will clarify our later discussion, if we sketch out here the broad framework within which we have operated. Unavoidably, this sketch will be highly progràmmatic and we hope that any judgement on its effectiveness (or lack of it) will be reserved until after the more detailed, empirical exposition of later chapters.

In our view, therefore, the limitations of many of the traditional analyses of urban change derive from their failure to relate what happens in particular towns, cities and regions to the essential features of the social system which gives rise to such local change. Hence the specific locational patterns of economic and social activity in a capitalist society (such as Britain) should be interpreted in a manner consistent with a prior conceptualization of the workings of capitalist commodity production and the process of accumulation; the inherently antagonistic class relation between capital and labour; and the role of the state in mediating this antagonism and securing the appropriate framework for capitalist development.[4]

Figure 1 summarizes the key dimensions of such a conceptualization. The three *columns* indicate the elements of capitalism as a social system which, as we have suggested, should be seen to underlie specifically urban forms of change and crisis: production, class relations and the state. The three *rows* suggest distinct levels of increasing specificity in relation to these urban phenomena. Clearly, an adequate analysis must be able to explore the linkages between the

[4]Clearly, it is impossible to spell out in detail the nature of these – admittedly controversial – arguments here. For reasons which should become apparent later, this does not detract from our essential analysis. Our approach, however, broadly coincides with that spelled out by Urry (1981a).

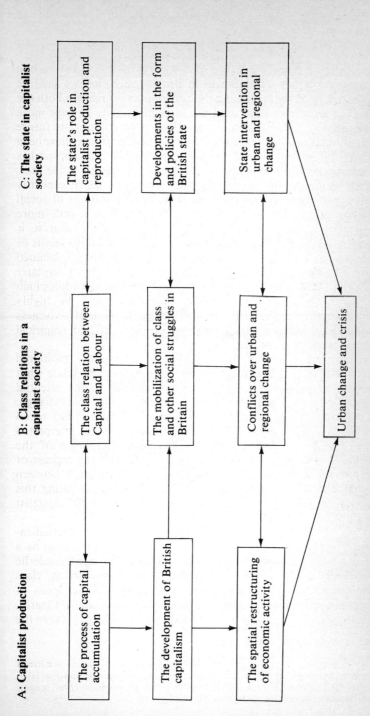

A: Capitalist production

B: Class relations in a capitalist society

C: The state in capitalist society

The process of capital accumulation

The development of British capitalism

The spatial restructuring of economic activity

The class relation between Capital and Labour

The mobilization of class and other social struggles in Britain

Conflicts over urban and regional change

The state's role in capitalist production and reproduction

Developments in the form and policies of the British state

State intervention in urban and regional change

Urban change and crisis

Figure 1:   The political economy of urban development

columns and the rows and we have indicated some of these in the figure. Equally, it must be able to trace out the data necessary to do empirical justice to the framework of theory. Our later chapters are, of course, far from complete statements in this respect; they are rather initial explorations of the kind of urban analysis we think is needed. In what follows here, we seek to present the essential features of each element in Figure 1 and to explain how subsequent chapters will expand upon them.

Capitalist production

The process of capital accumulation

The basic form of capitalist production may be represented by the exchange $M \rightarrow C \begin{cases} MP \\ LP \end{cases} \rightarrow P \rightarrow C' \rightarrow M'$. Hence, money (M) is advanced as capital (C) in order to expand it. Capitalists use M to buy materials and equipment (the means of production, MP) and labour-power (LP). These are combined in the process of production (P) to make commodities (C'), which are then sold on the market, realizing money (M') once more. The point of this industrial circuit of capital is that M' should be greater than M: the difference between the two represents the capitalist's profits. Firms which are able to achieve at least normal profits on capital advanced (C) will reconstitute the commodity producing process in new rounds of productive activity; those which fail to do so cannot remain viable in the long run and will go out of business.

Capital is organized into individual units which are constantly in competition with one another. Accordingly, each firm has to struggle to minimize its costs of production and to maximize its profits. This competitive pressure makes necessary the ploughing back of at least part of the excess of M' over M into a continuous process of expansion and streamlining of the production process, which in practice means that there is a tendency for firms to substitute capital for labour, thereby increasing labour productivity. In this way, then, commodity production is enlarged through the process of accumulation.

However, it should not be thought that this process of accumulation proceeds in a smooth and unproblematic manner. On the contrary, as Mandel (1975) suggests, accumulation follows a course of ' . . . successive phases of recession, upswing, boom, overheating, crash and depression . . . ' (1975: 438). These crises derive from the fact that capitalist production is characterized by a tendency for the rate of profit to fall, thus necessitating the mobilization of counter-tendencies to restore levels of profitability, by opening up new forms of technology and work organization, exploiting new source of raw materials, developing new markets and so on.

So far, then, we have been concerned only with the – admittedly dominant – *industrial* circuit of capital. Two further circuits may be identified, with corresponding fractions of capital. Hence, commercial capital is involved in supplying commodities to and realizing the outputs of production (M → C → M') thereby maximizing the efficiency of the sphere of circulation. Whilst financial capital concentrates that part of money-capital (M) which is not directly engaged in industrial or commercial operations, thereby reducing to a minimum the amount of capital that needs to be held in a liquid form as working capital; its circuit may thus be represented as M → M'. The significance of these distinctions is that, in reality, there is no reason to suppose that the activities of these fractions of capital will mesh together smoothly.

The development of British capitalism
It is important to understand, however, that these immanent characteristics of the capitalist mode of production are expressed in concrete patterns of development which vary considerably between different societies. Hence, the second level of our theoretical framework involves the analysis of the development of *British* capitalism, albeit in its international context and in terms guided by the more abstract account of the accumulation process which we have outlined.

Accordingly, as we shall see in Chapter 2, it is certainly the case that Britain's economic problems in part reflect an international crisis due to the tendency of the rate of profit to fall, which has dominated the world economy since the ending of the long boom of the 1950s and earlier 1960s. However, Britain's problems are equally the result of a *long-term* failure to restructure British industrial capital and to meet foreign competition. Hence, it has tended to achieve *relatively* low profits and/or to depend on below-average wages. Moreover, these failings have been reinforced by specific features of British society: the hegemony of financial over domestic industrial capital; the defensive strength of organized labour; and the nature of state intervention.

The spatial restructuring of economic activity
These broad patterns of development in the British economy, in turn, set the context for urban and regional change within Britain. Hence, in general terms, spatial or territorial structure is integral to the social processes of capitalist production. On the one hand, space constitutes a framework within which commodity production and the accumulation process take place: it constitutes a distribution of natural resources and social conditions which are themselves used in

production. Moreover, the use of land and its resources is subject to a characteristic set of rules of property ownership, which confer on landowners a substantial element of control over access to many of the useful effects of land. On the other hand, spatial structure is itself partly the *outcome* of the social processes of capitalist accumulation. Hence, patterns of growth and decline of capital both create new spatial structure and themselves are conditioned by those spatial structures which were the result of earlier periods of capitalist development (Dunford and Perrons, 1983).

More specifically, these general conditions imply that the *particular* pattern which accumulation has taken in Britain should be interpreted as embodying changes in both the organization of the processes of production and the spatial distribution of the activities of which these processes are comprised. Hence, there is a characteristic historical movement in which successive phases of accumulation have generated new forms of economic activity and corresponding spatial structures, with each phase being conditioned by the circumstances created in earlier ones.

Accordingly, as we saw earlier, Britain's nineteenth-century economic growth was based in large part upon the success of a set of dominant industries, organized in particular ways and concentrated spatially in the coalfield areas of 'Outer Britain'. The emergence of a new phase of accumulation – which became especially apparent during the years between the two world wars – was defined by switches of investment into new industrial sectors, utilizing new technologies and work organization and whose locational requirements were best fulfilled not in the traditional industrial regions, but rather in the South East and the Midlands, the heartland of 'Inner Britain'. As we shall show in Chapter 2, the process of accumulation in Britain since 1945 has continued to necessitate extensive industrial restructuring. Moreover, as in the earlier periods to which we have referred, this restructuring has involved substantial shifts in the spatial structure of economic activity. And it is these shifts which underlie the observable patterns of regional growth and decline, the collapse of manufacturing industry in inner-city areas and so forth.

Such developments, however, do not occur naturally or inevitably. Rather, capitalist development both gives rise to and is determined by antagonistic social relations: the second key dimension of our theoretical framework.

Class relations in a capitalist society

The class relation between capital and labour
The process of capital accumulation sketched earlier implies class antagonism between capital and wage-labour. The increase in value

realized in the excess of M' over M derives from the fact that, whilst the whole of the value of the means of production (MP) which is used up in production (P) is passed on to the new commodities (C'), the value of labour-power (LP) is usually *less than* the value added by the labourer in the course of production (P): that is, the application of labour-power in production enables the capitalist to derive surplus value. In consequence, it is part of the necessary function of the capitalist to organize the processes whereby such surplus value is achieved; in contrast, labour attempts to force up real wages above the level necessary for its own reproduction. Moreover, this conflict is intensified as a result of the accumulation process. The substitution of capital for labour and associated changes in the organization of production are likely to be opposed by labour (as they are perceived in terms of unemployment, cuts in living standards and so forth), as well as underpinning the crisis tendencies previously noted (through the removal of the only source of value).

However, the acknowledgement of this essential relationship of conflict between capital and labour over the production and appropriation of surplus value, does not imply a narrow, economic reductionism. For, as Urry (1981a) shows:

> [c]lasses only exist within civil society – the form that they take is given, first, by the current patterns of capital accumulation and relations between the functions of capital and labour; second, by the forms of gender, age, racial, regional and national interpellation within civil society; and third, by the forms of political organisation and state apparatuses. There are no pure classes determined economically – capitalist relations, with a particular division of antagonistic functions of capital and labour, are manifest *within civil society*. (1981: 66)

What this implies, therefore, is that the *actual incidence* of class struggles and the *form* which they take cannot be deduced from the functional contradiction between capital and labour, but depend also on processes of mobilization and organization structured in civil society.

Furthermore, there are other bases of social conflict and struggle, which are not directly determined by capitalist relations of production and which may assume equal or even greater significance within a particular society. Hence, for example, there are numerous class groupings which cannot be unambiguously identified in terms of the basic class relation of capitalism, but which nevertheless occupy a common position in relation to the means of production and which may constitute the social base of mobilization and struggle; examples of such 'classes-in-struggle' (Laclau, 1979) include the traditional petty bourgeoisie, the 'new middle class', landlords and the lumpenproletariat. More widely too, the structure of civil society is such as to yield a diversity of dimensions around which struggles may be mobilized and conflicts focused, but which are unrelated to class relations. Such popular-democratic struggles, then, involve the organization of 'the people' in terms of, for example, gender, generation, race, region or place of residence and, of course, interact with the realization of genuinely class struggle in the manner noted earlier.

The forms taken by these various types of struggle differ considerably. However, what is most significant is that the actual pattern taken by the accumulation process and the associated reorganization of capitalist production within a given society is crucially dependent upon the variety of struggles and conflicts which we have outlined. Whilst it is clearly possible to specify what is necessary for the continued accumulation of capital, the fulfilment of such conditions is by no means guaranteed: it is dependent upon the outcomes of class and other social struggles and is therefore *indeterminate*.

The mobilization of class and other social struggles in Britain

In the same way that a necessary level of analysis relates to the specific features of accumulation in Britain, so class relations and other social struggles have assumed a form which is determined by the particularities of British society and its history. Indeed, as we have already begun to indicate, the pattern followed by economic development in Britain is in large measure the result of such relations.

Hence, for example, the circumstances of Britain's nineteenth-century economic growth generated a radical disjuncture between financial and industrial capital; moreover, the investment activities of the former have not been in the best interests of large sections of the latter and it has proved impossible to establish any real political unity between the two (a disunity accentuated, of course, by the individual, competitive nature of industrial capital itself). Similarly, the early development of trades unionism in Britain yielded a social force with powerful defensive strength, which has been especially significant in the determination of post-war economic change. Again, Britain's post-Imperial settlement has involved the considerable immigration of workers and their families from former colonies and their progressive ostracization within the social structure of modern Britain; thus creating conditions for social conflict which are of special importance to the contemporary urban situation. And, of course, further examples of such major social cleavages will form a central part of our discussion in subsequent chapters.

Conflicts over urban and regional change

Spatial structure is also central to the determination of class and social struggles more generally. Given what we have said about the spatial differentiation of productive activity, it is not surprising that the actual realization of class struggles should be conditioned by processes of mobilization which are often quite specific to particular localities. Hence, for example, certain areas (such as the South Wales coalfield or Clydeside) have histories of relatively militant and combative relations between labour and capital, which are the product of a wide range of conditions (not exclusively within the sphere of production) characteristic of those areas; and, of course, other localities have quite different records of class struggle. Moreover, the spatial structure of production may itself become a focus of such struggle. The process of accumulation implies the growth of some areas and the decline of others and hence conflicts between capital and labour may frequently take the form of struggles over the fate of given *localities*. In this way, changes in the location of production are themselves partly the outcomes of class struggles, in precisely the same way as other elements of industrial restructuring.

Equally, however, such locality-based struggles may take alternative forms to class conflicts. Indeed, it has been argued that a focus upon what is happening in a particular place (whether local area, region or wider geographical unit) has the effect of *displacing* distinctively class struggles (Urry, 1983). An example here is the emergence of regionalist and nationalist movements in Britain and elsewhere, concerned to safeguard their areas, on a basis which effectively cuts across lines of class division (for example, Rees and Lambert, 1981). However, the principal influence of such non-class social groupings is likely to be exerted through the intervention of the state in the organization of production and reproduction.

The state in capitalist society

The state's role in capitalist production and reproduction
The state has become a pervasive influence in the economies of *all* capitalist societies. Its *normal* functions extend far beyond its well established role as guarantor of the conditions of exchange – through its control of money, the legal system, etc. – and now include both a substantial involvement in ensuring the reproduction of labour power – by means of the educational system, health services, welfare payments and so forth – as well as major direct intervention in the organization of the accumulation process itself – through the whole panoply of modern economic policies.

However, this does *not* imply that these uniformities are underpinned by a capitalist state with an invariant relationship with capitalist relations of production (Jessop, 1982 gives an exhaustive review of such theories). It is clearly the case that the nature of the state cannot be divorced form the actual structure of productive relations which is characteristic of capitalist social formations. The competitive nature of capitalist production and the consequent tendencies to crisis, create the context in which the state is the only possible vehicle through which the appropriate conditions for extended accumulation may be ensured. And this, in turn, is reflected in the assumption of the kinds of functions which we have noted. However, it is significant that there is *actually* an extremely wide variation in state forms and policies between different capitalist societies: Britain is different from the United States, which is different from France or Japan, and so on.

Developments in the form and policies of the British state

What is most significant here is that the specific forms taken by the state in different capitalist societies and the actual types of intervention which they pursue are crucially determined by the outcome of the class and other social struggles to which we have referred. Hence, for example, to understand properly the emergence of what Jessop (1980) refers to as the 'Keynesian-welfare state' during the first post-war decades in Britain, it is necessary to understand the *particular* configuration of class and popular-democratic forces which constituted the social base for such a development (about which we shall say more in Chapter 3). Similarly, the implementation of policies of a determinate kind – say, the creation of the National Health Service in 1946 or the nationalization of the coal mines in 1947 – cannot be comprehended adequately without relating them to the pressures exerted by class and other social groupings constituted in civil society. Indeed, during the contemporary period, the state and the determination of state policies have become probably the central arena in which social struggles are carried out.

Furthermore, the effects of such struggles in terms of patterns of state intervention are crucially mediated by the form and operation of the state itself. Hence, the state itself is an active agent in *constituting* a sufficient basis of support for a given line of policy development. Given the prevalence of some kind of democratic norms, then particular regimes will themselves engage in attempts to ensure the combination of class and other social groupings into a 'power bloc' in support of their policy programme. In addition, such attempts will frequently involve activities at the level of ideology in the construction of particular definitions of the nature of economic and social problems, appropriate solutions and so forth (Middlemas, 1979 gives a detailed historical account of such developments in Britain).

Equally, however, the form and operation of the state condition the capacities of different social groupings to use the resources of the state in pursuit of their objectives. Relationships between class and other social struggles and the nature of state intervention are shaped, at least in part, by considerations such as the form of interest representation within the political process (for example, parliamentarism versus corporatism); the *internal* relationships between different parts of the state (for instance, between the executive and the bureaucracy or between the central and local state); and the incidence or otherwise of 'fiscal crises' and other resource-related issues.

Moreover, these relationships are made more complex by the increasing role which has been played by the state in reproduction. This role arises from the fact that the competitive nature of capital is such that it is only very rarely in the interests of any individual capital to bear the costs of reproducing its own labour power. Hence the state has come to undertake the provision of the necessary conditions and to ensure that all capital-units bear some of the costs, through the taxation system. What this means is that much of the conflict over reproduction is expressed through struggles over state policy. And these struggles, in turn, have a determining influence upon the kinds of policies which are pursued. However, it should be noted that there is no reason for mobilization of this kind to occur exclusively or even primarily on class lines. Again as we saw in earlier discussion, the emergence of urban policy in Victorian and Edwardian Britain, for example, was not directly conditioned by conflicts between capital and labour. Rather, it was the outcome of struggles between land- and property-owners and a wide variety of other social groupings, although in a context set by the contemporary state of accumulation and the class antagonisms thereby implied. Also, of course, there is no guarantee that the conditions which are necessary for appropriate reproduction are actually fulfilled.

State intervention in urban and regional change
A significant dimension of the state's general role in the development of the British social formation relates to the latter's spatial or territorial structure. Particular forms of state intervention have developed whose objectives are the facilitation of given patterns of restructuring of both production and reproduction and the management of their consequences; and clearly these include those policies concerned with regional economic development, the distribution of land-uses, property relations, aspects of housing and infrastructural provision, the regeneration of the inner cities and a wide range of other issues. Neither the form nor the effects of such policies can be considered separately from the wider character of state intervention of which they are part. However, as we have begun

to indicate, they are shaped by class and other social struggles, whose focus is specifically spatial. Moreover, these policies are produced in a *social* process of policy-making within the state, which mediates the effects of social struggles. And a major part of this policy-making process involves the prioritization of certain issues and their definition in characteristic ways; hence, for instance, the current emphasis upon the economic regeneration of inner-city areas through the encouragement of private-sector investment.

In summary, then, we have argued that a proper analysis of urban development and policy – and of the present urban crisis more specifically – requires an account constructed around three closely inter-related dimensions: the accumulation process; the state; and, most importantly, class and other social struggles. Each of these dimensions may be conceptualized at different levels, ranging from the most generalized examination of the capitalist mode of production, to the more specific analysis of developments within British society, and, finally, to the delineation of particular spatially focused changes within urban Britain. The following chapters present our attempt to apply this framework to what has happened in Britain during the period since the Second World War.

The structure of the book

The schematic presentation of our theoretical framework in Figure 1 also provides the key to the structure of the remainder of the book. In Chapter 2, we give a summary account of the course taken by accumulation in Britain since 1945. In particular, we describe three phases of post-war accumulation: the long boom of the 1950s and the 1960s; the accelerating economic decline of the later 1960s and first part of the 1970s; and the intense economic crisis of the late 1970s and 1980s. And we show that each of these phases generated corresponding patterns of urban and regional change. In terms of Figure 1, then, this represents our attempt to spell out the first column. Chapters 3, 4 and 5 comprise the heart of the book and present an analysis of the state intervention in urban and regional change which was characteristic of each of the three phases of accumulation which we have outlined. These chapters accordingly present our account of the third column of Figure 1. Throughout, however, we shall be concerned to emphasize the centrality of class and other social conflicts to both patterns of accumulation *and* forms of state intervention; and this is signalled by the central position of class relations in the second column of Figure 1. Moreover, given our particular concern with state intervention, the ways in which such conflicts have been mediated through political processes and the internal operation of the state itself will provide a special focus of this discussion.

This focus upon the state is *not* intended, of course, to suggest that state action has exerted the most significant influence upon the actual pattern of urban change. Indeed, much of our discussion will be concerned to demonstrate the real limits of state intervention during the post-war years. Rather, it is indicative of our view – which may certainly be regarded as reformist – that it is through *alternative* forms of state activity that the greatest potential for new forms of urban development lie. Furthermore, the development of such alternative forms is dependent upon a proper understanding of past and existing state policies. These are the issues which are picked up in Chapter 6, where we use our general conclusions from the preceding discussion as the basis for an evaluation of the posibilities of resolving the current urban crisis on terms which serve the interests of those who are most disadvantaged by it.

2

Capital accumulation and urban development in post-war Britain

Central to our theoretical approach, then, is the view that the form taken by urban development cannot be understood properly without consideration of its relationships with the process of capital accumulation. The patterns of growth and decline of Britain's towns and cities have reflected the exigencies of the particular trajectory taken by British economic development. The conflicts of interest between class and other social groupings which have been integral to this development have likewise exerted a determining influence over the character of urban change in Britain. Whilst – most crucially for our purposes – the state, as well as its specifically urban policies, have been a key arena in which these class relations have been expressed.

We have already begun to explore these issues empirically in our re-evaluation of the 'Whig interpretation' of the origins of urban policy during the late Victorian and Edwardian periods. Moreover, the severity of Britain's economic crisis in the years between the two world wars served to underscore the essential interdependencies between accumulation and patterns of urbanization. Hence, although what happened at this time embodied, in part at least, no more than an intensification of trends which had been immanent in the British economy since the last quarter of the nineteenth century, the spatial unevenness of the crisis created a radically altered context within which the future of Britain's urban areas had to be considered.

On the one hand, therefore, those industries which had provided the essential impetus to the growth of the great urban centres of 'Outer Britain', especially during the period after 1860 (textiles, coal, iron and steel, shipbuilding and so forth), stagnated or declined during the 1920s and 1930s. Their relative inability to absorb technological changes and to adapt to new market possibilities underpinned a declining international competitiveness. This was compounded, of course, by the development of new industries abroad and the loss of foreign markets which followed from the adoption of policies of protection. It was the dependence of these industries on world trade which had made possible their growth and prosperity; it was this same dependence which implied their collapse in a world in which barriers against this trade were being increasingly strengthened (Pollard, 1962). In addition, after 1925, this relative loss of foreign markets was aggravated by the over-valuation of the pound, which, in turn, is explicable in terms of the dominance of financial capital over the British economy and the centrality of sterling to international financial markets (Hobsbawm, 1968).

What these developments implied, however, was that those areas which were the centres of these traditional industries came to be wholly dominated by mass unemployment and economic depriva-tion, in spite of the substantial outward migration of workers and their families. In particular, the years of the Great Depression between 1929 and 1932, when the long-term decline of the traditional industries was further aggravated by the collapse of world trade in manufactured goods and primary products and a reduction in world output of about a third, saw levels of unemployment in the industrial regions reach truly astronomical proportions (Hobsbawm, 1968).[1]

On the other hand, the inter-war years also witnessed the substantial *growth* of new industries, producing new types of product, which were for the most part dependent upon the development of home-based consumption through mass markets. Hence, for example, the electricity-supply industry, motor-car manufacture, electrical goods, pharmaceuticals and so forth, all recorded large increases in output and contributed significantly to the overall growth in industrial production during the 1920s and 1930s. In addition, some of the traditional consumption-good industries – such as food-processing, clothing and furniture manufacture – recorded moderate rates of expansion; whilst the building industry was one of the fastest growing sectors of the inter-war economy (Pollard, 1962).

Most importantly, however, these new industries sought out their most profitable locations in precisely those areas of 'Inner Britain' (in the South East and the Midlands) which were least affected by the decline of the staple, nineteenth-century industries. Owing to technological changes, and particularly the increasingly widespread availability of electrical power, they were not tied to coalfield locations and could set up production near to their major markets. Moreover, many of these new plants located in the smaller towns on the edges of the major urban centres, where land was plentiful and

[1]Hence, for example, in 1931–1932, 43 per cent of cotton operatives were unemployed, with an overwhelming concentration in the mill towns of the North West. Similarly, after 1925, seldom fewer than 25 per cent of miners were unemployed, with especially high rates in the older coalfields, such as South Wales. Whilst unemployment amongst steel-workers reached 48 per cent and that amongst ship-building workers 62 per cent by the early 1930s (Hobsbawm, 1968).

cheap, and wages tended to be lower than in the established urban cores. Hence, together with the development of new forms of transportation, both of goods and people, which became available at this time and the massive expansion of owner-occupied housing, they contributed substantially to the suburban growth which was a central feature of the inter-war years (for example, Hall *et al.*, 1973).

In this way, then, the pattern of capital accumulation characteristic of the 1920s and 1930s was imprinted upon the development of Britain's towns and cities during these years. Moreover, as we noted earlier (and in Chapter 1), it was the juxtaposition of growth and decline in different parts of Britain, and the social relations which underlay them, which set the context for the emergence of new forms of state intervention during and after the Second World War; and we shall pursue these issues in some detail in Chapter 3.

For the purposes of the present chapter, however, we shall extend our analysis of capital accumulation in Britain into the period after 1945. Just as in the earlier eras which we have considered, what has happened in Britain's urban areas since the Second World War has reflected the contours of the wider processes of British capitalism's development. Accordingly, the analysis presented here will provide the essential context for our discussion of the evolving forms of state intervention in urban change – culminating in the current preoccupation with the inner-city crisis – which will provide the focus for the later chapters of the book.

British capitalism in its international context

The restoration of capital accumulation in the decades following the Second World War was made possible by the growing *internationalization* of industrial and financial capital. Accordingly, the development of British capitalism during this period has been conditioned – even more so than previously – by its location within a *world-wide* capitalist economy. We shall therefore examine this wider context, before turning to the specificities of the British situation.

In the immediate aftermath of the war, American capital secured a pre-eminent position as a result of its industrial strength (its production was twice that of the rest of the world in 1945), the great demand for investment capital, machinery, and finished products in Europe and Japan during post-war reconstruction, and the paramount position of the dollar in the international monetary system (which had been negotiated at the Bretton Woods Conference in 1944). Hence, under American dominance, the necessary conditions were established for the growing international mobility of industrial and financial capital, marked most clearly in the growth of (especially United States-based) multinational companies and the closely associated overseas investments of the large banks (Mandel, 1975). In particular, a stable international monetary system, the increasing liberalization of trade and investment, and military and political cooperation amongst the major capitalist powers were secured with the creation of major, supranational institutions, such as the International Monetary Fund (IMF), the World Bank, the General Agreement on Tariffs and Trade (GATT), the North Atlantic Treaty Organization (NATO) and so forth.

It was these circumstances, then, which laid the basis for the long post-war boom of the 1950s and earlier 1960s, during which all the capitalist economies recorded unparalleled growth in output.

Table 2.1 The long-run growth of advanced capitalist countries

	Rate of growth of output per head of population	Rate of growth of stock of means of production
	Annual average percentage	
1870–1913	1.5	2.8
1913–1950	1.1	1.6
1950–1970	3.8	5.6

Source: Glyn and Harrison (1980), p. 5

More specifically, the increasing application of advanced methods of production and work organization (in which the multinational companies played a leading role) secured large rises in labour productivity. In addition, raw materials – and, in particular, oil – were plentiful and cheap. Whilst the state management of the business cycle and organized wage-bargaining, as well as the ready availability of labour (in the shape of former agricultural workers, immigrants and women previously not in employment), ensured that wages increased broadly in line with labour productivity. All of these contributed to the creation of an especially favourable context for capital accumulation. At the same time, however, the increasing role of capitalist states, both in the provision of industrial infrastructure and in reproducing labour-power, further improved the conditions for expansion. And the extension of credit facilities enabled the massive growth of consumer expenditure, which provided outlets for the marketing of new commodities (especially consumer durables) and, together with the generally low levels of unemployment, enhanced the widespread climate of prosperity (Mandel, 1975).

However, by the mid-1960s, this especially favourable configuration of conditions for economic expansion was beginning to break up. Since this time, the international economy has entered a period of ever-deepening crisis: output has alternated between decline and stagnation; unemployment has risen steadily; inflation has become a persistent feature of the advanced capitalist economies; and the international monetary system has been thrown into turmoil (for example, Mandel, 1978). Underlying these trends has been a fall in the rate of profit enjoyed in the major capitalist economies.

Table 2.2   Rates of profit for industrial and commercial companies

| | Percentage before tax | | | | |
	1960	1965	1970	1973	1975
UK	14.2	11.8	8.7	7.2	3.5
USA	9.9	13.7	8.1	8.6	6.9
France	11.9	9.9	11.1	10.2	4.1
Japan	19.7	15.3	22.7	14.7	9.5
Italy	11.0	7.9	8.6	4.5	0.8
West Germany	23.4	16.5	15.6	12.1	9.1

Source: Gyln and Harrison (1980), p. 12

The explanation of this declining rate of profit (and, indeed, the collapse of the long boom more widely) is highly complex and need not detain us here (the issues are discussed at length in Mandel, 1975 and 1978). However, significant influences certainly included the increasing difficulties encountered in further raising rates of labour productivity, without major transformations in the organization of production and the growing capacity of organized labour to resist productive innovation, whilst at the same time pushing up the level of real wages, thereby contributing to inflationary pressures. These basic tendencies, in turn, were exacerbated by the mounting problems encountered by the capitalist states in financing their facilitation of the reproduction of labour-power (leading to the emergence of 'fiscal crises'); the collapse of the Bretton Woods monetary system as a result of the relative decline of the economic power of American capital; and the 1973 rise in world oil prices.

However, capital has not been passive in the face of these problems. It is important to understand that the period since the later 1960s has been marked by tendencies to *counter* the decline in profit rates. Hence, in some industrial sectors, there has been quite substantial reorganization of production, which has involved the introduction of new forms of technology and closer control over the labour process; as, for example, in the – albeit limited – introduction of the automated assembly-line in the motor-car industry. More widely, of course, the least profitable and productive elements have been eliminated as firms have gone bankrupt and/or been absorbed by more effective ones, in a process of centralization of capital. These developments, in turn, have generated intense competition between individual capitals, as each firm battles for its survival.

One particular form of industrial restructuring which has been especially significant has involved the relocation of production facilities to the low-wage countries of the Third World – the 'New International Division of Labour' – thereby opening up possibilities (especially in certain sectors, such as electronics and clothing) for restoring profitability by the reduction of wage costs. Equally, however, the Third World has come to constitute a significant new *market* for many of the industries of the advanced capitalist economies; as well as continuing to fulfil a more traditional function as a supplier of cheap raw materials and energy sources. Moreover, these developments have been paralleled by trends in financial capital, which are most clearly manifested in the growing indebtedness of many Third World countries to foreign banks (Jenkins, 1984). The point here is that all of these trends should be seen as possible counters to the decline in rates of profit.

Clearly, we should expect to see these general patterns of economic development during the post-war period reflected in the British experience of these years. However, the particularities of Britain's situation have given rise not simply to a characteristically British pattern of accumulation, but also to a uniquely severe set of economic problems. It is to a consideration of these that we turn in the next section.

The post-war problems of British capitalism

One element in the determination of the characteristic pattern of Britain's post-war economic development has been the particular problems created by her nineteenth-century – and, more precisely, Imperial – legacy. Crucial factors here have been the traditional role of sterling as a major international reserve and trading currency and the loss of Empire combined with massive defence commitments overseas. Moreover, even after the former problems were largely solved through the diversification of British financial capital into Eurocurrency operations during the 1960s and the dramatic reduction of Britain's military role East of Suez at the same time, the British economy remained dependent upon foreign trade for its economic survival. As we shall see, all of these have exerted major constraints on the process of capital accumulation, especially in setting the agenda for state economic policy (Gamble, 1981).

However, these factors have only served to compound the continued, long-term decline of British industrial capital, which, as we have indicated, has its origins in the last decades of the nineteenth century. Although the effects of this decline were to some extent masked by the extraordinary conditions of the long boom, since the

1960s (and in a most acute form since the mid-1970s) they have become all too starkly apparent and account for the fact that the contemporary economic crisis in Britain is much more severe than in most other countries. Moreover, it is in this general context that we should seek to locate the important changes which have taken place since the 1960s in both the internal form and strategies of the British state and its external relationships (marked most clearly by British entry to the European Economic Community (EEC) in the early 1970s) (Jessop, 1980).

As we have already begun to show, the key to understanding British industrial capital's long-term decline lies in its failure to match internationally competitive norms of industrial investment (at least domestically), of technological and organizational innovation and, in consequence, of labour productivity. Table 2.3 gives an indication of the severity of this failure during the period since the Second World War.

Table 2.3   The rates of growth of industrial productivity (Gross Domestic Product per man-hour)

	Average annual compound growth rates		
	1870–1913	1913–1950	1950–1976
UK	1.1	1.5	2.8
USA	2.1	2.5	2.3
France	1.8	1.7	4.9
Japan	1.8	1.4	7.5
Italy	1.2	1.8	5.3
West Germany	1.9	1.2	5.8

Source: Maddison (1979), p. 195

During the post-war period, the results of this failure have been that established industries have not been modernized in ways that would enable them to compete with foreign competitors; whilst those industries for whose products world demand has been expanding have developed relatively slowly in Britain (for example, Pavitt, 1979). The overall effect has been that Britain's Gross National Product (GNP) has grown chronically slowly (averaging less than 3 per cent annually) relative to the other advanced capitalist economies.

The full impact of these trends, however, did not become apparent until the 1960s, when British trade began to be redirected from the protected markets of the Commonwealth towards the European economies. Up until this time, then, British capital had been sustained not only by its highly favourable trading relations, but in addition by supplies of cheap food and raw materials, also from the

Commonwealth. Moreover, of course, it took some time for the economies of continental Europe and Japan to recover from the effects of the war (Hobsbawm, 1968). Since then, however, Britain's share in total world exports has declined sharply (from 16.5 per cent in 1960 to 9.7 per cent in 1979; in 1950 the equivalent figure was 25.5 per cent), as its true competitive weakness has been exposed. Equally, there has been a marked increase in the volume of imports; and import penetration has become significant even in sectors which, during the 1950s, had been dominated by domestic products (as, for example, in consumer durables and industrial equipment goods) (for example, Caves and Krause, 1980). In consequence, one of the besetting problems of the British economy – especially during the later 1950s and 1960s – was its balance of payments (an issue we shall return to later).

More latterly, the effects of North Sea oil (amongst other factors) have reduced balance of payments problems. And the focus of concern has shifted – in particular since the mid-1970s – to the threat posed by import penetration and failures in export markets to the very survival of large sections of British manufacturing industry. More specifically, it has been argued that the collapse of British manufacturing has undermined the capacity to earn sufficient foreign exchange through exports to pay for the imports of food, fuel, and raw materials on which the economy depends (Cambridge Economic Policy Group, 1977). What is more certain is that there has been an enormous loss of jobs from the manufacturing sector, much of which, of course, had grown up during the inter-war period (as we saw earlier). Hence, by the mid-1970s the manufacturing industries of Britain employed some 1,300,000 fewer people than they had 10 years previously: a decline of just over 15 per cent. Subsequently, this decline has steepened, with lay-offs from manufacturing reaching unprecedented levels by the early 1980s (for example, Blackaby, 1979). Moreover, it is also clear that the effects of 'de-industrialization' have been felt in other sectors of the economy too: thus, the internal employment problems in primary product industries have been severely compounded by falling demand from manufacturing (as, for example, in the coal industry); whilst services jobs, after a sustained period of growth (over 1,500,000 new jobs were created between 1970 and 1980), have begun to decline too (Massey and Meegan, 1982).

However, one of the paradoxes of this dismal record of British industrial capital is that during these same post-war years which we have been discussing, there has been a substantial *growth* in British multinational companies, with extensive investment and trading interests overseas (especially, of course, in former Imperial territories). Now, as we have indicated, the internationalization of the world capitalist economy has been one of the principal features of the post-war period: and, equally, this trend has been dominated by American capital. Nevertheless, the proportion of British firms operating six or more foreign subsidiaries had increased from a fifth in 1950 to a half in 1970; and all of the largest 100 British manufacturing companies had become multinationals by 1970. Moreover, by the same year, 11 of the world's 100 largest businesses were British, compared with only 18 for the whole of the EEC; whilst of the 200 largest non-American companies, 53 were British, 43 Japanese, 25 West German and 23 French (Gamble, 1981).

Accordingly, although there has been a substantial growth in investment by foreign-based multinationals in the British economy (particularly in sectors such as mechanical and electrical engineering, chemicals, transport equipment and so on), it remains the case that this is exceeded by British investment overseas. Indeed, this British overseas investment was never less than 17 per cent of that in domestic manufacturing through the 1970s, and in some years topped 30 per cent: levels which were far greater than those for other advanced capitalist economies, with the exception of the United States (Gamble, 1981).

Clearly, these investments abroad have facilitated the penetration of foreign markets and have often given rise to export orders. However, the activities of British multinationals have also contributed substantially to the failures of the home-based economy. The leading sector of British industrial capital has sought to retain its strength and competitiveness by operating *internationally*, rather than by expanding from a secure base at home. And this has been an important reason for the inability of British industry to match the levels of output growth, investment, productivity and exports of its foreign competitors. Hence, the distinction between the *internationalized* and *domestic* sections of British industrial capital has been a crucial determinant of Britain's economic problems.

Closely related to this overseas orientation of a major part of British industrial capital, has been the key international role played by financial capital (and particularly 'the City'). As we outlined earlier, the circumstances of Britain's nineteenth-century economic growth gave rise not only to the distinctive dislocation between the financial and industrial sectors, but also to the predominance of the former, based on its servicing of the world-wide economy (Hobsbawm, 1968). In spite of the radically changed circumstances of the post-war period, there was nevertheless a concerted attempt to maintain this key position at the centre of the world capitalist system, which was reflected not simply in the activities of the British multinationals, but also in the international financial, shipping and insurance services provided by the City. In addition, at least until the 1960s, Britain was also committed to extremely high levels of overseas military spending, which were deemed commensurate with her role in the international political system.

What this implied was that the central objective of state policy became the preservation of the stability of sterling, so that it could continue to function as a top international reserve currency and as a major medium of international trade. And this, in turn, necessitated the attempt to avoid deficits on the balance of payments, in order to maintain confidence in sterling. However, the latter could not be achieved by imposing restrictions on the free flow of capital and portfolio investment overseas; or by reducing military expenditure. Therefore, successive governments deflated the domestic economy in order to reduce demand for imports. At the same time, the need to maintain levels of employment at home and to finance state expenditure limited the possibilities of such a policy, with the result that the British economy of the 1950s and 1960s came to be characterized by a unique series of 'stop – go' cycles, with alternating periods of expansion and stagnation (for example, Brittan, 1971).

The effects of these cycles were disastrous. On the one hand, they failed to halt the long-term decline in the roles of sterling and Britain in the international system. This was reflected in a growing association between financial and industrial capital (at least in its internationalized sector), as, for example, City institutions acquired increasing equity stakes in industrial and commercial enterprises; and, during the 1960s, the diversification of the City into the fast-expanding Eurocurrency and Eurobond markets. On the other hand, they intensified the weaknesses of domestic industry. As the periods of 'go' got shorter and those of 'stop' longer, so it became increasingly difficult for firms to improve levels of investment, productivity and output. In addition, despite the devaluations of sterling between the mid-1960s and mid-1970s, the prices of British exports remained *comparatively* high; whilst the inevitable rise in the prices of imported goods fuelled domestic inflation.

Moreover, the priority attached to the interests of the internationally orientated sector of industrial capital and, more especially, the financial sector, severely restricted the potential for a state-induced programme of *modernization* of domestic industry. Even when circumstances changed somewhat during the 1960s and 1970s, the continued dominance of these class fractions served to limit the scope for such state intervention, as is demonstrated in the failures of 'indicative planning' during the 1960s and industrial reorganization policy during the 1970s (issues to which we shall return in later chapters). More recently, of course, the intensification of the economic crisis has further restricted the scope for state intervention and has provided the context for a substantial reorientation of the direction of government strategy, clearly exemplified in the programme which has been pursued by the Conservative administrations since 1979.

A further element in the explanation of Britain's particularly severe economic problems during the years since 1945 has been the peculiar character and *defensive* economic power of the organized labour movement. Again in consequence of nineteenth-century economic development, trades unions have developed in Britain with high levels of membership in industry, an absence of religious and political divisions that might undermine union solidarity during disputes and strong organizaiton at shop-floor level. This, in turn, has enabled at least the better organized workers to establish significant elements of control over the labour process; and this has been manifested in restrictive practices concerning demarcation, apprenticeships, manning levels, work rates, overtime and so forth, as well as in shop-floor resistance to the reorganization of production (Friedman, 1977). In consequence, industrial capital has been reluctant to re-equip and restructure, and has often preferred to invest overseas where labour was more compliant; and we have already charted the effects of these trends.

Moreover, of course, the commitment of post-war administrations to the maintenance of full employment through Keynesian demand management and to the provision of a substanial Welfare State, further strengthened the power of organized labour (as well as being, in part, a reflection of that strength). Hence, during the 1950s and 1960s, conditions of relative labour-shortage greatly increased the incidence of plant- and company-level bargaining over wages and the terms of industrial reorganization. This resulted in an enhanced ability on the part of labour to resist reductions in real wages; and, thereby, compounded the difficulties experienced by industrial capital (Glyn and Sutcliffe, 1972). In addition, the expansion of state expenditure and employment, which was made necessary not only by electoral pressures, but also by the demands of Keynesian economic management, gave rise to a considerable increase in taxation levels. To the extent that this fell upon industry, it heightened profitability problems. Conversely, insofar as the major burden was shifted on to earned income and consumption (and this was the major trend), it fuelled trades union militancy and industrial disputes; and this was so, despite the continued attempts of the unions to keep up the level of the 'social wage'. Accordingly, given the continued slow expansion of the economy, by the later 1960s, the British state was beset by both a 'crisis of industrial relations' and an emergent 'fiscal crisis' (Jessop, 1980).

As we shall see in later chapters, attempts to resolve these crises, as well as to modernize British industry, have preoccupied successive governments since the end of the long boom. More recently, however, the intensification of Britain's industrial decline has substantially changed the terms on which such attempts have been made. Most crucially in the present context, the massive increase in unemployment through the 1970s has undermined the strength of the trades unions. This – amongst other factors – has opened up the possibilities both for the direct control of the power of organized labour and for the major redirection of state expenditure. What is less clear, however, is that either of these strategies has effected any long-term improvement in the performance of British capital.

In summary, then, Britain's contemporary crisis has been determined *both* by deep-seated trends in the international economy *and* quite specific features of the British social formation. Hence, the decline of the rate of profit at the international level since the end of the long boom has set the essential context for British economic development and precludes a purely domestic solution to Britain's crisis. At the same time, the latter has assumed especially acute proportions, given the failures of British industry *relative to* its immediate rivals. These failures, in turn, have been seen to be rooted in the characteristic class relations of British society: the dominance of financial and international industrial capital; the defensive strength of organized labour; and so forth. It remains, therefore, for us to explore the ways in which these general patterns have manifested themselves in the urban development which has been characteristic of post-war Britain. Our analysis at this stage will be somewhat preliminary, setting out only the general issues; we shall return to many of the points raised in later chapters.

Post-war patterns of urban and regional restructuring

Our purpose in this section, therefore, is to establish how the *general* processes of capital accumulation which we have described, have worked *unevenly across space*. In the same way as in earlier periods, the years since the Second World War have been marked by profound differences between the regions and localities of Britain in patterns of investment and disinvestment; employment growth and decline; consequent levels of prosperity and economic hardship; and so forth. These patterns, in turn, have set the context for the movement of population, the amount and distribution of house-building, the development and redevelopment of the urban infrastructure and the provision of state facilities generally. In short, then, Britain's post-war urban experience has been conditioned by the spatial manifestations of the accumulation process; accordingly, what has happened in the inner cities cannot be comprehended in isolation from developments elsewhere in, say, surburbia or the peripheral industrial regions. Moreover, as we might expect, the phases of accumulation which we have noted generally have been clearly reflected in the changes in towns and cities with which we are principally concerned here.

The period of the long boom

As we showed earlier, the 1920s and 1930s were remarkable for the severity of the disparities between the peripheral regions of 'Outer Britain' and the Midlands and the South East. However, the expansion of demand resulting from the Second World War served to revive the economies of the traditional industrial regions; whilst the direction of key elements of manufacturing (for example, of munitions) away from the strategically vulnerable regions of Britain by the war-time government further reduced the inter-war disparities. In addition, of course, bombing damage severely disrupted the economic functioning of many urban centres, especially in the newer industrial concentrations of 'Inner Britain'; as well as destroying substantial residential areas (for example, Pollard, 1962).

Nevertheless, the period of the long boom through the 1950s and earlier 1960s saw the reappearance of major regional inequalities, along lines which paralleled those of the years before the Second World War. It is true that immediate post-war reconstruction during the 1940s generated high levels of demand for the products of the peripheral regions. Moreover, after the resolution of the economic crisis of 1948 to 1951, the generally favourable conditions of the 1950s were reflected in the continued expansion of output and low levels of unemployment in these regions. However, it remains the case that the principal focus of the most dynamic elements of industry during these years remained in the regions of 'Inner Britain', where the inter-war growth had also been centred.

Accordingly, the established industries of the peripheral regions expanded during the period of the long boom by taking on labour and operating existing capacity to its fullest extent. Generally, where investments were made this involved the simple replacement of out-moded and defunct technology: a process of making good the earlier absence of investment, rather than securing substantial increases in productivity through the introduction of wholly new production methods (Hudson, 1983). Moreover, of course, these regions remained crucially dependent upon a relatively narrow range of industries. Here, the role of coal was central, as, at this time, the British economy as a whole continued to be based upon this single fuel source. Equally, however, other traditional industries were relatively buoyant; hence, for example, iron and steel and shipbuilding were able to expand in response to both general economic conditions and more specific circumstances, such as the Korean War of the 1950s. Nevertheless, there *was* some growth in sectors which were new to these areas. Certain types of manufacturing (such as chemicals, electrical engineering, motor-car components and so on), many of which had moved to the regions of 'Outer Britain' under the influence of the regional policies of the 1930s, war-time decentralization of production and the strengthened regional policies of the period between 1945 and 1948, were able to increase output quite dramatically, with large rises in labour productivity, frequently associated with the employment of women entering (peace-time) occupations for the first time (for example, Morgan, 1982).

Generally, then, these circumstances implied *historically* low levels of unemployment in the traditional industrial regions during much of the 1950s. This, in turn, accorded very well with the priorities of the organized labour movement, which was extremely anxious to avoid any return to the economic desolation of the 1930s, and served to ensure generally high levels of compliance with the strategies of capital and the state; reinforced, no doubt, by the rising real wages of the period (Rees and Lambert, 1981). However, such unemployment levels were only made possible by the considerable movement of population away from these regions to the South East and the Midlands, where labour shortages were severe. It is this fact which provides the key to the real dynamic of the long-boom economy.

The essential point, then, is that the industries which constituted the *core* of the British economy's expansion during the 1950s were, for the most part, concentrated in the regions of 'Inner Britain'. As we have seen, it is here that they had located during the 1920s and 1930s, when their growth had been restricted by the generally low levels of demand of those years. However, the rapidly expanding home-based consumer markets of the long boom, as well as Britain's relatively favourable external trading relations, created the conditions in which they could expand output and employment significantly (although this expansion was somewhat constrained by the policies of 'stop – go', as we mentioned earlier). Hence, the Midlands and the South East became the centres of the modern growth industries, such as electrical engineering, motor-car manufacture, pharmaceuticals, etc., which embodied some of the most advanced and productive elements of the British economy; and, not surprisingly, unemployment in these areas fell to very low levels indeed, averaging only around 1 per cent. Therefore, despite what we have said about the historically favourable conditions of the peripheral industrial regions, they remained *relatively* disadvantaged; and – however difficult for 1980s observers to believe – their unemployment rates of some 3 per cent came to constitute, by the end of the 1950s, an important reassertion of the 'regional problem' (for example, McCrone, 1969).

These changes in the industrial structure of Britain were mirrored in major shifts in patterns of urban development too. We have already referred to the movement of population from the 'Outer Britain' of the North and West to the South East and the Midlands. Allied to the overall increase in population during the 1950s (by some 5 per cent between 1951 and 1961) and the rising rate of household formation, this clearly imposed substantial pressures on the existing urban centres, focused in the more prosperous areas. Accordingly, most sizeable towns faced quite acute housing shortages during the earlier post-war years. In consequence, large amounts of existing housing stock, much of it in the inner urban areas and scheduled for slum clearance before 1939, had to be retained; and it was not until the 1960s that any very significant inroads were made on this problem (English *et al.*, 1976). However, at the same time, there was a sustained boom in housebuilding, which maintained the trend towards suburban expansion, which we have seen was a major feature of the inter-war period. Initially, this was concentrated in the state sector. However, fuelled by the rising levels of real wages which the economic expansion of these years made possible, it soon became a boom in owner-occupied housing, provided by private builders (Merrett, 1979 and 1982). And, moreover, it set in train a substantial rise in house prices and, in most parts of the country, those for land as well (Cox 1984).

It is also clear that the phase of accumulation expressed in the long boom created the conditions for the substantial restructuring of the central areas of many of the larger towns and cities, in particular, of the Midlands and the South East (although by no means exclusively so). The extent of this restructuring is indicated by the fact that, by 1962, about a third of urban areas with more than 5,000,000 inhabitants, a half of those with 40,000 to 100,000 inhabitants and a quarter of those with 20,000 to 40,000 inhabitants were involved in redevelopment schemes (Cox, 1984). Some of these reflected the growth of the slum clearance programme towards the end of the 1950s. However, the majority reflectd much wider economic trends. Hence, the rapid expansion of the tertiary sector generated a growing demand for offices; whilst the burgeoning consumer economy – central to the long boom itself – was reflected in the creation of new, larger retail outlets, in maximally accessible locations. And these, in turn, enabled the spawning of a new industry – property development – which was to exert an important influence upon post-war change more generally (Marriott, 1967).

Furthermore, rising levels of prosperity also made necessary the reconstruction of the transportation networks of many urban areas. Car-ownership increased dramatically during the 1950s: a reflection of the importance of the motor-car industry to the long-boom economy. Indeed, the number of vehicles on the road rose from

2,300,000 in 1940 to 9,400,000 in 1960; and commuting became an established part of the daily lives of a substantial proportion of the population. As the government report, *Traffic in Towns* (Buchanan, 1963), was to recognize, the effect was to render obsolete much of the existing transportation infrastructure, thereby necessitating enormous state expenditure on its redevelopment. Much more widely, of course, all of the urban restructuring during this period was supported by extensive state expenditure and thus contributed to the general rise in public spending during these years (Ball, 1983).

Economic decline and restructuring

If the expansionary dynamic of the long boom produced determinate patterns of urban and regional change, so the onset of economic decline during the 1960s likewise created characteristic forms of spatial development. Hence, as we might expect, the effects of the ending of the long boom were felt earliest in the traditional industrial regions of 'Outer Britain'. In particular, the late 1950s saw the beginnings of major reductions in employment in shipbuilding and coalmining, both, of course, concentrated in these areas (for example, Hudson, 1983; Morgan, 1982). However, it is important to emphasize – and we shall reiterate the general point later – that there was a *diversity* of processes involved in these changes. In the former, problems of profitability arose as a result of the failure of the British industry to compete successfully with foreign producers, using more modern techniques: as we have seen, the paradigm post-war experience of domestic manufacturing. But in coalmining, the fall in employment resulted directly from the decision of the British state to capitalize upon the availability of cheap oil on the international market, by converting to a multi-fuel economy; thereby – it was hoped – reducing the energy costs of the large part of manufacturing industry. This implied the reduction of total coal output and, more specifically, the closure of high-cost pits, which had especially severe consequences for those coalfield areas in which these pits were concentrated. In South Wales, for example, employment was reduced from 93,000 jobs in 1959 to 38,000 in 1970, with the closure of no less than 87 collieries (Francis and Smith, 1980).

However, through much of the 1960s and earlier 1970s, the effects of these job losses in traditional industries were offset by the *growth* of employment in the peripheral industrial regions in new types of manufacturing and the services sector. These changes, then, reflected complex, general processes of reorganization in the British economy, in the face of the mounting crisis which it was experiencing (and which we sketched earlier). But what is crucial for our present purposes is that these broad patterns of national economic change had profoundly differing effects on different parts of the country and it was these local effects that provided the immediate context for urban and regional restructuring during these years.

To begin with, let us consider employment decline. We have already noted the loss of jobs in some of the traditional industries of the peripheral regions, during the 1960s in particular. However, superimposed upon these changes, was an increasingly significant loss of jobs from the manufacturing sector: hence, manufacturing employment fell from some 36 per cent of the total workforce in 1961 to only some 28 per cent by the end of the 1970s. Most importantly, the spatial consequences of this decline were very different from that of the older industries. Hence, employment losses were *not* concentrated almost wholly into particular regions, but were much more pervasive. Nevertheless, it remains the case that those areas which were most heavily dependent upon manufacturing, correspondingly, were most severely affected.

For example, manufacturing employment in the North West fell from the early 1960s, gradually picking up speed to lose 20 per cent of its manufacturing jobs between 1966 and 1976. Even the West Midlands, one of the heartlands of growth industries during the long boom, lost some 10 per cent of its manufacturing jobs during the 10 years after 1965 (Cambridge Economic Policy Group, 1982). Most striking of all, however, were the effects of the decline in manufacturing on the large urban centres. Nowhere was this clearer than in London, where 200,000 manufacturing jobs were lost every five years between 1961 and 1976 (Massey, 1983a). As Hall *et al.* (1973) have indicated, London's experience was simply an early and intense expression of a more general trend and we shall consider it in greater detail later.

However, it should not be thought that employment decline was the only result of the changes in industrial activity which took place during this period. Certain sectors of the economy, of course, expanded. And, more significantly, what economic activity there was, became reorganized in a way which implied for certain types of locality quite dramatic growth and development. Indeed, as we have mentioned, the traditional industrial areas benefited in this way.

The crudest expression of this spatial reordering of economic activity is in terms of an 'urban – rural shift'. Hence, for example, Fothergill and Gudgin (1982) conclude from their extensive empirical analysis:

> The decline of cities and growth of small towns and rural areas is the dominant aspect of change in location of manufacturing industry in Britain and other Western industrial economies. The strength and pervasiveness of this urban – rural shift has been remarkable, and there is every prospect of it continuing. . . . The larger and more industrial a settlement, the faster its decline. At the two extremes, London lost nearly

40 per cent of its manufacturing jobs between 1959 and 1975, while the most rural areas increased theirs by nearly 80 per cent during the same period. (1982: 68)

Other commentators have noted that superimposed upon this general pattern is a regional differentiation, with the previously largely non-industrial areas of southern Britain having displayed a particular dynamism (Hall, 1981). Indeed, by the 1970s, the notion of a British 'sun-belt' (by analogy with the enormous growth which has taken place in the southern and western states of the United States) had achieved some currency, to describe the broad corridor running from Bristol and Southampton, along the line of the M4 motorway, and up to Cambridge.

The key here is provided by the changes which occurred in the organization of capitalist firms. As we have noted, in response to competitive pressures, there has been a long-term tendency toward the growth in the size of firms. However, in face of the problems of the 1960s, this intensified to the extent that Prais (1976) writes in terms of the emergence of the 'giant firm'; and the growing importance of the multinational companies was a further manifestation of this tendency. These changes were paralleled by often dramatic restructuring of the production process, frequently involving more intensive capitalization. And this, in turn, enabled the splitting up of large industrial complexes and the distribution of separate functions within the production process to their *individually* most appropriate locations (for example, Lipietz, 1977).

One consequence of these changes was the increasing separation of the 'higher-order' functions of conceptualization and control – planning, design, administration, marketing and so forth – from the actual production of commodities. Moreover, such 'head office' activities tended to concentrate geographically in London and the South East: for example, by 1977, 350 of the top 500 British companies had their headquarters in this part of Britain. And this, as we shall see, was associated with major changes in the urban structure of the metropolitan area.

However, in terms of actual production itself, the *trend* was the opposite. There was a relative shift not only outwards from the central cities to the suburbs and smaller towns of the rural areas; but also away from the South East and the Midlands toward the 'Outer Britain' of the North and West. Generally, then, capital's attempts to counter the decline in profit rates, which we saw earlier was a central feature of the phase of accumulation ushered in by the end of the long boom, involved the growing *centralization* of capital, combined with the geographical *decentralization* of production units. In this way, then, capital's reorganization was experienced quite differently by distinct types of locality.

Of course, these broad trends subsume a variety of changes in different industries and even in firms within the same industry (Massey and Meegan, 1982). Hence, for example, it is in industries such as telecommunications, parts of electrical engineering, and electronics that the processes which we have outlined were most clearly exemplified. Here, as the production process moved towards increasing mechanization or techniques involving major assembly stages, so there were shifts in the sort of labour required. As Massey (1983) puts it, '[t]he archetypal shift [wa]s from male manual workers classified as skilled to female assemblers classified as unskilled or semi-skilled.' (1983: 23)[2] What this implied in geographical terms was that firms were no longer constrained by the concentrations of traditional 'skilled labour' in the urban manufacturing centres, especially of the Midlands and the South East, and were able to seek out new types of worker, frequently worse paid and organized, in new types of locality. In addition, therefore, to raising levels of productivity, the introduction of such new methods of production had the effect of breaking up urban concentrations of *organized* labour, based around traditional, male-dominated trades unions, thereby further easing capital's problems.

In other instances, however, change in the labour process were less significant. In the clothing industry, for example, given growing competition from low-cost imports, it was the availability of traditional, female labour which was the prime determinant of the decentralizaton of production, at least by the larger firms. By shifting to smaller towns, trading estates and even sometimes quite isolated areas in the peripheral regions, such firms were able to capitalize upon the availability of older, married women in such places and, equally, to evade competition for workers from, in particular, the tertiary sector in the established urban centres (Massey and Meegan, 1982).

Even in the tertiary sector itself, however, there was a major dispersal of at least the *more routine* aspects of clerical and other administrative work; largely in response to the fact that both clerical wages and office rents decline rather sharply in suburban and more peripheral locations. Perhaps most notable here was the shift of many thousands of jobs in the central departments of the Civil Service to regions such as South Wales and the North East of England, mostly during the period of rationalization and modernization of the state bureaucracy in the late 1960s and early 1970s. (Winckler, forthcoming 1985). But there was also a striking shift in the private sector; although here it was the outer suburban

[2]In this context, it is worth noting that women increased from some 30 per cent of the total workforce in 1961 to over 40 per cent by the 1970s. Much of this increase was accounted for by married women going out of the home to work.

areas, rather than the peripheral regions, which were the principal recipients of new jobs. Of course, neither of these trends involved the abandonment of the central urban areas by office activity; not only was the sector as a whole expanding substantially at this time, but also the higher levels of administration remained largely centrally concentrated (Pickvance, 1981).

What this *diversity* of specific trends implied, then, was the emergence of often very local patterns of change, with each area experiencing the effects of economic reorganization in quite distinct ways. Moreover, the results of such changes in any given locality were determined not simply by the *current* 'round of investment', but also by the residue of earlier ones (Massey, 1978). Hence, for example, the effects of productive decentralization during the 1960s and early 1970s on communities such as those in South Wales were quite different from those in, say, Mid Wales, as a result of the differing economic and social structures produced in the *historical* dependence of the former upon coalmining and the latter on agriculture (Rees, 1984).

Nevertheless, for analytical purposes, certain broad dimensions of spatial restructuring can be identified. Hence, certainly by the mid-1970s, the effects of the changes we have sketched were apparent in the general growth of employment in non-urban areas. However, within this, it is important to distinguish between the experience of the so-called 'sun-belt' and that of the peripheral regions.

In the former, expansion was most striking in new industrial sectors and especially in scientific and technological development, in which research played a major role. This was so both for the research and development sections of the major corporations, as well as for a wide variety of independent 'business services' (such as computer consultancies) and high-technology industries. The jobs created in such sectors tended, of course, to be in the higher echelons of the occupational hierarchy; moreover, as a result of the functional separation within the production process which we described earlier, there was a tendency for the higher levels of management to concentrate in this region also. Hence, the 'sun-belt' emerged with a distinctive social status, as well as industrial structure (Massey, 1983a).

In the peripheral regions, on the other hand, and more specifically in the centres of traditional heavy industry, the loss of jobs from these sectors was, to a considerable extent, balanced by employment growth in consequence of the decentralization of production and some services. Moreover, this expansion was reinforced by the development of smaller firms in these areas, often sub-contracting to the branch-plants of larger enterprises. Indeed, by the mid-1970s, a number of commentators were pointing to the convergence in conventional indicators of regional inequality (unemployment and activity rates, income levels, migration rates, etc.) as confirmation of the economic progress made by 'Outer Britain' (for example, Keeble, 1977). However, what this convergence disguised was the emergence of new forms of regional disparity. Hence there was a growing gap between centres of management and control, and areas whose industrial development was externally controlled and whose employment structures were dominated by relatively unskilled and low-paid jobs. Moreover, these latter regions were increasingly characterized by a reduction in the coherence of their productive systems, as the new branch-plants often produced only parts of products and had very limited intra-regional linkages (Dunford, 1977).

Equally, of course, what appeared as the *relative* improvement in the condition of the peripheral industrial regions, in part simply reflected the *national* decreases in manufacturing employment and their concentration in the inner-city areas, especially of the South East and the Midlands. This latter phenomenon tended to cut across conventional regional distinctions, but was, nevertheless, perhaps the most striking consequence of the reorganization of capital during these years. Table 2.4 gives an indication of its extent.

Table 2.4 Employment decline in the inner cities by sector

Sectors	'000s 1951	Index 1951 = 100 (Figures in brackets = indices relative to the UK average) 1951	1961	1966	1971	1976
Primary	13	100	91(98)	78(101)	58(96)	50(93)
Manufacturing	1785	100	92(88)	80(77)	68(67)	52(57)
Private service	1749	100	111(97)	108(86)	94(79)	88(67)
Public services	1280	100	101(96)	102(91)	103(85)	106(80)
Total	4827	100	101(94)	96(87)	86(79)	79(72)

NB. The inner areas considered comprise those of London, Birmingham, Manchester, Liverpool, Tyneside and Clydeside.

Source: Cambridge Economic Policy Group, 1982, p. 42

It was in these inner-urban areas, then, that within given industries there were the greatest concentrations of the oldest factories, employing outmoded production techniques and with chronically low levels of labour productivity. Accordingly, such areas were the most vulnerable in any capital reorganization aimed at countering declining rates of profit through raising productivity; whether by means of plant closure, of increased capitalization and productive innovation, or of transfer of production to other sites with reduced labour inputs (Massey and Meegan, 1978). Certainly, Dennis (1978) concludes from his study of manufacturing employment trends in London that, between 1966 and 1974, 27 per cent of job loss was the result of firms moving; 44 per cent of plant closure; and 23 per cent of labour-shedding by firms remaining *in situ* (although a number of these subsequently closed). Equally, most inner-city areas were highly unattractive as sites for the establishment of *new* firms (for example, Cameron, 1973); and, as we have seen, what growth did occur, tended to be located in suburban or more rural areas. Moreover, many firms which remained in the inner cities – especially in activities such as clothing, furniture-making, toy manufacture, etc. – were able to impose regimes of long working-hours, low wages, and poor work conditions upon a labour-force often drawn from highly exploitable social groups, such as women and the ethnic minorities (Community Development Project, 1977a). And, of course, it was these trends of industrial change – together with the rising unemployment which they occasioned – which prompted the state's recognition of an 'inner-city problem' during the mid-1970s (an issue we shall say more about later).

Not surprisingly given these developments, the 1960s also saw a major decentralization of population. In particular, the inner areas of the major urban centres lost large numbers of people as a result of migration trends (and in spite of relatively high levels of natural increase). Hence, for example, the population of the urban cores of cities with a 1971 population over 1,000,000 – London, Birmingham, Glasgow, Liverpool, Leeds, Manchester and Newcastle – fell by some 9 per cent between 1961 and 1971 (Kennett and Spence, 1979). Conversely, of course, the suburbs and more rural areas recorded substantial population gains; although this trend was complicated somewhat by the continued regional distinction between the North and the South of Britain, where (with the notable exception of London) population growth tended to be generally more dynamic.

The effects of these population shifts were heightened, moreover, by the composition of the migration flows. Accordingly, it was generally the more affluent, more self-sufficient and more marketable groups who were in a position to leave the inner areas. Certainly, the proportion of those in the upper socio-economic groups in cities has declined; and, as we have seen, this decline is, to some extent, mirrored in the emergence of the 'sun-belt' (although the general increase in managerial and professional groups, as well as intermediate non-manual groups, has been significant here too).[3]

[3]Generally, non-manual workers rose from 38 per cent of the total workforce in 1961 to nearly 47 per cent by the middle 1970s. Moreover, it tended to be the higher status occupations which expanded fastest (Warwick University Manpower Research Group, quoted in Massey, 1983a).

On the other hand, those with lower-than-average incomes, young adults and the relatively old have all increased proportionally in the cities (Hall, 1981).

Likewise, of course, the later 1950s and 1960s were years when considerable numbers of immigrants from Britain's former colonies in the West Indies and the Indian subcontinent settled in the inner areas of a number of British cities.[4] The processes by which this immigrant labour-force became segregated into the older inner-city neighbourhoods have been extensively documented (for example, Rex and Tomlinson, 1979). What is important to note here is that the availability of certain types of jobs was a central part of their movement. Although demand for immigrant labour occurred across quite a wide range of industries, the jobs themselves tended to be uniformly low-paid, frequently involved shift-work and were hence unattractive to the white work-force. And it is clear that the incidence of such employment in certain urban areas was closely related to the pattern of industrial reorganization and change which was characteristic of this period (Smith, 1977).

More generally, however, the relationships between the movement of population and that of employment are less clear-cut. Hence, Hall *et al.* (1973) suggest that the former began somewhat before the major decentralization of jobs; although by the later 1960s, the two movements were more closely synchronized. What this indicates, then, is that there was no simple causal mechanism by which population followed jobs to the less urban areas. Indeed, in certain circumstances, population growth itself creates jobs, especially in certain of the service, such as education or health-care.

What was also of significance in determining the outward movement of population as a whole, was the fact that the supply of new owner-occupied housing – in good condition, at the right cost and of an appropriate size for family use – was overwhelmingly concentrated in the suburbs and more rural areas. Hence, by the middle 1960s, some 200,000 new private dwellings were being started each year; however, given the substantial availability of public infrastructural investment, the locational preferences of the building firms were focused on green-field sites in the non-urban areas (Ball, 1983). In addition, of course, the continued rise in the prices of

[4]*Residents in Great Britain born in the New Commonwealth (including Pakistan)* (thousands)

1951	1961	1966	1971	1981
218	541	853	1151	1513

Source: Castles *et al.* (1984) p. 43
Geographical concentration into particular urban regions was extremely significant, with London and Birmingham playing the most prominent role.

housing and land through the 1960s and early 1970s, reinforced the difficulties of lower-income groups in breaking into the housing market; thereby, accentuating the social divisiveness of home ownership.

At the same time, the acceleration of the slum clearance programme was *forcing* the movement of many thousands of families to the suburban overspill estates built by many local authorities during these years. Moreover, the land which was thus released in the central areas tended not to be redeveloped to such high housing densities (even in high-rise schemes). Indeed, increasingly, it was not redeveloped at all; and certainly by the 1970s, with the reduction in national building programmes, demolitions were exceeding local authority construction in all but one of the conurbations outside London (Jones, 1979).

These decentralizing pressures in the sphere of housing were strengthened by the effects of town-centre office and retail development schemes, which continued throughout the 1960s in response to the generally rising demands of the tertiary sector. By the end of the decade, however, these demands – especially for office space – intensified and the property development sector entered a period of quite remarkable boom, during which commercial property rents and values increased massively. Accordingly, investment in property development mushroomed, with both the mainstream financial institutions of 'the City' and the secondary banks playing a particularly prominent role: so much so, indeed, that it was widely argued that manufacturing industry was being starved of funds at a time of mounting industrial crisis (for example, Massey and Catalano, 1978). However, the boom proved short-lived and the market collapsed during 1973–74, incurring enormous losses for many investors and leaving many office blocks empty. In the event, this was merely a prelude to the wider intensification of urban problems, as the national economy has plunged into the heightened crisis of the later 1970s and 1980s.

The economic crisis of the later 1970s and 1980s

As we have seen, the years since the mid-1970s have been marked by a deepening of Britain's economic problems. Most striking has been the rapid increase in rates of unemployment, as manufacturing industry has gone further down the road of de-industrialization and even the previously expanding services sector has begun to contract. And once again, of course, these general trends have been fully reflected in patterns of urban and regional development.

A useful starting point in examining these patterns is provided in Table 2.5, which shows the spatial distribution of male unemployment on the eve of the 1981 urban riots (Hamnett, 1983).

Table 2.5   Urban and regional rates of male unemployment in England in April 1981

Area	Male unemployment as % of all men (Figures in brackets = male unemployment as % of economically active men)
England	10.0 (11.0)
North	14.5 (16.2)
Tyne and Wear Metropolitan County	16.5 (18.5)
Newcastle/Gateshead Partnership	16.8 (18.9)
North West	13.0 (14.5)
Greater Manchester Metropolitan County	12.6 (14.0)
Manchester/Salford Partnership	21.4 (25.0)
Merseyside Metropolitan County	17.8 (20.0)
Liverpool	21.6 (24.4)
Liverpool Partnership	23.1 (26.0)
West Midlands	12.7 (13.9)
West Midlands Metropolitan County	15.7 (17.2)
Birmingham	16.7 (18.5)
Birmingham Partnership	18.7 (20.7)
Yorkshire and Humberside	11.2 (12.4)
East Anglia	8.1 (8.8)
East Midlands	9.0 (9.9)
South East	7.8 (8.6)
Greater London	9.3 (10.3)
Inner London	12.8 (14.4)
Lambeth Partnership	13.7 (15.5)
Hackney/Islington Partnership	15.1 (17.0)
Docklands Partnership	16.1 (18.3)
South West	8.2 (8.1)

Source: Hamnett (1983), p. 9

One feature of this distribution which emerges very clearly is that, whatever the situation in the mid-1970s, by the early 1980s there had been a reassertion of something approaching a traditional 'regional problem'. Hence, male unemployment in the northern part of England (the North, North West and Yorkshire and Humberside) was significantly above the national average and well in excess of that in the South East and its adjacent regions, East Anglia, the East Midlands and the South West. Moreover, if the figures for Scotland (12.3 per cent) and Wales (12.9 per cent) are added, then the familiar distinction between 'Outer' and 'Inner Britain' seems re-established. What had changed was that the level of male unemployment *nationally* had risen significantly; and, more specifically, the West Midlands had moved into the 'Outer Britain' category, as a result of the especially dramatic collapse of manufacturing industry in this region (losing some 160,000 from its manufacturing workforce between 1979 and 1981 alone (Cambridge Economic Policy Group, 1982)).

This re-widening of the gap between the older industrial regions and much of the rest of the country partly results from the vulnerability of those manufacturing plants established in these areas as a result of the 1960s decentralization of production, to the effects of the intense recession of the later 1970s. In particular, such areas have suffered not only from the general reduction in demand, but also from the increasing competition from the *really* low-wage areas of the world, such as Mediterranean Europe and certain Third World countries (for example, Hudson, 1983).

In addition, however, some of the traditional industries of these regions have entered a period of severest crisis. Most spectacular here has been the British steel industry, which has recorded extremely large job losses, as it has – belatedly – attempted to reorganize in the face of a changed world pattern of steel production and the especially dramatic collapse of demand from the British steel-consuming sectors of manufacturing. Hence, for instance, the steel-producing areas of South Wales lost some 12,000 jobs in consequence of the 1980 redundancy programme, with resulting sharp rises in local unemployment rates (for example, Morgan, 1983).

The second general point to emerge from Table 2.5 is that the broad regional picture we have sketched is complicated by the further deterioration of employment in the inner areas of the major urban centres. Hence, the highest levels of unemployment are recorded in the inner cities (represented in the table by the Partnership areas designated under the inner cities policy initiatives of the late 1970s). And this is true even for those inner urban areas which are part of the *generally* prosperous South East region. In part, of course, this reflects the continuation of the trends in the distribution of manufacturing employment which we have identified as characteristic of the 1960s and earlier 1970s. However, their effects have been exacerbated by general conditions since the later 1970s, when demand, output and employment have all fallen substantially across the economy as a whole. In addition, the cities have been adversely affected by the recent changes in the services, where the longer-term decline in the private sector is no longer cushioned by public service employment increases (as may be inferred from Table 2.4). These shifts are likely to exert marked effects on female unemployment, which otherwise has been broadly coincident with that of men during this latest period of economic crisis: it is notable, for example, that the *number* of women in employment in 1982 was below that for 1964 (8,500,000 compared with over 9,000,000) (Massey, 1983a).

Other social groups have been especially hard hit by the general rise in inner-city unemployment during the present recession. Hence, for example, Thrift (1979) points out in his review of urban employment problems that the incidence of unemployment is significantly higher amongst unskilled workers. Similarly, young people face acute difficulties in getting work; as do the members of the ethnic minorities. It is highly instructive, for instance, that a recent survey by the Commission for Racial Equality revealed that six out of every 10 black teenagers and four out of every 10 Asian teenagers were unemployed (Commission for Racial Equality, 1982).

However, the mounting employment problems of the inner cities are marked not simply in levels of unemployment, but also in the continued deterioration in the *quality* of the jobs which remain. Hence, the growth in part-time work, home-working and sweat-shops in such areas is as much an indication of the effects of the economic crisis as high rates of unemployment are (Friend and Metcalfe, 1981). Indeed, some commentators have written (perhaps somewhat simplistically) in terms of the development of a 'secondary labour market' in the inner urban areas. For example, Scott (1982) argues:

[M]uch of the metropolitan labour force, even today, remains effectively unorganized, and this is above all the case in the so-called secondary labour market that is invariably found in and around the cores of large metropolitan areas. . . . The secondary labour market is characterized by low-wage immigrant and ethnic workers, and is typically associated with high female participation rates in the work force. It is also marked by abnormally high incidences of unemployment. As a corollary, industrial wage rates at present tend to be lower in inner city areas than in any other part of the metropolis. (1982: 115)

In short, then, an essential part of recent economic change in the inner cities has been the intensification of highly exploitative *forms* of work. Moreover, such forms are made possible by the availability of marginal workers, who have concentrated into the inner areas as a result of the socially differentiated flows of population which we outlined earlier (and which, it should be noted, have slowed somewhat during most recent years).

All in all, therefore, the period of heightened economic crisis since the later 1970s has been characterized by a rapid further deterioration of the situation in Britain's inner-city areas. Moreover, much more widely, towns and cities have stagnated, as the recession (with its high interest rates and falling real wages) has discouraged investment in either property development or house-building. Perhaps most crucially of all, state expenditure on most aspects of urban development has been severely curtailed during these years as well, thereby imposing a further brake upon urban change. It is to understanding this emergent role of the state in urban and regional development that we devote what remains of this book.

3

Post-war reconstruction, the long boom and the denial of planning

In the previous chapter, we presented an analysis of the emergence of the contemporary urban crisis from long-standing processes of industrial and employment change, shifts in the structure of city populations and the re-shaping of housing provision and the built environment more generally. Whilst there is certainly no unanimity in the literature, we sought to indicate our own view that these patterns of urban change have been rooted in deep-seated shifts in the economic and social condition of Britain; shifts which, in turn, are best understood by reference to certain essential features of capitalist social relations.

This chapter begins our exploration of the role of the state in all this. As we suggested earlier, it is clear that the state has come to exert a pervasive influence upon the organization of capitalist societies such as Britain. More specifically too, a significant element of the state's activities has attempted to shape processes of urban and regional change, through, for example, regional economic policy, land-use planning, housing policy and so forth. Accordingly, the relationships between such state intervention and the actual patterns of development which we have described (in Chapter 2) constitute a central topic of analysis, which will concern us for most of the remainder of the book.

Here, however, we shall focus upon what is frequently referred to as the 'post-war planning system'. This was the policy-system which derived from a series of war-time Commissions and Committees, whose recommendations were, in large part, enacted in a major legislative programme by the Labour administrations between 1945 and 1951, the highpoint of social reconstruction after the Second World War. It has been characterized as the first thoroughgoing attempt to improve the social and economic condition of the people of Britain as a whole, by means of the control of the geographical distribution of employment and population, the planning of land-uses and development, the provision of better housing and physical environments, and so on. It remained the principal means by which the state sought to eradicate what were seen as the problems of

Britain's towns and cities throughout the 1950s and earlier 1960s. Only as the long boom finally ended were wholly new forms of state intervention attempted.

Now, again as we have suggested earlier, the conventional 'Whig interpretation' argues that there was a persistent disjuncture between what had been intended for this planning system and what it actually achieved. This failure, moreover, is represented as the consequence of the *technical* shortcomings of planning intervention and, thereby, as necessitating its reform and improvement. Indeed, this was what actually happened during the later 1960s and early 1970s, as we shall see in subsequent chapters. However, again as we have indicated, we are sceptical of the simplicities of such a 'Whig interpretation'. Accordingly, in what follows, we present a reassessment of the post-war planning system, in a manner consistent with our earlier, theoretical discussion.

Hence, it is certainly the case that only to a very limited extent were the objectives which were publicly espoused for post-war planning actually fulfilled. But it does not follow that this was indicative of some sort of technical failure on the part of policy-makers or professional planners. Rather, the system of planning which was developed during these years was itself the product of the conflicting interests of class and other social groupings, as these were mediated by the political parties and other organizations, and the state itself. These interests, in turn, reflected – in some sense – the exigencies of the particular phase of accumulation embodied in the period of reconstruction and the long boom. Accordingly, the *effects* which post-war planning yielded may be comprehended only by reference to the social processes by which such conflictual interests were worked out. Moreover, once it had been created, the post-war planning system itself became an arena within which these conflicts were expressed.

The genesis of post-war planning

Donnison (1980) provides an admirably succinct account of the legislative basis of the post-war system:

> [T]he Town and Country Planning Act of 1947 . . . gave Counties and County Boroughs a duty to regulate nearly all development of land . . . .
> [It] was the most important in a series of five Acts, passed within seven years, which together created a planning system that has not been fundamentally changed since. The others were the Distribution of Industry Act 1945 giving powers to regulate the location of industry and to attract industrialists to chosen regions; the New Towns Act 1946 providing for the building of new towns by public development corporations; the National Parks and Access to the Countryside Act 1949 giving planning authorities powers to run countryside parks with advice

from a central commission; and the Town Development Act 1952 enabling big cities, with help from central government, to collaborate with smaller towns which are prepared to take some of their people. (1980: 3–4)

Moreover, this system has been characterized in terms of a *coherent* set of objectives, which in effect describes a desired future pattern of urban and regional development, to be achieved by the policy instruments contained in the new legislation (for example, Hall *et al.*, 1973). These can be summarized under three headings:

(i) *Regional balance* by means of the redirection of industrial development away from the relatively prosperous South East and Midlands toward the depressed 'Outer Britain' of the North and West. The central policy instruments were, of course, the locational controls and incentives introduced by the Distribution of Industry Act (and subsequently confirmed in the 1947 Town and Country Planning Act); although certain of the non-metropolitan New Towns were also intended to stimulate economic growth in depressed areas.

(ii) *Urban containment* entailing an end to sprawling suburban growth and the preservation of the countryside and agricultural land. The Development Planning and Control systems of the 1947 Town and Country Planning Act were to be the primary policy instruments. The declaration of 'Green Belts', initially around London, but extended in 1955 to all major cities, reinforced the Development Plans, by their presumption against permission for new development. And future population growth would be directed away from the existing conurbations (especially London) to the planned developments in the New Towns and elsewhere.

(iii) *The reconstruction of the urban centres* to provide much higher levels of physical and social amenity than had been the case previously: for some towns and cities, moreover, the need for reconstruction was literal because of extensive bomb damage. Hence, large-scale slum clearance and central area redevelopment were planned to specified standards of physical design. And again, the New Towns would provide decent homes and jobs for those families who could not be rehoused in the transformed urban areas.

The main dimensions of this system were clearly set out by Lewis Silkin, the Minister of Town and Country Planning, in his remarkable two-hour speech in the debate on the Second Reading of the Town and Country Planning Bill in 1947. It is worth quoting him at some length:

[T]he objectives of town and country planning . . . are to secure a proper balance between competing demands for land, so that all the land of the country is used in the best interests of the whole people . . . [Land will be needed for] the housing programme, including the clearance of slums and the rebuilding of blitzed areas, the redevelopment of obsolete and badly laid out areas, the dispersal of population and industry from our large, overcrowded cities to new towns . . . .

On the other hand, town and country planning must preserve land from development. A high level of agricultural production is vital. More land must be kept for forestry . . . . And it is important to safeguard the beauty of the countryside and coast-line [in order to] enable more people to enjoy them . . . .

. . . these conflicting demands for land must be dovetailed together. If each is considered in isolation, the common interest is bound to suffer. Housing must be so located in relation to industry that workers are not compelled to make long, tiring and expensive journeys to and from work. Nor must our already large towns be permitted to sprawl, and expand, so as to eat up the adjacent rural areas and make access to the countryside and to the amenities in the centre of town more difficult. Green belts must be left around towns, and the most fertile land kept for food production. The continued drift from the countryside must be arrested . . . . [B]etween the wars, industry tended to concentrate in the South of England, with the result that towns in the South, especially London, grew too large for health, efficiency and safety, while some of the older industrial areas suffered chronic unemployment. (Official Report, 1946–47, Volume 432; Second Reading of the Town and Country Planning Bill, 29 January 1947, Column 947 *et seq.*)

This lucid declaration of intentions appeared to reflect in a straightforward way the pressing problems of the day, which had been carefully examined first by the Barlow Commission on the Distribution of the Industrial Population (1940); then by the Scott Committee on Land Utilization in Rural Areas (1942); and by the Uthwatt Committee on Compensation and Betterment, which also completed its work in 1942.

What these reports had done, in effect, was to present a sober – but quite categorical – *exposé* of the essentially uncontrolled urbanization of Britain which had culminated in the crisis of the inter-war years. The catalogue should be familiar from earlier discussion: economic collapse, population loss and community decline in the traditional industrial areas; economic expansion for much of the period in the South East and the Midlands, where the growth of new types of manufacturing and services created labour shortages, a rising population, rapid urban growth and consequent congestion and overcrowding. In these same areas, urban sprawl and 'ribbon development' were eating into prime agricultural land and destroying the countryside; and the planning legislation passed after 1909 was quite incapable of preventing such trends because of the massive compensation payments to land-owners which were entailed (Cullingworth, 1979). Accordingly, during the 1920s and 1930s, some 1,000,000 acres of land in Britain were converted from agricultural to urban use: and this represented a 50 per cent increase on the previous total acreage of British towns (Best, 1981). Moreover, the boom in private, speculative building which fuelled ·this urban expansion was, of course, *directly* beneficial only to selected social groups. As Merrett (1982) puts it, the bulk of new housing was bought ' . . . by households of a very mixed social composition including the regularly employed and better paid manual and clerical workers, teachers, government employees, families with small and medium-sized businesses, and the class of executive and management personnel.' (1982: 14) At the the same time, in the major cities and increasingly in the traditional industrial areas, in spite of the slum clearance efforts of the 1930s, there was a delapidated and unhealthy housing stock (English *et al.*, 1976).

Clearly, then, in that it was agreed that these problems were the result of *uncontrolled* development, the official inquiries were unanimous in their recommendations that intervention by the state could remove them. Moreover, there was considerable consensus over the *form* which such intervention should take.

Hence, it is frequently argued that in framing their precise legislative proposals, the inquiries were powerfully influenced by the 'Town Planning Movement', which by this time had coalesced around the Garden Cities and Town Planning Association (GCTPA) (renamed the Town and Country Planning Association (TCPA) in 1942) and the Council for the Preservation of Rural England (CPRE), established in 1925. Certainly, Patrick Abercrombie and Hermione Hitchens, both central figures in the GCTPA, appear to have exerted a major influence over the Barlow Commission and, thereby, much of the debate leading up to the passage of the 1947 Town and Country Planning Act. F.J. Osborn, another stalwart of the Association, suggests in a letter to the great American urbanist, Lewis Mumford, that GCTPA views were put forward within the Commission in a concerted way. He writes:

> [W]hen [Abercrombie] was a member of the Barlow Royal Commission I redrafted for him some of the key paragraphs of the majority report and drafted some of his own minority report – but it was all very 'hush-hush' and both of us were kept hard at this underground work by Mrs W.L. Hitchens . . . . She and Abercrombie did get the wording of the main recommendations considerably strengthened, but not enough to avoid the necessity of the minority report. (Mumford and Osborn, 1971: 271)

Again, Patrick Abercrombie (1945) was commissioned to prepare the *Greater London Plan* of 1944, which encapsulated the key assumptions about urban containment, new town development for overspill population and inner-city reconstruction, and subsequently provided a model for other towns and cities to follow.

We should be careful, however, over the precise nature of the concerns of the Town Planning Movement. It drew, of course, upon the tradition of propaganda and advocacy which could be traced back to the environmental and land reformers of the Victorian period. Indeed, many of the characteristic concerns of those reformers continued to preoccupy their inter-war and even post-war inheritors. Hence, theirs was a quintessentially *Victorian* vision of the connectedness of the physical environment, the health of the populace and the smooth future development of society. Certainly, in spite of the progressiveness of many of their ideas, they should not be viewed as conventional socialists or even radicals. In fact, by the 1930s, disquiet over the decline in the birthrate had focused the antipathy of the Town Planning Movement towards urban life into an almost moral (and to present-day observers distinctly *un*progressive) concern with the eugenic properties of Britain's towns and cities. As Lewis Mumford put it in a letter to Osborn, '. . . the big city not merely devours population, but because of its essential nature prevents new babies coming into the world.' (Mumford and Osborn, 1971: 61)

Similarly, in governmental circles, much of urban policy was conceived in terms of its effects upon the nation's health. It was, after all, the *Unhealthy* Areas Committee (our emphasis), established by the Minister of Health in 1920, under the chairmanship of Neville Chamberlain, which first officially proposed the creation of 'garden cities'. Similarly, the Barlow Commission, appointed in 1937, a few months after Chamberlain had been made Prime Minister, took as one of its major themes the state of health of the urban population. As Hall *et al.* (1973) comment:

> Thus we find a considerable paradox, on which more than one observer commented at the time. The central principles and objectives of urban and regional planning were developed in England around the turn of the century, at a time when the modern social sciences scarcely existed. They then remained in a more or less fixed state for over 40 years, during which they had little practical effect but increasing intellectual influence, culminating in the Barlow Report of 1940. From that, the influence had a critical effect on the way the planning system was set up at the end of the Second World War, and on the general policy objectives of that system: planning, when it came to effective power in England, was working with ideas that were over 45 years old. (1973: 41–2)

This 'Whig' emphasis upon the continuities between the post-war planning system and earlier currents of urban reform is important. However, we should certainly guard against overstating the influence of the Town Planning Movement. Whatever the continuities, it must be remembered that the historical moment at which the planning system was finally ushered in, was highly distinctive: the aftermath of a societal war which engendered an enthusiasm for social reform and reconstruction almost without parallel (for example, Addison, 1975). Cullingworth (1975) in his *Official History of Environmental Planning*, emphasizes the extent to which there was a widespread, *popular* enthusiasm for the adoption of urban and regional planning:

> To those living in the blitzed cities of England during 1941 the relevance of (planning) was obvious, and a warm public welcome was assured for a bold and comprehensive scheme which would strike the imagination and offer to those contemplating the ruins of their homes some assurance that the government certainly meant business in the severely practical task of rebuilding the damaged cities (1975: 15)

And again:

> The war-weary public increasingly expected bold and imaginative planning which would – as with a military operation – succeed in achieving the building of a better Britain. Public imagination and determination in favour of this planning for a better Britain constituted a force which it is now difficult to appreciate. Mingled with an attitude nigh to comtempt for pre-war inadequacies, public attitudes were reflected in the continuous barrage of parliamentary questions during the early and mid forties. (1975: 252)

Moreover, Backwell and Dickens (1979) show that the war-time administration, and in particular the Ministry of Information, was well aware of the potential of urban and regional planning in offering an apparently non-controversial, apolitical means of reconstructing post-war society and, accordingly, used it extensively in their propaganda.

It must also be emphasized that the creation of the post-war planning system, based upon the *legislative* framework which we have outlined, was the product of a *political* process, in which the Town Planning Movement could be only partially involved. McDougall (1979) has made the same point in her stimulating account of the 1909 Housing and Town Planning Act, where similarly many analyses within the 'Whig tradition' fail to recognize the central significance of the interests represented in Parliament and, indeed, the state bureaucracy.

However, Donnison's (1980) brief account of the origins of the 1947 Town and Country Planning Act *does* take as its starting point the parliamentary arena. Hence, he writes in terms of Lewis Silkin's achievement in translating into parliamentary terms the very broad base of support which had been secured for planning in the country as a whole: support which embraced not simply the Town Planning Movement, but also health and housing reformers, farmers, country land-owners, commuters, local authorities, the labour movement, the tourist industry and so forth. But what made this apparently widespread consensus possible was that each of the groups involved could see something different in the proposed system; each could interpret it as being in their particular interest.

What is welcome here is the acknowledgement that the creation of the planning system involved the appeal to the power and influence of real social groupings and organizations in pursuit of what they conceived to be their material interests. Whatever the influence exerted by the Town Planning Movement over the formulation of the legislation adopted, it is important to stress that other visions of the planning system and its operation were implied within the coalition which made it possible. More particularly, any consensus was limited to the particular form of planning embodied in the legislation, rather than extending to any general agreement as to the need for a strongly interventionist state role. And, of course, there were certainly articulate, contrary voices of *laisser-faire* conservatism and liberalism, which were deeply suspicious of any central planning or any intervention in the working of the free market.

Given this, then, it is not at all surprising that the planning system which was created was limited in its scope and ambition. The extent of its limitations becomes crystal clear if we examine the actual effects of the operation of the system, rather than what was believed or claimed that it could achieve.

The achievement of post-war planning

In this section, therefore, we want to examine some of the effects of the urban planning legislation of 1945 to 1952. The principal source of information we shall use for this is the encyclopaedic study of post-war planning by Hall *et al.* (1973): in many ways, the exemplar of the 'Whig interpretation'. Certainly, it is a study which allows an assessment in terms of the three aims which we outlined in the previous section: urban containment; the reconstruction of urban centres; and regional balance. However, it also highlights other effects which take us some way toward a more thoroughgoing evaluation. To the extent that the planning system failed to achieve its publicly stated aims, then we need to ask why this should have been so. And this will lead us to a reappraisal which justifies the title of this chapter.

The containment of urban growth

Hall *et al*. (1973) conclude that the containment of urban growth was indeed achieved during the first post-war decades. However, it was only partly the result of conscious policy. More central, they argue, was the capacity of agricultural and rural preservationist pressure groups to resist the encroachment of urban development. Whilst urban local authorities were themselves loath to decentralize population out of their areas, with consequent rate losses. Most significantly, however, containment both produced and was then reinforced by soaring land prices.

We shall return to the subject of land prices later. However, a major part of the containment strategy was for overspill population to be located in the New Towns. What was their fate? Twelve New Towns were designated in England and Wales between 1946 and 1950: eight around London; two in the North East; one in South Wales; and Corby in Northamptonshire. Moreover, as numerous commentators have pointed out, they became probably the best-known aspect of post-war urban planning in Britain (for example, Schaffer, 1972). And certainly, it was intended that they should play a *central* role in the new urban and regional structure which the planning system was to produce, particularly in respect of the residential problems of the inner-urban areas. Furthermore, essential to the social rationale for the New Towns – typical of the post-war reconstruction programme – was that they should be ' . . . self-contained and balanced communities for working and living.' (Reith Report, Cmnd. 6876, 1946).

Numerous studies have now shown that in terms of 'self-containment', the first generation of New Towns can be reckoned only a partial success. Whilst on 'social balance', commentators have noted the fuzziness of the very concept. Certainly the New Towns did not correspond to some national average in terms of the distribution of population between different occupational categories. However, it is not clear what this means in terms of the class structures of the New Towns (Aldridge, 1979).

Much more certain is the under-representation of the ethnic minorities and the massive preponderance of younger people (Deakin and Ungerson, 1972). In the latter case, of course, although such a skewed age distribution may have created problems of medical, educational and welfare provision, at least the New Towns provided an exceptionally good housing market for first-time buyers. The corollary, however, was that they contributed only marginally to the solution of the housing problems of the poor of the inner cities, and the experience of the ethnic minorities was in this sense indicative of that much wider range of disadvantaged groups. Indeed, as Ebenezer Howard himself had recognized, the necessity for the New Towns to be successful in terms of attracting industry and providing good housing *implied* this failure to tackle the problem of the urban poor, unless much higher levels of housing subsidy had been forthcoming from the state.

More generally, however, what Hall *et al.* (1973) emphasize is the *numerical* insignificance of the contribution of the New Towns to the post-war housing programme and the resolution of the cities' problems. If the supposed architects of the British planning system envisaged that these planned communities would be a principal form of urban development, they were to be sorely disappointed. Even in the South East, where the New Towns were concentrated, only a little over 7 per cent of the housing programme went into the New and Expanded Towns; in the rest of England and Wales up until the mid-1960s, it was actually less than 2 per cent.

What this failure meant was that the effect of urban containment by means of highly restrictive development plans and green belt policy was to produce a pattern of residential development which was concentrated either into the private sector, in numerous small towns and villages away from the urban periphery; or into high-density, often high-rise, municipal building within the existing boundaries of the cities and larger boroughs. And, as we noted earlier, it was the former which accounted for the larger part of house-building after the immediate post-war years; which, in turn, yielded high returns for the construction firms. What must be emphasized, however, is that this pattern was very different from that envisaged at the inception of the planning system, when public-sector, planned development had been central. As Hall *et al.* (1973) note, ' . . . the new suburban communities of owner-occupied houses in the small towns and villages cater[ed] for a narrow spectrum of social classes. Coupled with the concentration of municipal housing in the cities, the result [wa]s the development of publicly sanctioned, publicly subsidized *apartheid* . . . . ' (1973: 397)

The reconstruction of the urban centres

If urban containment was, at best, only the most qualified of successes, what of the linked aim of central area reconstruction? From the mid-1950s onwards, the main thrust of local housing policies in the cities was slum clearance and over the next 10 years or so vast acreages of Victorian terraced housing were cleared away and a new generation of municipal estates put up in their place.

Yet here too there is need of qualification. Firstly, as we saw earlier, high-density, high-rise housing tended to predominate both in the cleared and redeveloped sites and in the peripheral estates which were needed to rehouse those moved from the inner areas to allow clearance to proceed. If in terms of room space and facilities this housing was a great improvement on the slums they replaced, access to jobs, schools, shops and health facilities were not necessarily improved; and municipal housing became more and more unpopular with those who had to live there. As Dunleavy (1981) has shown most recently, in part this was due to the unsuitability of high-rise flats for families, the quality of construction, the costs of heating, the inadequacy of repairs and the characteristically directive style of local authority housing management: all of which fed into a more diffuse sense of 'loss of community'.

But, perhaps of even greater importance, it soon became clear that slum clearance would not in fact eradicate all substandard housing from the towns and cities of Britain. English *et al.* (1976) have described the fundamental weaknesses of the clearance programme as envisaged during the 1950s and early 1960s. Quite simply, the government had no idea of the scale of the problem which they were attempting to solve and, partly in consequence, the programme was hopelessly under-resourced. It soon became apparent, therefore, that the rates of demolition and replacement building were much too slow to keep pace with the growing number of houses defined as unfit. In addition, having cleared the slums, many local authorities found themselves unable to finance redevelopment, and this led to what became known as 'planners' blight' (for example, Dennis, 1972). Ultimately, the increasing recognition of the inadequacies of the policy, combined – and this was crucial – with severely limited funding by successive administrations in the face of the mounting economic problems of the later 1960s, resulted in a shift toward the improvement of *existing* housing as the central element of housing strategy for the inner urban areas. However, this reorientation by no means provided the key to an effective housing programme in the cities and, indeed, left many central sites derelict and undeveloped.

In sum, then, by its very nature the slum clearance programme by-passed a substantial section of those in the weakest position within the housing market. Despite the very often highly dramatic reshaping of many towns and cities through clearance and redevelopment (where it occurred), there remained large numbers living in the poorest housing conditions, often in the privately rented sector, whom the process of urban development had simply not affected. And, of course, the housing disadvantage experienced by these people was frequently one of the many exploitations to which they were subject.

In other respects too, urban planning was intimately involved in the far-reaching changes to the existing fabric of British cities which we have shown were taking place during these post-war years. Hence, Hall *et al.* (1973) observe that the Development Plans of the period served largely to confirm existing land-uses, themselves the product of previous eras. Accordingly, they proved very effective in discouraging the decentralization of offices, shops and major civic and other public buildings from their traditional locations. Certainly, most county boroughs were loath to lose valuable commercial properties from their rate base. Indeed, on the contrary, local authorities frequently *promoted* central area redevelopment, with a view – amongst other things – to bringing valuable commercial values to reinforce their rate funds. As the post-war years went on, this kind of redevelopment became increasingly significant in the process of urban change, with its new industry, property development, increasingly dependent upon extremely close links with the planning system. In fact, by the end of the 1950s, when suitable development sites in prime central areas were becoming much scarcer, cooperation between the public and the private sector in urban renewal was essential, if the profits of developers and builders were to be maintained (Cox, 1984).

Now, as we have seen, these kinds of development – the modernization of commerce and retailing, involving a new style of office and shop building – clearly reflected the massive changes in the structure of employment in the tertiary sector characteristic of the long boom. And it is thus significant that the system of Industrial Development Certificates (IDCs) introduced by the 1945 Distribution of Industry Act and the 1947 Town and Country Planning Act, were wholly ineffective in respect of these changes because they focused entirely on manufacturing industry. Nevertheless, the question remains of how these policy instruments operated more generally to achieve the remaining objective of post-war planning: regional balance.

Controlling the geographical distribution of employment growth

The central means of controlling the spatial pattern of industrial growth – the IDC system operated by the Board of Trade – was not generally used to achieve specified distributions of employment *within* urban areas. To the extent that the latter was attempted, it was overwhelmingly the responsibility of local authority planners, utilizing the routine development control machinery to separate out non-conforming land-uses. However, this constituted rather an insignificant influence upon industrial change, especially for firms already established in the localities in which they wished to expand (Hall *et al.*, 1973). Hence, the principal impact of post-war planning over industrial development *within* Britain's towns and cities during these years was through its provision of public services and infrastructure: a point of some significance given the established trend toward decentralization from inner-city locations to suburban ones, which we noted earlier.

However, again as we have noted, superimposed upon these changes at the urban level was the wider pattern of regional growth and decline; and, indeed, for most contemporary commentators, 'regional balance' was directly complementary to 'urban containment'. The first point to note here is that the IDC system was not used with equal vigour throughout the period. It was strictly operated only between 1945 and 1947, when the balance of payments crisis and the conditions attached to Marshall Aid necessitated a relaxation of restrictions on the location of export industries in the prosperous regions (Pollard, 1962). This relaxation was continued after the election of the Conservatives in 1951; and the 1950s were generally years in which little attempt was made to direct the regional pattern of industrial location.

What is extremely difficult, however, is to evaluate the effects of these various stages of policy. Certainly, as we have indicated, until 1948, industrial expansion and factory building were very marked in the depressed areas. In addition, when the controls were relaxed, manufacturing employment growth once more became largely concentrated in the industries of the South East and the Midlands (McCallum, 1979).[1]

However, it does not follow that this pattern of development was *simply* attributable to the influence of regional policy: for example, in the years immediately after the war, factory premises were provided in many of the Development Areas in converted munitions factories, whilst elsewhere they were in very short supply as a result of building controls; similarly, the Development Areas had ready supplies of labour, in contrast to the shortages elsewhere in Britain (for example, Morgan, 1982). More generally, the fact that unemployment in the Development Areas remained much lower than in previous periods at least up until the 1950s, owed little to regional policy, as it was not being operated with any vigour during these years; and much more to the relative prosperity which we have seen was associated with the general conditions of the long boom. Furthermore, the relatively dynamic part of the economy remained concentrated in the South East and the Midlands, as the more modern types of manufacturing capitalized on the general economic expansion up until the mid-1960s. The result was thus a widening gap between the increasingly congested metropolitan centres and the declining industrial areas. In short, then, there was little indication that regional balance – a central plank of the Barlow Commission's

---

[1]More than 51 per cent of approved new industrial floorspace located in the Development Areas between 1945 and 1947. However, only 19 per cent located in these areas between 1948 and 1951, and 17 per cent between 1952 and 1955 (McCallum, 1979).

recommendations and the *raison d'être* of the IDC system – was being achieved, at least up until the 1960s, when the emphasis of policy changed significantly.

All in all, it is difficult to discern in the actual operation of post-war planning much movement toward the fulfilment of the objectives of the system, as these were outlined in the previous section. Certainly, whatever the optimism of the reconstruction programmes, there was no indication that Britain's towns and cities were being shaped into humane and civilized environments, in spite of the general prosperity associated with the long boom. However, to begin the task of explaining these real outcomes, it is necessary to return to perhaps the central issue in the development of urban policy during this period: land values.

Land values and development planning

As we have seen, land reform had been a persistent theme amongst Victorian and Edwardian reforming circles and had given rise to heated political controversy. Not surprisingly, then, the Barlow Commission recognized the problem that any shift to planned urban development necessarily denied development profits to some, whilst it generated them for others. Hence, given that such planning was deemed essential to the resolution of urban problems, it recommended the nationalizaton of development rights; and the Uthwatt Committee was appointed to investigate the detail of this classic contradiction between the public and the private interest.

The Uthwatt Report (Cmnd. 6386, 1942) rejected what it recognized as the 'logical solution' – outright land nationalization; compensation payments would be too expensive and the inevitable political opposition too troublesome. It recommended instead the vesting of all rights to develop land in the state and the nationalization of all land as and when it was actually built upon. Owners of nationalized land should be paid at current-use value (that is, before development). And all development after nationalization should be in accordance with development plans, even when undertaken by private developers.

It was something like this that was implemented by the 1947 Town and Country Planning Act, although it tried to avoid land nationalization altogether by introducing a betterment levy instead. Hence, any development or change of land-use required planning permission from the local authority; compensation was to be paid to owners for the loss of their development rights from a fixed fund of £300,000,000 (£2,500,000,000 at 1980 prices); a Central Land Board was to administer the raising of a 100 per cent betterment levy on any increment in land value arising through no action of the land-owner; and local authorities were empowered to acquire land at its existing use-value, that is with no regard to its potential, future value.

It is now generally accepted that the financial provisions of the 1947 Act were never really effective (for example, Cullingworth, 1979). They were in any case scrapped by the Conservative government in 1953; the Land Board was dismantled and the operation of the land market was restored. Only local authority land purchases were excepted and this hopeless anomaly – which in effect created a dual market in land – was removed by the 1959 Town and Country Planning Act. However, given the continued operation of planning controls, this was only in a partial sense a revival of the free market. And, hence, land-owners whose property had been granted planning permission thereby stood to receive 'windfall gains'.

These changes, together with the abolition of the building licence system in 1954, made it extremely difficult for local planning authorities to shape land-use changes within a pattern of rational urban development. Most spectacularly, commercial development – in the form of offices, shopping centres, hotels and so forth – came to dominate the restructuring of the central areas not only of the major conurbations, but also smaller towns and cities across the whole of Britain, as we have already indicated. Moreover, as Ambrose and Colenutt (1975) have shown, these sorts of developments were often seen to be at the expense of manufacturing industry and of working-class housing in the inner-urban areas, giving rise to a mounting tide of local protests.

Closely associated with these developments was the dramatic rise in land prices from the mid-1950s onwards (Massey and Catalano, 1978). This affected all types of land, but was especially acute in the case of urban uses. And, it is claimed, this had a marked effect upon housing markets, with steep rises in prices. Hence, Hall *et al.* (1973) conclude:

> The 1947 Planning Act worked as a system of physical controls but failed lamentably as a system of fiscal controls. Since the repeal of the provisions of the 1947 Act concerned with development values, no effective measures have been taken to check the rise of land prices and the system of physical control which remained has actually served as a key component in the inflationary spiral. The system has been directly inflationary by putting a price tag on land zoned for residential development; and by making it expensive in terms of time and money for developers to get permission to build on land not zoned for development. Thus containment has been achieved partly at the cost of rising prices. (1973: 395–6)

It is here that they see the most dramatic denial of the publicly espoused objectives of post-war planning.

What this brief consideration of development land values highlights is the fact that the operation of urban and regional planning

during the post-war years had distinctive *distributional* consequences: some people gained and others lost out as a result of the
functioning of the planning sytem. It is worth pursuing this issue in
somewhat greater detail, in that it casts new light on the results which
urban planning achieved.

The distributional consequences of post-war planning

In the conclusion of their study, Hall *et al.* (1973) themselves attempt
to identify some of the major distributional consequences of urban
planning during the post-war decades; and in this go beyond most
'Whig' accounts. Hence, they single out three groups who
disbenefited. Firstly, they argue, 'the aspirant rural or suburban
dwellers' lost out: as a result of urban containment, many families
who sought a rural life had to settle for a suburban one; whilst
suburbanites were housed in homes that provided worse quality
accommodation than did the suburbia of the 1930s. Moreover, given
the increasing separation of residence from other urban facilities,
these suburbanites faced deteriorating accessibility, manifesting
most clearly in long and stressful journeys to the urban centre.
Secondly, a price was paid by all those tenants who were housed in
high-density, high-rise municipal developments because of the
shortage of building land. In particular for families with children,
such developments were inferior to the council housing estates of the
1930s, where the great majority of houses had gardens. Thirdly,
there were those lower-income families who lived in privately rented
housing in the big cities. As we saw earlier, they were simply passed-
by in the process of urban change; the planning system had almost
no effect upon them and they had to endure some of the worst
housing conditions of all.

They also identify some groups who benefited from the operation
of urban policy. The residents of the New and Expanded Towns
enjoyed well designed housing and a general level of urban
environment which few speculatively built developments could
match. We might add that, at least for the earlier New Towns, there
were sufficient jobs to occupy most of the population of working
age. 'Existing rural inhabitants' also profited. They did so partly
because, as most of them were owner-occupiers, the value of their
property rose in the general inflation of house prices. More
significantly, it is argued, they enjoyed the benefits of undisturbed
access to the countryside. Indeed, it is further suggested that
'[o]rganized politically in the rural counties, and in the rural
districts, they have been responsible for the successful policy of
urban containment. The story of urban development in post-war
England, is the story of their triumph.' (1973: 431) Whether this
claim is wholly justified is a moot point. Certainly, Hall *et al.* (1973)

themselves show that there were other diverse and powerful groups who did extremely well out of the planning system.

Hence, by far and away the most dramatic gains were made by those who had a substantial stake in the land and property markets. Those owners whose land was granted permission to develop, reaped the reward of 'unearned increment'; although, of course, simply granting permission did not ensure actual development and the realization of the enhanced value. Equally, those with interests in the development process gained large profits, part of which derived from the context for development created by the planning system. There can be few more telling illustrations of this than Marriott's (1967) claim that ' . . . a relatively large number of individuals became extremely rich via property development between 1945 and 1965. I have listed 108 men and 2 women, each of whom must have made on my calculation at least £1 million in this golden period.' (1967: 1–2) Similarly, the corporate sector of the construction industry was able to capitalize upon the massive scale of urban development through the very size of its operations and extensive land-bank holdings (Ball, 1983).

Much more generally, however, there were benefits for those who owned wealth in the form of property rights, which arose from the general inflation of land and property prices. As we have already suggested, Hall *et al.* (1973) attribute this directly to the planning system's restriction of land supply, with rising land prices feeding through to housing and other property. Ball (1983), on the other hand, emphasizes the effects which planning had in raising total development value through the removal of 'negative externalities' (such as congestion, non-conforming land-uses and so on) and, of course, through state expenditure on the built environment (in the provision of infrastructure, servicing facilities, etc.). Hence, the rise in land values which occurred may simply reflect the distribution of such financial benefit in favour of the private land-owners. Similarly, the rise in prices of housing land was, in part at least, the expression of the land-owners' ability to share with developers and builders in the profitability of housing development.

Whatever the causation, land prices rose very sharply, especially after 1957, to the undoubted benefit of those who owned it. Likewise, people who purchased houses during the 1950s have seen the value of their property double every decade since, with almost no corresponding increases in mortgage outgoings. Undoubtedly, the growing split which was thus implied between owner-occupiers and those in other tenure categories exerted major effects on social and political relations through into the 1960s and, indeed, beyond (a point we shall return to later).

It is also clear that there were other major beneficiaries of the operation of urban and regional policy who may be identified from the foregoing analysis. For example, there were the private manufacturers who were permitted to establish new industries or expand existing ones in those locations which were most favourable to them, irrespective of the wider social implications; and with new services and infrastructure provided by the state. Equally, there were the large retailers whose supermarkets and multiple-outlet undertakings allowed them to pay handsome rents for modern premises, thereby enabling them to absorb or otherwise ruin smaller, traditional firms. And clearly, other such beneficiaries could be identified.

Clearly, this is to do nothing more than scratch at the surface of the analysis of post-war planning's distributional consequences. However, it is perhaps sufficient to indicate that the planning system did exert a considerable influence upon the changes which were taking place so rapidly in British society during the decades which followed the Second World War. Moreover, there is a sense in which this influence was *systematic*; it *tended* to reinforce inequalities and disparities which were longstanding features of the British social structure and which assumed particular forms during the period of the long boom, irrespective of the general levels of prosperity.

In part, this has to be represented in terms of what the planning system failed to do. Hence, for example, the disparities and inequalities between regional economies were *not* significantly reduced by regional planning during this period. This, in turn, had the profoundest consequences for the traditionally working-class and 'bonded' communities of large parts of 'Outer Britain' (Williams, 1983); consequences which by the later 1950s and 1960s were to be measured not simply in terms of economic stagnation and the outward migration of population, but also in the chronic debilitation of the social and political institutions which these communities had once supported. And viewed from this perspective, of course, these were effects upon the *class* structure (for example, Rees and Rees, 1983).

However, comparable results were achieved by what the planning system *did* do too. Slum clearance and central area redevelopment broke up the great concentrations of working-class families in the inner areas of the cities and likewise undermined the culture and organizations which had thrived there. Indeed, some commentators have suggested that the slum clearance of the 1950s and 1960s in effect completed the task of dispersing what was perceived as a dangerous urban proletariat, which had been started by the Victorians (Dennis, 1968). And certainly, slum clearance contributed substantially to the changes in the *political* character of Britain's cities during these years, which – as we shall see later – have become apparent only subsequently. Neither, it seems likely, were the compensations of improved living conditions for individuals and families adequate: undoubtedly many families were delighted to leave squalid slum housing; however, many were sorely dis-appointed by what replaced it.

Most significantly, however, as we have indicated, the operaton of urban and regional planning during these long-boom years had the effect of reinforcing the disparities between those who owned land and other forms of property and those who did not. Most spectacularly, of course, this is reflected in the enormous profits made by those with relatively large holdings of this kind and by those who were professionally involved in the process of property development and speculative building. Equally, however, important sectors of industrial and commercial capital benefited both from state provision of services and infrastructure and from the broadly *permissive* planning system which had emerged by the 1950s. Moreover, it is relatively straightforward to translate these results into terms of the class structure.

Much more complex, however, were the effects of the widening division between owner occupiers and those in other tenure categories. It has been suggested that this division came to exert a powerful influence over the general character of social relations in post-war Britain. Certainly, we can agree with Karn (1981) that ' . . . more than any other service, housing influences many other aspects of social life: status in the community; contact with relatives and friends; quality of schooling; access to jobs; recreation facilities; aesthetic and social qualities of the environment.' (1981: 15) It is perhaps not surprising, then, that the growing separation of owner-occupiers from others – in terms both of the value and of the physical location of their homes – allied to the growth in the absolute size of the owner-occupied sector, should have been accorded such significance.

Most interesting are the arguments that there is a close relation-ship between housing tenure (and other forms of consumption) and wider political changes. Hence, for instance, Dunleavy (1979) suggests that 'consumption cleavages' – such as that between owner-occupation and state provision of housing – may cut across traditional class allegiances. In particular, the fragmentation of manual workers and their families between different consumption sectors and the ideological structuration of different modes of provision weakens the traditional links between the working class and the Labour Party.

Whether this is so or not, it is certainly the case that during the 1950s there were widespread *beliefs* that the changes taking place with regard to home-ownership were contributing significantly to the 'embourgeoisement' of the more affluent sectors of the working class; a trend which was thought to be reflected in the electoral dominance of the Conservatives after 1951 (Abrams and Rose, 1960). Given this, the policies with respect to owner-occupation pursued under the Conservative administrations after 1951 are entirely comprehensible. Moreover, one does not have to accept the arguments set out by Dunleavy (1979) in full, to appreciate the profound effects on class structure and political activity brought about by changes in the sphere of housing (and consumption more generally): effects which were again disruptive of the established social structures of working-class communities.

What this sort of analysis implies, then, is that if we are to understand the reasons why the planning system yielded the results which we have begun to sketch, we need to construct a thoroughgoing *politics* of urban and regional policy during the immediate post-war decades. Moreover, such a politics should be consistent with the real consequences of this policy, rather than those statements of aspiration and intent which were the commonplace of government pronouncements and professional debate.

Post-war planning reconsidered

For many conventional accounts of post-war planning, the obvious way of explaining the system's performance has been to focus upon its *technical* inadequacy. One version of this type of analysis is provided by a publication of the Royal Town Planning Institute (1976):

> First, though careful projections of population growth were made, they could rest on the comfortable assumption that future levels were unlikely to be very different from those then obtaining; a medium or long-term plan to redistribute population was not to be complicated by large future increases in total population. Second, an economic 'steady state' was expected, with no great economic growth, ... This explains, for instance, why forecasts of future car ownership were too low. Third, it was assumed that centralist powers of control were going to be effective: in particular, a good deal of residential building would be through state or local authority enterprise, and industrial location would be controlled. (1976: 102)

The clear lesson of such an account is the need for a planning which is *institutionally* and *technically* more competent; and this is certainly what the Royal Town Planning Institute was anxious to conclude, as befits a professional body which is characterized by an 'apolitical technicism' (Ball, 1983: 201).

In fact, there is considerable strength in the argument that the institutional form which the planning system took did limit its effectiveness. For instance, both the Barlow and Uthwatt Reports talked in terms of a central planning authority, which was the only means by which major decisions on location and land-use could be taken with a view to the 'national interest'. However, what was actually implemented was much more decentralized, with considerable local autonomy through the Development Plans produced by individual county and county borough authorities; this made regional and national coordination difficult, without making plan-production genuinely democratic.

Moreover, it is apparent that the principal impulse to new development derived not from the state, but from the private sector. In particular, as we have seen, after the scrapping of building controls and the financial provisions of the 1947 Act, the urban planning system was unable to do more than attempt to *control* aspects of land-use, rather than positively to promote its change: it was reactive to the private sector, rather than itself initiatory. Hence, with the exception of the numerically insignificant New and Expanded Towns, private enterprise speculative building rapidly became the norm of green-field, residential development. Local authority and central government activity in this sphere was confined to the redevelopment of the inner urban areas, where private developers would not consider residential development on grounds of cost. What the latter *were* keen to do in such areas, of course, was to redevelop for office and other commercial purposes, with the consequences which we have outlined. Even if we consider the planning of economic activity, the reality fell far short of the Barlow Report's recommendation (and more particularly those of the two minority reports). IDC controls and the subsidies for location in Development Areas could only be operated in response to demand from private industry. This gave little scope, therefore, for shaping positively industrial development, even had there been the will to do so (which for much of the 1950s, of course, there was not).

Indeed, it is doubtful whether it makes much sense to think in terms of a post-war planning *system* at all, in spite of the conventional usage. It is certainly the case that the majority recommendations of the Barlow Commission, as well as the two minority statements, recognized the essential interdependency of the control of industrial location and that of the urban environment: hence, any effective planning would have to encompass both dimensions. However, the fact is that the planning of economic development (to the extent that there was any) was kept institutionally separate from other aspects of planning. Hence, responsibility for the pattern of industrial location was jealously guarded by the traditional ministries, the Board of Trade and the Treasury. And this obviously made the integration of policies much more difficult.[2]

[2]For example, as Douglas Jay pointed out at the time (in 1946), there was the clear potential for conflict between regional economic policy, attempting to redirect industrial development and employment growth to the less prosperous regions, and the London New Towns, unless very stringent controls were operated to ensure that the

Clearly, then, we can agree that these features of post-war planning were central to the results which it produced. However, in our view, far from providing evidence of unfortunate oversights and technical blunders on the part of government (as 'Whig' commentators suggest), this kind of planning appears to have reflected with some consistency the social and political conditions in which it was created. It is only from this perspective, we think, that the sorts of consequences which we have outlined are comprehensible.

Urban planning and post-war reconstruction

It should be remembered that the series of Acts upon which post-war urban and regional policy was based, was the product, in large measure, of the preparatory work undertaken by the war-time coalition government. Indeed, as we have already shown, it was a central element in a much wider programme of post-war reconstruction. A number of consequences follow from this.

The whole of the programme of reconstruction had to be based upon *consensus*: this was a necessary condition of the continuance of the coalition and the effective prosecution of the war. As Cullingworth (1975) has made clear, at the inception of the reconstruction programme, the entire emphasis was upon generating *national unity*: for example, the Cabinet Committee on Reconstruction Problems, set up in 1941, was charged with producing plans which ' . . . should have as their general aim the perpetuation of the national unity achieved in this country during the war, through a social and economic structure designed to secure equality of opportunity and service among all classes.' (R.P.(41)3; quoted in Cullingworth, 1975: 6) To this end, the various Reconstruction Committees which followed were deeply engaged with bodies outside government itself – and in particular with the employers' organizations and the trades unions, but with local authority associations and voluntary organizations as well – in order to secure their cooperation. Necessarily, then, party political conflict had to be kept to a minimum (Middlemas, 1979).

In fact, the stability of the coalition was severely tested over the Beveridge Report (Cmnd. 6406, 1942), which elaborated a scheme for social insurance against illness, poverty and unemployment, plus proposals for a national health service, family allowances and the maintenance of full employment. It was, of course, strongly supported by Labour back-benchers. But the Labour members of the coalition were forced to heed the strong reservations of Churchill

firms moving to the latter really did come from the congested areas of London, rather than elsewhere in the country. Some 20 years later, when Jay had actually become the Minister in charge of the Board of Trade, he could make the same point with equal validity in respect of the second generation of New Towns.

and other of their Conservative colleagues. What these stresses meant, of course, was that other reconstruction policies had to avoid even a hint of political controversy.

This is well illustrated in the kinds of policies adopted with regard to planning, which consistently fudged their potential political impact. For example, in the discussions which eventually led up to the 1944 Town and Country Planning Act, the issue of compensation and betterment simply could not be resolved finally. As Cullingworth (1975) says, ' . . . agreement on the compensation-betterment issue and on the system for controlling development had not been reached. It should not be forgotten that at the root of the problem lay the fact that these essentially political issues were being tackled by a coalition government.' (1975: 111) The compromise which eventually emerged required the personal intervention of Churchill and the setting up of a special committee under Attlee's direction. The end product still drew the following comment from Lewis Silkin: he called the Bill a:

> miserable and mean measure which represents a victory by the land owning interests over the public interest. If the Labour Party accepts it, even in principle, it will be guilty of having betrayed the hopes of all who have placed their trust in our movement . . . . It will have passed a sentence of death upon comprehensive planning for generations to come. (quoted in Foot, 1975: 472)

Ironically, of course, Silkin himself was to introduce a Bill aimed at 'comprehensive planning' only three years later. This too, however, was only very partially successful, as we have seen.

It is also clear that the relationship between the planning of industrial location and other aspects of planning was a highly contentious one. Again, Cullingworth (1975) provides the relevant evidence:

> This distinction [between economic and other aspects of planning] was not so clear in the public mind as in the mind of some ministers . . . and the anxieties arising from this fact, in view of the serious political implications of total economic planning as distinguished from town planning, brought about delay, hesitation and timidity in government decisions which seemed incomprehensible to the critics. (1975: 16)

And similarly:

> Ministers might discuss, debate and compromise but, in this extraordinary war-time period, the lines of debate were largely settled by civil servants. The effective opposition [to the creation of an all-inclusive planning apparatus] was not a political party, but the Treasury and a host

of departments who saw threats to their traditional areas of responsibility. (1975: 253)

In short, then, the peculiar circumstances of the war-time coalition meant that it was possible to go so far, but no farther, in the development of a planning system.

However, it could be argued that whilst this may have been true of war-time itself, it did not apply following the overwhelming return of Labour to office in 1945. And, of course, it is true that, for example, the 1947 Act went beyond what had been possible in its 1944 precursor. Nevertheless, there remained considerable *continuity* between the deliberations of war-time and what was actually implemented during the post-war years (Addison, 1975). At one level, Booth (1982) has demonstrated the extent to which regional policy after 1945 owed its character to the experience gained in the organization of production during the war itself. At another, there was, in some ways, remarkably little party political conflict over the passage of the planning legislation. Hence, for example, even though over 1400 amendments were tabled to the 1946 Town and Country Planning Bill and the Conservatives eventually voted against, this was by far the most controversial of the various pieces of planning legislation and opposition was actually focused upon the *technical detail* of compensation payments, rather than matters of principle.

We should make clear, however, that our argument is that this relative absence of political controversy derived from the nature of the legislation itself: essentially the product of the highly constrained politics of the war-time years. Interestingly, this conclusion appears to be consistent with the contemporary commentary on the land-use planning issue of D.N. Chester, later to become a doyen of Oxford political scientists, made when he was a member of the Economic Section of the Cabinet Office in 1945:

> The State leaves the actual ownership of the land in private hands but takes away the profit motive, the mainspring of private enterprise, by nationalizing the development value. If I were labelling the scheme, I would call it 'bastard Tory reform' . . . . We feel that the scheme should either go a little further in the way of socialization or should not go so far as to take the profit incentive out of private ownership. Any in-between system is likely to get the worst of both worlds. [Minute from D.N. Chester to the Lord President on C.B. (45)6, 27 October 1945, Treasury File L.B. 171/46/03; quoted in Cullingworth, 1975: 259]

However, we think that we need to go further than this to account for the nature of the post-war planning system and its effects. For it was crucially significant that this somewhat consensus legislation was made possible by the *general* political conditions which characterized the period.

Class interests and the post-war planning system

As we saw earlier in this chapter, one version of the political processes through which the planning system was created is provided by Donnison's (1980) notion of an alliance of a wide diversity of interest groups in support of the relevant legislation. What he does not make explicit, however, is the theoretical basis of his analysis. In fact, it is clear that the perspective which he adopts is broadly that of pluralism: to simplify somewhat, the state is viewed as responding to the pressures of competing interest groups and the electorate more widely; and these pressure groups are seen as exerting an apparently equal influence within the political process (for a review of these and related issues, see Lukes, 1977). Hence, for example, we may legitimately conclude from Donnison's account that the Town Planning Movement was as influential as the labour movement in determining the 1945 Labour administration's policies with respect to urban and regional development.

Such a conclusion, of course, is unconvincing in the extreme. At a general theoretical level, pluralist analysis has been subjected to the severest criticisms (Lukes, 1977). Moreover, the analysis applied in this particular context is difficult to reconcile with the results which the operation of the planning system during the decades after the Second World War actually produced. As we have already argued, these results worked systematically to disadvantage certain sections of the population and to advantage others. Therefore we think that it is reasonable to look for systematically unequal influences upon the political processes by which planning policy was formulated and implemented.[3]

Hence, for instance, we find that in its evidence to the Barlow Commission, the Federation of British Industries (FBI) – an umbrella organization for industrial capital – argued powerfully against the adoption of thoroughgoing powers to control the location of industry and population, and conceded only the need for the state to encourage redistribution, especially in the particular circumstances of London. To quote from the Commission's Final Report (1940):

> So far as industry itself is concerned evidence was given by, amongst others, the Federation of British Industries; this evidence was prepared with the assistance of a number of constituent members to whom a questionnaire had been sent. With regard to existing concentrations of

[3]This does not imply, however, that we may infer the determinants of state intervention from an analysis of its beneficiaries: all state policies may have unforeseen consequences.

industry and industrial population, the view was expressed that these could not be broken up without the gravest of risks. The Federation were opposed to compulsion on industrialists in the matter of location, but at the same time they were prepared to accept a policy of 'discouragement' of settlement in certain areas and 'encouragement' of settlement elsewhere. In the case of London a new industry or industrial establishment, unless it could make out a special claim, might be 'urged' to go elsewhere, and the Federation believed that that would be effective. (1940: 190)

The Trades Union Congress (TUC), on the other hand, presented a case for the establishment of a national authority ' . . . to exercise both positive and negative forms of control over the location of industry . . . . ' (1940: 191) However, it declined to specify the *form* which such control should take; nor the *aims* which it should pursue, beyond that of the 'public interest'.

These views have to be related, of course, to the pattern of development characteristic of the inter-war decades. The FBI was dominated by the representatives of the 'new industries', which, as we have seen, had expanded very rapidly and had every expectation of continuing to do so during the post-war boom (the Barlow Commission itself made all this clear). The necessity of state intervention was recognized, if for no other reason than to maintain at least some demand amongst the populations of the depressed regions and to take account of the unique problems of London. It should be remembered, of course, that the costs to the state of the rapid suburbanization (especially around London) during the 1920s and 1930s were increased by its unplanned nature. It may well be that the FBI was convinced of the need of limited planning in order to improve the efficiency of service and infrastructural provision for new development. However, continued profitability and the drive to accumulation would only be impaired, it was thought, by any extensive paraphernalia of locational control.

The trades unions, in contrast, were clearly impelled to advocate a greater degree of state intervention, given the plight of their traditional constituencies in 'Outer Britain'. However, the TUC in particular had accepted the case for the 'modernization' of British industry along American lines during the 1930s and, in consequence, it was difficult for it to press a *form* of state policy which would threaten the interests of the 'new' industrial capital. Moreover, it was generally the case that the most concerted opposition to the 'corporatist' strategy which had been adopted arose from within the labour movement in precisely those areas of economic decline which stood to gain most from the work of an effective and thoroughgoing system of urban and regional planning (Middlemas, 1979).

In these senses, then, there was a considerable coincidence of interests between the FBI and the TUC and the dominant sectors of industrial capital and labour which they, respectively, represented. It is, of course, also the case, as we have already shown, that the system of planning which was instituted after 1945 and, more especially, which was implemented during the 1950s, was entirely compatible with these positions: negligible controls, combined with substantial state subsidy of urban and industrial development.

Again as we have seen, one consequence of the failure to control the location of industrial development was the progressive encroachment of industry and its attendant population into the countryside. This, of course, was widely perceived as a major problem during the inter-war years. Moreover, the restrictions imposed on city-centre development, immediately following the recommendations of the Uthwatt Committee, appeared likely to accentuate the trend. As Backwell and Dickens (1979) have pointed out, this inevitably gave rise to a conflict between industrial capital and rural landed interests. In particular, the encroachment of industry would have the effect of raising wage levels in the rural areas to the detriment of the profitability of traditional agriculture. Indeed, Backwell and Dickens (1979) go on to suggest that the decision to set up the Scott Committee to investigate the problems of industrial development in the countryside represented the attempt by the landed interests to resolve this conflict on their own terms. Hence they point to the fact that Lord Justice Scott not only himself approached Lord Reith – then the Minister responsible for planning – to ask that the inquiry be established, but was also a member of the executive of the CPRE, which was broadly representative of the conservationist objectives of the landed and agricultural lobby.

Moreover, the recommendations made by the Scott Committee appear to have borne out successfully the intentions of these landed interests, particularly in the well known presumption against the change of agricultural land-use, unless it could be justified in terms of the national advantage. However, as Wibberly (1965) amongst others has shown, the actual operation of the post-war planning system in this respect was much more complex. Insofar as development was prevented in rural areas, it tended to be residential development. Indeed, the Scott Committee itself made it clear that industrial growth was inevitable on the edges of existing urban areas and in small towns in the countryside. And these, of course, were precisely the sorts of location which were highly attractive to some of the most advanced sectors of industrial capital itself (as we showed in Chapter 2). As Backwell and Dickens (1979) conclude:

The Scott Report, while originally concerned with rural conservation, was thus in the event a means for reconciling competing capitalist class interests while (through appealing to the apparently classless symbol of conservation) still finding widespread approval. It is difficult to assess whether landed capital in any sense 'lost out' from this legislation, but if any fraction of landed capital did suffer, it was perhaps small agricultural capital (which lost decision-making power over the urban or rural development of their land) and not the large landed estates. (1979: 12)

However, what would appear much more clear-cut is the fact that those fractions of capital which were involved with *urban* development *were* threatened by the rigorous planning restrictions imposed in towns and reconstruction areas by war-time controls – following the Uthwatt recommendations – and, of course, initially appeared to be by the 1947 Town and Country Planning Act itself.

What should be borne in mind here, however, is the limited capacity of these sections of capital to resist such encroachments at this time. Hence, for example, private landlords had been experiencing increasing difficulties throughout the inter-war period: no less than six official committees had testified during these years to the landlords' poor and declining situation. The havoc wrought in many urban areas by the blitz accentuated these problems by the straightforward destruction of property and by legislation which removed from tenants the need to pay rent for damaged lodgings. Hence, the war-time measures enabling the purchase of sites in such city-centre areas by public authorities, and compensating at 1939 prices must have appeared extremely attractive to many landlords renting out property in wrecked or still vulnerable urban areas.

These same blitz conditions, however, offered positive opportunities to other property interests, which were enabled to buy up bombed sites with a view to redeveloping then once the war was over (Marriott, 1967). At the time, such activities achieved a widespread notoriety. For example, even *The Economist* (in February 1941), having referred to the problems associated with high compensation payments before the war, welcomed the Uthwatt Committee in the following terms:

> Now there is every indication that a movement is on foot which will intensify these old difficulties when the problem of replanning the bombed areas comes to be resolved. Land in these districts is being bought to sell again for redevelopment, and the speculators are plainly determined that, if the community is to have new cities, it will have to pay through the nose for them. It is the best of news, therefore, to learn that Lord Reith, the Minister of Works and Buildings, is working on plans to frustrate these pirates. [quoted in Backwell and Dickens, 1979: 14]

Even so, in spite of this mobilization of popular sentiment against the activities of these property development 'pirates', it is remarkable that once the very special conditions of war-time had passed, there was a progressive retreat from the state control of the development of land. The war-time controls on building and development *were* stringent, especially in the reconstruction areas of the city centres. Equally, the 1947 Act did impose restrictions upon the profits to be made from the development process through the betterment levy and other financial provisions; although it did allow substantial compensation payments to land-owners for their loss of development rights. However, as Marriott (1967) has shown most clearly, the war-time damage to the urban centres created opportunities for development on a massive scale in the conditions of the post-war boom. Moreover, the increasing general strength and influence of land and property interests during these years – with the infusion of funds from financial capital as a whole – were paralleled by the progressive retreat from the implementation of the 1947 Act and, as we have seen, the ultimate abandonment of its financial clauses, once the Conservatives (the traditional representatives of these interests) had returned to office in 1951 (Cox, 1984).

In this way, then, the *form* which the post-war planning system took may be interpreted in terms of the influences and pressures exerted by particular class groupings, pursuing their interests through the policy-making process. And hence, the results which were achieved by planning intervention (which we sketched earlier) are also best understood in the light of these interests.

The post-war settlement and urban and regional planning

These influences upon the processes by which the post-war planning system was created were conditioned, of course, by the general form of the British state during this period. Hence, for example, Jessop (1980) was written in terms of the emergence of the 'Keynesian-Welfare State' in the aftermath of the Second World War. As he puts it:

> By this term, I refer to a state in which the principal forms of intervention in economy and civil society are macro-economic demand management within a mixed economy together with maintenance of the external conditions of capitalist production ('Keynesian') and which also operate a redistributive and/ or insurance based welfare state oriented to the social reproduction of the 'people' via intervention at the level of the individual citizen and/ or his (or her) dependants ('-welfare state'). (1980: 86)

It is impossible to understand this new form of state except by reference to the economic and political conditions of the inter-war period and of the Second World War. Of major significance here was the fact that the Labour Party, whilst firmly established as the principal opposition to the Conservatives, was severely affected by the failure of the General Strike in 1926 and, more particularly, the collapse of the second Labour government in 1931 and the defection of several of its leaders to the Conservative-dominated National Government. Hence, during this key period, and in particular from the mid-1930s onwards, both the Labour Party itself and the labour movement more generally came to be dominated by their right wings. This was especially significant as it was in these years that the Labour Party for the first time worked out a coherent programme of policies which it would implement on its assumption of office. The right-wing dominance meant, not surprisingly, right-wing policy programmes (Howell, 1976).

This trend was further accentuated by the experience of the war-time coalition: not only were the Labour leaders constrained by the 'responsibilities' of government office, but the whole strategy which had been adopted was one of whole-hearted cooperation in the war effort in return for government concessions to working people. The point was, however, that the gains which were secured were, for the most part, those which raised no issues of political principle (Middlemas, 1979).

Equally, however, the inter-war years signalled the manifest failure of orthodox economic policies, based on 'balanced budgets' and 'sound finance', to promote economic growth and full employment. Hence, within the Conservative Party during the 1930s there had been a persistent conflict between those who maintained a belief that the state's role should be a minimal one and those who had come to see that state intervention was necessary in order to ensure that a stable society could be maintained, that private enterprise could continue to function and so on. As Harris (1972) puts it:

> The two pressures – from 'free enterprise' and from the 'reorganizers' – found the government uneasily balanced between. Yet through the 1930s, the Government seemed to lean increasingly towards the second. More might have been possible if the government had had any clear idea of where it was going, of what central priorities should guide it. As it was 'rationalization' (of industry) often seemed no more than outdoor relief for big business. (1972: 45)

However, again the experience of the war-time coalition in managing many aspects of the economy and social life not only confirmed views on what policies were possible, but also had the effect of enabling the 'interventionists' to gain the upper hand within the Party; strengthened, of course, by the defeat of the 'old guard' in the 1945 General Election.

More generally, the conditions of the 1920s and 1930s encouraged far-reaching reassessments of economic and political strategies, not simply within the political parties, but also in the trades union movement, the City and industry, the civil service and intellectual circles (for example, Middlemas, 1979). Hence, there was a general movement in favour of a settlement between the classes, and state intervention in the interests of economic growth and improved social conditions for the whole people. This ideological shift was confirmed in the reconstruction programmes of the war-time coalition (as we saw earlier) and also, of course, by the election of the Labour administration in 1945.

It was the latter which laid the institutional basis for the mixed economy and the welfare state. What this implied, however, was certainly not a transition to some form of socialism, whatever the mythology of certain elements of the Labour Party (for example, Crosland, 1956). Rather, as we have seen, it was the expression of a quite widely held consensus. This is not to deny the achievement of the post-war Labour administrations, but simply to characterize that achievement precisely. Accordingly, capitalist social relations went largely unchallenged, and the scope of state intervention remained limited. For example, even Labour's nationalization schemes, although opposed by the Conservatives and many industrialists, paid generous compensation to former owners; whilst state take-over enabled the major reconstruction of key infrastructural and industrial sectors, as well as facilitating more general demand management. Certainly, the latter, acting only at the level of the general economy and involving no direct controls on either capital or labour, provoked little opposition from financial and industrial capital or their political representatives in the Conservative Party (Jessop, 1980). Therefore, when Labour was defeated in 1951, the incoming Conservative government was careful to retain the institutional basis of the post-war settlement and the commitment to the Welfare State and full employment.

This is not to say, however, that there were no changes brought about after 1951. In fact, the Conservatives themselves had changed very rapidly after 1947. Again Harris (1972) summarizes the situation clearly:

> no sooner had the radicals consolidated their position, than they were faced with a broad shift in public opinion which, beginning in 1947, produced a surprising refurbishment of forms of pluralist thought, a 'neo-Liberalism' . . . . Ironically, the Conservative Party of 1951 was more Liberal than it had been ever since the 1920s. (1972: 77)

Hence, within the limits of the post-war settlement, this shift in the dominant ideology within the party was reflected in the kinds of policies which were espoused during the 1950s. The removal of physical controls over the economy was accelerated; iron and steel and road haulage were de-nationalized; and greater emphasis was placed upon indirect economic controls based on the manipulation of market forces (leading ultimately to the 'stop–go' cycles noted earlier) (Harris 1972).

In this way, therefore, the nature and scope of urban and regional policy during these years reflected with some precision the *general* form of state intervention. Hence, the post-war planning system embodied limited – but by no means wholly insignificant – attempts at state *regulation* of urban and industrial development, which were widely recognized as necessary to overcome the problems of the inter-war period and which expressed a particular kind of settlement between, on the one hand, capital and labour and, on the other, different fractions of capital (as we suggested in an earlier section).

By the 1950s, however, whilst in principle the general framework of policy remained intact, it had been modified substantially in ways which affected its actual performance markedly. Thus, the financial aspects of the 1947 Act were repealed; regional policies allowed to wane; no more New Towns were declared; the private housing market was expanded and the public sector relegated to slum clearance and special provision; and local planning was restricted to the facilitation of the changes needed by an expanding economy. What *was* unchanged, however, was the continued state subsidy of urban growth and industrial development through the provision of services, roads and other infrastructure; indeed, public expenditure on such items was running at some £1,100,000,000 per annum (at constant 1975 prices) by the mid-1950s and rose through the remainder of the decade and into the 1960s (Ball, 1983).[4]

Now it should be clear, this pattern of state intervention was wholly consistent with the conditions of the long boom. On the one hand, organized labour was able to secure rising real wages through collective bargaining, as well as the benefits of welfare state

---

[4]Ball's (1983) figures here refer to 'public non-housing expenditure on construction work'. He explains this category as follows:

Included in this category are projects associated with government administration, defence and the investment programmes of the nationalized industries . . . . Data do not exist to break down the various components of this global public non-housing category, yet it is to be expected that most does relate to the potential transformation of residential space, either directly, as in new town and urban renewal programmes, or indirectly by altering the potential residential attractiveness of particular locations through road building and other transportation expenditure or as part of residentially linked welfare programmes, such as schools, health centres and hospitals. (1983: 249)

expenditure. The plight of those who missed out on this general prosperity – the unemployed, the slum-dwellers, the residents of 'blighted' central areas and so forth–remained largely unacknowledged. On the other hand, industrial and financial capital, as well as landed and property interests (and these fractions increasingly coincided) were able to pursue the growth strategies appropriate to the circumstances of the long boom, largely free from state regulation, but with continued state subsidization.

Unsurprisingly, then, the social disparities and inequalities of both society generally and within the urban and regional system more specifically, were heightened during these years. Nevertheless, it was not until the failure of the long boom that the vulnerability of this pattern of state intervention was exposed and new initiatives became necessary.

4

Economic decline, modernization and the reform of planning

We have argued, then, that during the long boom the post-war planning system manifestly failed to achieve the results which had been claimed at its inception. The vulnerability of the older industrial regions remained unchanged; as became apparent with the sharp increases in unemployment rates (especially in Scotland and the North East) during the late 1950s. In contrast, the economic buoyancy of the South East and the Midlands acted as a magnet for population and these regions suffered the consequences of rapid urban growth and congestion.

These problems were accentuated by the inability of local authorities to create an ordered and rational pattern of urban development. Slum clearance and redevelopment programmes floundered. The public housing drive more generally both failed to eradicate shortages and produced accommodation which proved to be dramatically unpopular. At the same time, this failure to provide decent homes for the less advantaged groups within the urban population was thrown into the starkest relief by the obvious boom in other kinds of urban development. Hence, speculative building for owner-occupation proceeded rapidly; whilst investment finance and land were readily available for office and other commercial building in the central urban areas.

Equally, it was apparent by the 1960s that the land-use planning system, which lay at the heart of the post-war policy framework, was failing badly as a system of government. Development Plans, introduced in 1947 to provide the statutory basis for shaping urban change, had proved singularly ineffective in achieving the goals set for them. Not only did they take an enormously long time to pass through the whole bureaucracy of central and local government to the stage of implementation; but also they proved cumbersome and inflexible policy instruments (Cullingworth, 1979).

Most importantly, however, it came to be widely recognized that the structure of government within which this planning was carried out itself hindered the achievement of the system's purported objectives. Thus, for instance, those major towns and cities where urban problems were often most severe, were unable to plan development adequately because their surrounding regions were controlled by other local authorities, which frequently wished to pursue a set of different priorities. Indeed, the later 1950s had witnessed a number of celebrated, set-piece confrontations between major metropolitan centres and neighbouring shire counties (for example, Hall *et al.*, 1973).

These particular problems, however, were interpreted in the much wider context of a concern over the operation of the machinery of British government generally. The view was gaining widespread currency that the structure and methods of (especially local) government had failed to change and modernize in line with the dramatic shifts in the social and economic structure of Britain and in the role of the state itself during the period since the Second World War. Now, as Dearlove (1979) has shown, these concerns were consistent with a very long-established tradition of thinking about the nature of British local government. Nevertheless, from the late 1950s onwards, there was a rising tide of debate and analysis about local government – reflected in a formidable catalogue of official inquiries into diverse aspects of its reform – which eventually culminated in its wholesale reorganization during the early 1970s. And it was in this context, then, that the debate over the administration of urban and regional planning took place: in fact, planning was central to the wider debate, in that its effective implementation was frequently argued to be a principal criterion for evaluating proposals for local government reform (for example, Senior, 1969).

These somewhat disparate elements came together in the 1960s to comprise a searching indictment of the sort of urban and regional policy which had been created in the reconstruction programme of the immediate post-war years and implemented during the subsequent couple of decades. In its emphasis upon institutional and technical shortcomings, it was – in our terms – a characteristically 'Whig' critique. And, as we shall see later, it was mirrored by substantial reforms in state policy during the 1960s and early 1970s. In the form in which we have presented it here, this critique was very much the preserve of interest groups, professionals and politicians. However, we should not forget that for the ordinary citizen, his or her experience was the much more direct one of bureaucratic inertia, seemingly intractable housing problems, the continued deterioration of the urban environment and, as the 1960s wore on, increasingly poor economic prospects, especially in the cities.

Indeed, more fundamentally, it is important to bear in mind that what underpinned the 'Whig' concern with the administrative problems of urban and regional policy was the accelerating decline of the British domestic economy after the end of the long boom, which we noted in Chapter 2. What this, in turn, implied was a crisis of the Keynesian-Welfare State *generally*. Hence, the effects of Keynesian demand management on the organization of *production* – as we have seen, the root of Britain's economic problems – were slight. Increases in effective demand proved just as likely to finance capital exports and the import of consumer goods, to enable capital to engage in speculative activities or to raise prices, and to allow labour to raise its money wages, as they were to stimulate further production or industrial reorganization. Likewise, the Welfare State imposed an increasing burden upon public expenditure, thereby exerting upward pressure on taxation and inflation; and yet could do nothing to prevent the continued reproduction of the conditions to which it was bound to respond (that is, unemployment, low pay, sickness and injury, etc.). In our view, it is in this context that the attempts to implement new forms of state intervention during the later 1960s and early 1970s should be understood (for example, Jessop, 1980). However, as we shall see, whilst the failings of the Keynesian-Welfare State became increasingly clear, the development of more effective alternatives was constrained by the balance of class and other social forces characteristic of the contemporary British social structure.

New forms of urban and regional policy

Accordingly, the later 1960s and early 1970s witnessed major innovations in the form and pattern of state intervention generally; and, of course, these were reflected at the level of urban and regional policy. What is perhaps most striking about the latter is that the principal emphasis was placed upon developments in the *regional* economic structure and the need to promote more balanced development. In part, this derived from wholly national development priorities; however, the solution to the problems of Britain's towns and cities was to a large extent perceived as conditional upon successful regional policies (cf. Community Development Project, 1977a). Certainly, this emphasis contrasts with that of more recent years. However, we shall show that there were also significant changes in urban policy during these years, which established important preconditions for later developments (to be examined in later chapters). In what follows, then, we shall describe the new policies and attempt to assess their impact upon patterns of urban and regional change.

The reassertion of regional planning

As we saw in Chapter 2, the earliest indications of the ending of the long boom were the sharp rises in unemployment rates in the older industrial regions at the end of the 1950s. The first phase of governmental reaction to these problems clearly reflected their apparently 'regional' character and was summed up in the Local Employment Act, passed by the Conservatives in 1960. In many ways, this Act expressed the kind of thinking which had dominated the approach of Conservative administrations to regional policy throughout the 1950s. Although expenditure on regional policy more than doubled between 1960–61 and 1961–62 (McCallum, 1979), the concentration of subsidies into employment exchange areas suffering especially high unemployment made it clear that regional policy remained officially defined as a means of improving the *welfare* of afflicted localities, rather than as an instrument of strictly economic policy.

The ineffectiveness of this sort of approach was highlighted during the recession of 1962–63, as even Lord Eccles – the Minister responsible for the passage of the 1960 Act – was forced to acknowledge. There followed a series of essentially *ad hoc* initiatives, which were nevertheless indicative of a movement toward more thoroughgoing changes of approach. Hence, a Minister was appointed with special responsibility for the North East of England, which along with Scotland (which already had its own Minister), was hardest hit. More significantly, two 1963 White Papers, on Central Scotland and the North East respectively, both advocated major expenditure programmes on the urban infrastructure – New Towns, the transportation network and so on – within a framework of regional development plans based (rather loosely) on 'growth pole' strategy (for example, Keeble, 1976). Clearly, the necessary implication was a considerably expanded role for state intervention.

At the same time, growing concern was being expressed over the mounting problems of the major conurbations. One result of this was a number of regional planning studies – in the South East, the West Midlands and the North West, for example – whose principal focus was upon issues of congestion and the impoverished urban environment. Eventually, these studies provided the basis for the resuscitated New Towns programme of the later 1960s. More immediately, the growth of state concern over these matters was signalled only in the creation of the Location of Offices Bureau, to promote the dispersal of offices away from central London.

These localized initiatives occurred simultaneously with much wider reappraisals of government economic policy, which were ultimately to have profound effects on the direction of regional strategy. Thus, the National Economic Development Council (NEDC), itself established by the Conservatives in 1962, published two major reports during 1963 which set out the case for economic policies which would generate growth in the national economy and which attributed to regional intervention a key part in achieving this growth. Accordingly, it was argued that regional unemployment should no longer be regarded as simply a *welfare* problem, and expenditure to alleviate it as a drain on the rest of the country; rather unemployed people in the regions should be viewed as a *resource*, with a vital contribution to make toward national economic progress. At the same time, economic expansion in the older industrial regions would have the effect of relieving the pressures upon the congested parts of the country, with obviously beneficial results for the conurbations. In this way, therefore, '[a] national policy of expansion would improve the regional picture; and, in turn, a successful regional development programme would make it easier to achieve a national growth programme.' (NEDC, 1963: 29)

Morgan (1980) has argued that this was the first time that regional development policy had been formulated officially in truly Keynesian terms: some 20 years after the formal acceptance of Keynesian principles by the war-time coalition. Whether this is so or not, it is certainly remarkable that such a clear re-statement of the essential interdependencies between the problems of the cities and those of the wider regional economic structure and of the need for a nationally coordinated state strategy to eradicate them, should have been made so long after the publication of the Barlow Report. Moreover, the Finance and Local Employment Acts of 1963, by considerably strengthening the incentives available to firms locating in the Development Districts, appeared to go some way towards implementing this approach, at least in respect of the older industrial regions. However, as we shall see later, it was not until after 1964 that the strategy was to achieve its full influence.

Nevertheless, the explanation of this switch in policy by the Conservatives remains an important issue. At one level, of course, we need to look no further than short-term electoral considerations. Hence, McCallum (1979) has suggested – somewhat simplistically – that there is a direct relationship between the results of the 1959 General Election and the changes in regional policy. Nationally, the Conservatives recorded a considerable success, winning 58 per cent of seats, some 3.5 per cent more than in 1955. However, in Scotland, the worst affected of the 'problem areas', they lost substantially, dropping from a 51 per cent to a 44 per cent share of Scottish seats. In this way, the shifts in regional policy which we have sketched are interpreted as a 'pork-barrel' politics attempt to recoup electoral support in those regions hardest pressed economically.

Obviously, we should need to know a great deal more about the process of policy-making by the Conservative government before evaluating this sort of account: especially as the electoral swings in other hard-hit regions were much less dramatic than in Scotland. However, it is clear that rather different political pressures – especially from Scotland – *were* instrumental in directing some major investment decisions being taken by the government at this time. Perhaps the most celebrated of these was the then Prime Minister's – Mr Harold Macmillan – so-called 'judgement of Solomon' on the development of the steel industry. Hence, in November 1958, it was announced that government funds were to be made available to finance the building, not of the single, very large strip-mill which was expected, but rather two smaller ones, at Llanwern in South Wales and – surprisingly – at Ravenscraig in Scotland. As Warren (1970) has pointed out, it is difficult to make much sense of this decision except in terms of the sustained campaign which had been fought – to a large extent on exmployment grounds – by '[l]ocal authorities, the nation's MPs, the Scottish Trades Union Council and the Scottish Council . . . .' (1970: 271) In short, then, it is clear that, even by the late 1950s, the Conservative administration was prepared to intervene powerfully in regional development, particularly in response to political pressure.

However, such pressures acted upon a Conservative government and Party which contributed independently to policy development. Indeed, it has been suggested that the significance of the shift in policy priorities during the early 1960s itself derived in large measure from the contrast with the 'neo-Liberalism' of the administrations of the 1950s: that is, from a change *internal* to Conservatism (for example, Morgan, 1980). Thus, it is argued, the strengthening and redefinition of regional development policy respresented a clear break with the position that ' . . . such interference by the state distorted the working of the market and so the most economic distribution of resources as reflected in different costs in different geographical locations.' (Harris, 1972: 209)

This view, in fact, should not be overstated. As we saw in the previous chapter, there were always substantial sections within the Conservative Party which were opposed to 'neo-Liberalism' and remained faithful to other traditions of Conservative 'corporatism'; it is simply that these groups were not in a commanding position within their Party during the 1950s. In any case, it is important to distinguish between the rhetoric of 'neo-Liberalism' and the reality of policy. It was never the case that state intervention was abandoned during the 1950s; rather, within the limits of the post-war settlement, it was substantially reduced and reformulated. Moreover, it must be remembered that the essential precondition of even 'neo-Liberal' aspirations was economic expansion. It is significant that as the post-war boom slackened in the later 1950s, the government's response was not to move toward a more explicitly *laisser-faire* approach, but rather to return to the orthodoxies of state intervention and planning.

Indeed, it is striking that Harris (1972) emphasizes the essential pragmatism of the policy shifts which took place. In particular, the government appeared to be responding to pressures from major sections of industry to redirect economic policy in the face of the deteriorating international competitiveness of British domestic manufacturing. This pressure was clearly demonstrated at the dramatic 1960 Conference of the FBI, where, in the presence of the Chancellor of the Exchequer, the FBI President declared:

> Economic growth . . . should be our ever-present aim. In our priorities growth comes first, because given growth all else can follow – stable prices, high employment, exports, and a secure balance of payments. Therefore we must be readier to think and plan ahead: to redeploy our resources, especially labour: to be more mobile: and to respond to change and welcome it. (FBI, *The Next Five Years*, 1960; quoted in Morgan, 1980: 9)

Hence, major sections of industrial capital saw the adoption of a planning-based growth strategy for the national economy as essential to their interests. The dependence on monetary and fiscal policy which had been characteristic of much of the 1950s was proving hopelessly inadequate; new approaches were needed.

What was required, then, was the coordination of the strategies of the large private firms and those of the state; by means of planning, the diversity of efforts within the economy could be brought to bear upon the crucial task of international competition. More critically, however, what was needed (from the point of view of the FBI) was the restriction of the rise in real wages and thereby unit costs of domestic manufacturing. The trades unions would only accept such restraint, however, given the *quid pro quo* of the promise of steady economic expansion. As Morgan (1980) puts it, ' . . . the growth option seemed the only viable long-term means to offset working-class bargaining power.' (1980: 10)

The relevance of these arguments to our concerns is that the general strategy being pushed by the FBI implied a clear shift with respect to regional development policy too. In 1963 – before the major policy statements from the NEDC – the FBI issued its own guidelines for the future conduct of regional policy. These included higher financial incentives to locate in the depressed areas; a more rigorous application of IDC controls; the designation of growth areas; an increase and acceleration of public investment programmes to improve economic and social infrastructure in the problem regions; and the establishment of autonomous regional planning agencies, with industrial representation (FBI, 1963). The point here is that by reducing regional inequalities in the distribution of unemployment, the economy would then be able to sustain higher levels of aggregate employment, without generating wage inflation through the creation of tight labour markets, such as had been experienced in the conurbations of the Midlands and the South East.

In summary, then, the redirection of regional development strategy during the early 1960s cannot be adequately understood as some kind of natural response to specific economic problems. Rather, it should be interpreted in the context of much wider reorientations in economic policy generally, in response to a deteriorating British domestic economy. Moreover, the policy shift was an outcome of essentially political pressures exerted upon the Conservatives from key sections of industrial capital, which were themselves badly affected by economic decline, reinforced, it would appear, by regionalist lobbies. Nevertheless, at this stage, policy changes remained limited, and certainly nothing like an integrated strategy either for the national economy or urban and regional problems had emerged.

Political realignment and the emergence of 'indicative planning'

However, after the General Election of 1964 and the formation of a Labour government, a thoroughgoing 'growth through planning' strategy was adopted. The whole question of economic planning – including regional development – had been a central feature of the election campaign; with Labour laying great stress on the '13 Wasted Years' of Conservative mismanagement of the economy. In addition, there was a strikingly 'regional' dimension to the pattern of actual voting; compared with the 1959 Election, the Conservatives lost 28 per cent of their seats in Scotland, Wales and the North of England, whilst only 12 per cent in the remainder of the country (indeed, if the latter pattern had been the general one, they would have retained power) (Butler and King, 1965). It is perhaps not surprising, therefore, that changes in the organization of economic management featured strongly amongst the early activities of the new administration, with regional strategy playing a central role.

Most significantly, the Department of Economic Affairs (DEA) was created, under the direction of the then Deputy Prime Minister, Mr George Brown. It was intended that it would assume responsibility for the restructuring and modernization of the economy in the longer term; leaving the Treasury – traditionally the dominant influence in economic policy – with the remit of short-term, *financial* control (for example, Shanks, 1977). In addition, the Ministry of Technology was set up to implement the modernization programme; with the Industrial Reorganization Corporation (IRC) playing a key role in the rationalization of British industry and the creation of industrial enterprises which could compete successfully in the international economy. Finally, public expenditure was greatly increased with the intention of overhauling the infrastructure of the British economy, its communication network, its educational system and its health service (for an evaluation of these initiatives generally, see Beckerman, 1972).

Regional development was to be one of the central concerns of the DEA; with the significance of the regions' potential contribution to national economic growth again being stressed. A uniform set of official regions was established, to provide the basis for a new regional level of administration in the Regional Planning Councils and the Regional Planning Boards. The former, composed of businessmen, trades unionists, academics and so forth from the regions themselves, were to provide ideas and advice for the DEA on appropriate patterns of future regional development. The Regional Boards were made up of civil servants from the various government departments already working in the regions and were intended to coordinate their departmental activities and to provide the nuclei of integrated regional administrative centres (Sharpe, 1975). By means of this new governmental apparatus, then, it was envisaged that efficient administration would be paralleled by a kind of regional economic development, which not only coordinated regional with national policy objectives, but also tied together economic change with urban and land-use change at the more local level, integrating responses to urban and regional problems.

Further evidence of the new government's intent with regard to the regions was given in the immediate increases in expenditure on industrial estates and advance factories, and in the number of Development Districts. Moreover, IDC controls were tightened and the regulation of office development was introduced through the Office Development Permit (ODP) system (McCallum, 1979).

However, the clearest expression of the administration's aspirations came in its much vaunted *National Plan* (Cmnd. 2764, 1965). At the British level, it envisaged an economic growth rate of 25 per cent between 1964 and 1970, necessitating the planned reorganization of industrial investment, manning and training. The resulting improved efficiency and productivity would provide the basis for an export-drive, thus resolving the balance-of-payments problem, whilst maintaining the parity of sterling. In addition, a growth rate of this magnitude was calculated to presage a labour shortfall of some 400,000; and it was argued that some 50 per cent of this would need to be made up by means of vigorous regional policies and the consequent utilization of labour reserves. The resulting balancing-out of resources between regions would also facilitate national demand management. Under the past regimes of 'stop–go', expansionary policies had caused 'over-heating' and inflation in the more prosperous areas; whilst deflationary ones had produced unacceptably high levels of unemployment in the problem regions.

Here again, therefore, regional development policy was at the heart of more general economic strategy.

Now, as we shall see later, the *National Plan* failed to survive the severe economic crisis of 1966. However, regional policy continued to play a major role in Labour's strategy. The administration's parliamentary position was considerably strengthened at the General Election of 1966. And, in the same year, the Industrial Development Act introduced a grant for all investment in manufacturing industry, set at 20 per cent, except in the Development Areas where it was 40 per cent. The Development Areas themselves were an innovation, replacing the old, narrowly defined Development Districts with larger regional designations (which in fact included some 20 per cent of the total British population). In the following year, a Regional Employment Premium was introduced, as well as concessions on Selective Employment Tax, which together provided – on McCrone's (1969) calculations – an 8 per cent subsidy on the average firm's wages bill in the Development Areas. The net result of all these activities was that in real terms the Labour government's expenditure on regional aid during its last two years of office (1968–69 and 1969–70) was over four times what it was during its first two years; and nearly 12 times what it had been during the last two years of the previous Conservative administration (McCallum, 1979).

It has frequently been remarked that the adoption of these policies by Labour during the mid-1960s expressed the ideological dominance within the labour movement of a particular kind of revisionism (for example, Warde, 1982). Hence, the much publicized internecine strife which had beset the Labour Party during the 1950s had resulted in the majority acceptance of a policy perspective which emphasized economic efficiency and growth, within a mixed economy, as the cornerstone of social progress. It was growth – rather than redistribution – which would enable the eradication of poverty and the creation of a humane and civilized society, based upon equality of opportunity (the classic statement of this ideology is, of course, Crosland, 1956).

After his election to the leadership of the Labour Party in 1963, Harold Wilson's particular contribution was to apend to this generalized commitment a much more specific concern with the *means* by which economic growth was to be achieved: that is, by the application of expert knowledge of science and technology in the planning of economic restructuring and societal modernization (Warde, 1982). And it was this meritocratic message which was the centrepiece of the successful 1964 election campaign (Butler and King, 1965).

Not surprisingly, Labour's programme made a powerful appeal to the 'new middle class' of highly educated technologists, scientists, administrators and managers, who seemed to have most to gain; indeed, there was almost an inversion of the 'embourgeoisement' notions. Also, however, the more progressive sectors of industrial capital appear to have been won over, as might be expected given the shifts in the thinking of the FBI which we described earlier. Hence, Blank (1973) has pointed to the relative absence (compared with other general elections) of 'free enterprise' campaigns, organized by industrial companies, during the 1964 election. Clearly, what was crucial here was not simply Labour's promise of planned industrial expansion, but also its presumed superior ability to contain wage increases. Significantly, however, the *financial* interests of the City of London were much less enthusiastic about the programme. And it was these entrenched interests which, in large part, ensured the abandonment of the general 'growth through planning' strategy, in the attempt to resolve the persistent economic crises of the mid-1960s. We shall return to this later.

The reconstruction of urban policy

These changes in policy at the national and regional levels were paralleled by the major reshaping of urban policy too. Indeed, sometimes the interrelationships between the different types of policy were very close. For example, the New Towns programme was revived both as a means of ameliorating the deteriorating conditions of the conurbations (especially London), as well as providing a presumed stimulus to regional economic growth in areas such as the North East and Scotland (Aldridge, 1979). Equally, what began as central–local government conferences on the future availability of urban development land, soon became transformed into the full-scale regional studies of the mid-1960s (Cullingworth, 1980).

Nevertheless, whatever the intentions at the time of the setting-up of the Regional Economic Councils and Boards, in reality, the degree of integration between the planning of economic development, on the one hand, and land-use and urban change, on the other, was generally rather slight. Indeed, this was recognized formally during the early 1970s, when the regional planning machinery became simply a means of coordinating environmental services (the concerns of the Department of the Environment) at the regional level (Sharpe, 1975).

However, in terms of the general arguments which we are trying to develop, it is instructive to examine in some detail two aspects of urban policy change: the attempts made by the Labour administrations after 1964 to resolve the persistent problems of speculative development; and the closely related issue of the reform of the statutory land-use planning system.

The control of speculative development

As we have seen, the period of the long boom proved highly conducive to speculative development, both in housing and commercial property; and large profits stood to be gained thereby. Although the commercial property boom had slackened by the early 1960s, the restriction of the supply of offices which resulted from the imposition of the ODP system in 1965, contributed toward sharp increases in commercial property rents and values thereafter, which, moreover, went largely untaxed (Cox, 1984).

Not surprisingly, then, an increasing volume of finance was channelled into property and its development by industrial and commercial firms, insurance companies, pension funds and banks. And this investment activity is reflected in the sharp rise in the number of property firms quoted on the Stock Exchange, as well as the increase in deals in property shares (Marriott, 1967). These trends culminated in the massive property boom of the early 1970s, by which time the Conservatives had removed almost all constraints on profits from property development. As Cox (1984) puts it:

> A range of estimated figures from various sources indicate the scope of investment by the secondary and primary financial institutions in property between 1971 and 1973. Pension funds doubled their investment in real estate from £138 million to £360 million between 1966 and 1969. Quoted property companies raised £108.7 million on the Stock Exchange through capital issues in 1972 (when the whole of manufacturing industry raised only £223 million), and property unit trusts gathered a further £150 million between 1966 and 1970. . . . In 1973 insurance companies alone invested £572.7 million in property. . . . Even the larger industrial companies, like the Rank Organization and Reed International, became involved in property speculation and the financial institutions moved gradually to buy up property companies as they tried to ensure a larger share in profits for themselves. (1984: 165–6)

And as we might expect, there was widespread concern that British manufacturing industry was being starved of investment, because of the greater profitability of land and property speculation (Massey and Catalano, 1978).

In short, then, the development process became an increasingly charged political issue through the 1960s; not simply at the local level of opposition to a specific development proposal, but also nationally, with major elements of financial capital having a considerable stake in the maintenance of the *status quo*. All this, of course, caused considerable embarrassment to the Conservatives in government up until 1964 and for the Party in opposition thereafter. They had themselves been responsible for the policy changes with regard to land during the 1950s, as we have seen. However, they could not be immune to the widespread media claims that massive speculative gains were being made out of land and property transactions. Nor was it easy to reconcile an ideological commitment to owner-occupation with land policies which were widely argued to be pushing up house prices (Cox, 1984).

The principal response from successive Conservative Ministers to these conflicting pressures was to emphasize the relationship between high land prices and the *supply* of development land. State activity, therefore, should be directed to ensuring that adequate land was made available in those areas where development pressures were high. However, following the election defeat of 1964 and the consequent changes within the Conservative Party (most particularly the election of Mr Edward Heath to the leadership), pressure of circumstances was sufficient to induce a commitment to a special levy on betterment and speculative gains in land (Cox, 1984).

However, even this minimal undertaking was short-lived. The strenuous opposition which was mounted against Labour's Land Commission Bill (organized by, *inter alia*, Mrs Margaret Thatcher) coincided with a retreat from ideas of special levies and a renewed dependence upon the efficacy of ordinary fiscal measures: a trend which was, of course, entirely consistent with the emerging 'spirit of Selsdon' and the withdrawal from interventionism, which characterized the first two years of Mr Heath's administration after the General Election of 1970 (Blackburn, 1971). However, the removal of direct controls through the 1971 Land Commission Dissolution Act, added to the taking away of effective taxation of profits from land and property speculation and the more general expansion of the money supply, created ideal conditions for the property boom which we described earlier.

It may well appear that none of these difficulties should have troubled the Labour Party. Its commitment to planning as a means of rectifying the anomalies of the free market; its traditional opposition to financial interests; its concern to provide decent housing and urban environments: all these suggest that a strongly interventionist land policy should provide an important and popular part of the policy programme.

In fact, the influential policy statement, *Signposts for the Sixties* (Labour Party, 1961), did include a commitment to the nationalization of all 'dead ripe' development land by means of a Land Commission. Moreover, the Party's Election Manifesto in 1964 promised that a Land Commission would be established to buy development land at its value in existing use, plus a small surplus for the land-owner to facilitate the release of land. In this way, the Land Commission could ensure that development proceeded rationally and that no obstacles in the land market prevented the provision of housing to the mass of the population; thereby, contributing substantially to the solution of the increasingly pressing problems of the major urban areas.

The reality of the legislation passed by the subsequent Labour Government, however, was very different. The Land Commission *was* set up in 1967. But it was actually given the task of buying up development land for future release and of collecting a betterment levy of 40 per cent (which was to rise by stages to 50 per cent) from the seller at the time of development. The more thoroughgoing powers outlined in the Manifesto were relegated to some unspecified, future date. In effect, then, the Commission was simply to undertake the very slow process of building up a bank of land necessary for development and of reintroducing a modest levy on betterment: scarcely the innovations to restructure the land market thoroughly (Cox, 1984).

As has been indicated most clearly in the *Diaries* of Richard Crossman (1975), who served as Minister of Housing and Local Government between 1964 and 1966, the shifts in policy between writing the 1964 Election Manifesto and the 1967 Land Commission Act can be explained, at one level, in terms of conflicts which were wholly *internal* to the administration. Crossman himself became convinced of the unworkability of the Manifesto proposals and was – with good reason – fearful of the effects of their implementation upon his own housing programme. Accordingly, he mounted a sustained opposition to the proposals in Cabinet, of which the sponsoring Minister, Fred Willey of the Ministry of Land and Natural Resources, was not a member. However, he also suggests that the influence of the bureaucrats was very powerful too. His Permanent Secretary, Dame Evelyn Sharpe, was untiring in her criticism of the Manifesto proposals and successfully influenced not only Crossman himself, but also the Treasury. As Crossman remarks, the situation changed rather rapidly after the retirement of Sharpe and, equally significantly, the absorption of the functions of the Ministry of Land and Natural Resources (which was abolished) into Crossman's own Ministry (Crossman, 1975).

However, this is only to give one part of the story. Crossman's *Diaries* again give ample evidence of the pressure which was being exerted upon the Labour government to modify its proposals by corporate institutions which represented very powerful interests in the land development market. For example, the associations representing the building industry, as well as the building societies, had regular meetings with the Minister to voice their opposition in terms of the effects on the supply of new houses (which, they argued, would be severely constrained).

As Dunleavy (1981) has shown, these pressures coincided with a campaign on the part of the major building contractors on behalf of industrialized building approaches to the provision of housing. This campaign was clearly aimed at increasing productivity and, thereby, profitability, through greater control over building workers (Ravetz, 1980). However, it also implied the growth in levels of house-building, which would have been jeopardized by the land policies outlined in the Manifesto. Much more generally too, the interests of large sections of financial capital were inimical to any intervention by the state to secure a more thoroughgoing control over the development process; as is indicated by the patterns of investment in land and property speculation described earlier. And it should not be forgotten that such groups were in an especially powerful situation given the deepening financial crises confronting the government during the later 1960s.

Perhaps most significant of all, however, is the fact that even the more extensive powers set out in the 1964 Manifesto were limited and partial when set against the magnitude of the land and development problem. It was this inadequacy which provided the essential precondition for the retreat between 1964 and the framing of the Land Commission Bill. Thus, Massey and Catalano's (1978) comments on the later Community Land Act and Land Development Tax Act apply equally well to the 1960s proposals: it was never even envisaged that land as a whole was to be nationalized, but only development land; moreover, the latter was to be very closely defined in terms of certain specific land-uses. In short, then, even if the Manifesto programme had been implemented, there would by no means have been a revolution in the land market; and it is unlikely that even a sound basis for a more rational pattern of urban development would have been provided.

This is, of course, hardly surprising, given what we have already said about the dominant forces within the Labour Party during the period under consideration. It is arguable, therefore, that there was an inevitable link between the ascendancy of revisionism within the Labour Party and the almost wholly ineffective legislation on the land problem during the later 1960s; an ineffectiveness which Crossman (1975) himself was later to acknowledge.

Accordingly, the major emphasis of the Land Commisison came to be the facilitation of private-sector house-building, which was experiencing severe difficulties during these years, with falls in the numbers of private housing completions for the first time since the mid-1950s (for example, Ball, 1983). Of course, this did relatively little for the problems of the less advantaged urban residents; problems which were further exacerbated by the failures of Labour's public housing programme, following the public expenditure cuts of the later 1960s (Merrett, 1979).

The reformulation of land-use planning
As we should expect, these sorts of very general points were not very frequently made in the *contemporary* debate on the ineffectiveness

of the Labour policy. What was referred to, however, was the relationship between the failures of the land policy and the inadequacy of the land-use planning system (Cullingworth, 1980). In fact, the previous Conservative administration had already set in motion the reform of this land-use planning system by establishing the Planning Advisory Group (PAG), comprising representatives of the major professions involved in local government, to prepare appropriate recommendations.

PAG's report, *The Future of Development Plans,* was presented to the Labour government in 1965, and was highly critical of the exclusive emphasis on the physical ordering of land-use embodied in the 1947 system. It suggested the integration of land-use planning *sensu stricto* with the trend planning of population, employment, transport and other socio-economic change. Thereby, it was argued, planning would be better equipped to deal with the pressing problems of Britain's urban areas.

This was the general approach adopted in the 1968 Town and Country Planning Act. It was to be implemented by means of Structure Plans, setting out the broad patterns of development for a county area or major town, and Local Plans, which were to fill in the detailed spatial arrangements for local areas. Moreover, the preparation of both types of plan was to include the opportunity for the general public to scrutinize proposals and to lodge objections where necessary; and these undertakings with respect to public participation in the planning process were subsequently reinforced by the recommendations of the Skeffington Committee, which reported in 1969.

As a number of commentators have remarked, this reformulation of the land-use planning system passed almost wholly without party-political controversy. Crossman, the responsible Minister, remarked that '. . . there was one Bill, the Planning Bill, *created by PAG.* That's the Bill I adopted and I have no doubt we shall see it put through by my successor. But it isn't a Labour Party Bill. It is the kind of Bill which any government will pass in due course. . . .' (1975:621; our emphasis)

Whilst we would agree with Crossman that the 1968 Act was powerfully influenced by the debate amongst the professionals over the shortcomings of state policy with respect to urban development, this is not to say that the production of the legislation was somehow 'neutral' or 'apolitical'. Thus, Dunleavy (1980; 1981) has demonstrated that professional groups regularly exert an important influence in the process or urban policy formation and should therefore themselves be analysed as central political actors. Certainly, what is interesting in this case is the readiness with which the professional interests involved, accepted and promoted a characteristically 'Whig' view of planning, which stressed its *technical* competences to produce more rational patterns of urban and regional development. In fact, not only was this claim grossly inflated, but also it side-stepped fundamental issues of the distributional consequences of planning activity. And, of course, this became increasingly clear as the effects of the broader decline of the British economy on the condition of the urban areas grew more intense.

It is also important, however, to make connections between the type of land-use planning which was envisaged in the 1968 Act and the general political climate in which the Act was formulated. Clearly, the new planning which was aspired to was not simply a matter of a new formal structure for statutory activity. Rather, as the professionals were advocating, what was foreseen was a much more effective and efficient shaping of urban change by means of the application of more sophisticated and technically expert methods of planning: in the future urban planners would have to be the masters and mistresses of a powerful new battery of technical tools by means of which the appropriate forecasts and projections about urban and regional development could be made.[1]

This sort of approach is, of course, wholly consistent with the much more general trends towards a thoroughly technocratic style of politics which was characteristic of the Labour administrations of the 1960s (especially during the middle years of the decade) and, accordingly, was symptomatic of other policy innovations which were going on at the same time over a wide range of fields. It is thus especially important to understand that, as Warde (1982) has argued most cogently, the modernization of Britain which was the central plank of Labour's programme, was not simply a matter of restructuring the economy to new standards of technological efficiency, it also implied the thoroughgoing overhaul of the system of government and administration itself, so that the latter could match the expertise which was to be developed in the private sector. Only in this way would the economic growth and greater equality of opportunity which the Labour Party aimed for, be achieved. Hence, for example, Warde (1982) describes the views of Tony Benn, who as Postmaster-General (1964–66) and then Minister of Technology (1966–70) was a key figure in the technocratic trend within the Labour Party at the time:

> For Benn, Britain was characterized by traditionalism and amateurism; its institutions needed to be brought up to date. He argued the need for reform: of an 'amateur centralized Civil Service'; of a 'weak ill-equipped House of Commons'; of the 'creaking piecemeal structure of local government'; and of the legal system. (1982:97; quoting from A. Wedgewood Benn, *The Regeneration of Britain*, 1965).

[1]Numerous contemporary accounts give a flavour of this new perspective; see, for example, McLoughlin, 1969 or Chadwick, 1971.

We would suggest, then, that we need to interpret the reformulation of the land-use planning system as one small part of this much broader movement. The emphasis upon the exercise of technical expertise in the new planning was indicative of a whole theory of how government ought to be executed: in the same way that a planned economy would eradicate Britain's persistent economic problems, so a reformulated urban planning would resolve the growing problems of Britain's towns and cities. However, much more significant in the wider policy change, was the reorganization of the structure of local government, through which most urban and regional policy was actually implemented.

The reorganization of local government

Cockburn (1977), in a study of local government reform in the London Borough of Lambeth, gives a good idea of the sorts of consideration which were held to underpin this reform:

> in the late fifties, a period of structural development [in local government] . . . began. As the official architects of the reforms made clear, they . . . were impelled by economic change. Industrial development, population growth and a dramatic increase in the use of motor transport had caused towns to spill out far beyond the boundaries of the authorities meant to govern them. For a start much larger authorities were needed. Existing authorities were 'too small of area, population and resources, including highly qualified manpower and technical equipment' for the job they had to do, wrote Lord Redcliffe-Maud. Since the war the government had 'had to assume far more direct responsibility for the management of the economy'. Modernization was overdue. 'There is an evident contrast between this enormous increase in the activities of government and the extent and pace of change in government institutions' wrote the authors of the Kilbrandon Report on the Constitution. (1977:11–12)[2]

It is clear, then, that the perception of a close relationship between economic development and the need to overhaul the system of government and administration was no idiosyncrasy of the 1960s Labour programme. It was shared by the official and expert inquiries (admittedly, for the most part appointed by the Labour government itself), which were established to advise on the nature of the necessary reform.

Dearlove's (1979) definitive analysis has gone further in identifying more precisely the shortcomings which were attributed to local government in its traditional form. Firstly, as Cockburn (1977)

[2]The quotations are taken from, respectively, the Redcliffe-Maud Report, *Local Government in England* (Cmnd. 4039, 1969) and the Kilbrandon Report on the Constitution (Cmnd. 5460–1, 1973).

correctly emphasizes, there was the problem of the size of local authorities. They were widely held to be too small to enable proper planning (because of urban expansion) or to provide an adequate population base for the provision of specialist services. In addition, small authorities were unable to attract the highest quality of personnel. Secondly, it was believed that the calibre of local councillors was inadequate to ensure effective administration, in the face of the increasingly complex problems confronting local authorities. Thirdly, it came to be seen somewhat later that the first two problems could not be separated from questions of the efficacy of the internal management structures of local government: that is, from the means by which policies were formulated and implemented.

As we have already suggested, the principal vehicle for the articulation of these problems of local government was the official inquiries mounted during the 1960s. Nevertheless, there was no straightforward link between the recommendations of these various Committees and Commissions and actual changes in policy. This was especially clear, for example, in the case of the Redcliffe-Maud Report (Cmnd. 4039, 1969). Hence, the Report proposed two types of local government structure: a two-tier one, such as already operated in Greater London, for the major metropolitan areas of Manchester, Liverpool and Birmingham; and a unitary one for the remainder of the country, with each local authority covering a fairly wide 'city-region'. Brand (1974) has suggested that these recommendations were substantially acceptable to the Labour administration. However, before they could be implemented, the Conservatives were elected to office in the 1970 General Election. And in the 1972 Local Government Act, the new Conservative government actually put into effect a system which comprised two-tier authorities for the whole of the country: metropolitan counties and districts for the six conurbations of the West Midlands, Merseyside, Greater Manchester, West Yorkshire, South Yorkshire and Tyne and Wear; and plain counties and districts for the remainder.

A number of analyses have attributed these shifts to nothing more than the most basic party political considerations. McKay and Cox (1979) comment, for example, that '. . . the Conservatives would hardly regard with benevolence any measure which undermined the Conservative dominated counties.' (1979: 49) Likewise, *New Society* (1971) described the Conservative proposals as '. . . a pure political carve up, devoid of all justification in terms of social geography or of good planning.' (1971:259) Certainly, there is ample evidence that the relationships between residential segregation, local authority boundaries and political control have not escaped the attention of politicians; as Crossman's *Diaries* demonstrate quite clearly. Equally, there are a number of examples of ludicrous decisions on the new local authority boundaries, which seem justifiable only in terms of narrowly political considerations; perhaps the most glaring of which was the creation of the almost unviable county of Mid Glamorgan, thereby removing the certainty of permanent Labour control of what became neighbouring South Glamorgan.

However, important though these specific considerations are, they should not be allowed to divert our attention wholly from the determinants of the wider structure of reorganization. Hence, Dearlove (1979) reminds us of the considerable pressures which were exerted by organizations representing industrial and commercial capital to increase the voice of these interests in the running of local government, by creating larger authorities. He quotes, for example, from the evidence of Aims of Industry to the Redcliffe-Maud Royal Commission:

> Given the present pattern of local authority boundaries and social structures in England, industry's directors and executives rarely live in local authorities where industry is situated, and are even more rarely represented on these authorities . . . . The result is that industry goes without adequate representation locally. (1979:79; quoting from *Written Evidence of Commercial, Industrial and Political Organizations to the Royal Commission on Local Government in England,* 1969)

Similarly, the Confederation of British Industries (CBI) is reported as asserting that '. . . local councils only attract members from a limited section of the community and lack sufficient representation from industry and the professions, (1979:99; quoting from *Written Evidence of Commercial, Industrial and Political Organizations to the Royal Commission on Local Government in England,* 1969) Dearlove (1979) goes on to suggest that it is this which lay behind the call for an improved calibre of councillor.

It is also important to recognize that the need to control the total amount of public expenditure came to be seen as a means of tackling the persistent economic crises besetting successive administrations. As we have seen, the Welfare State imposed major burdens upon state spending, which in the context of Britain's poor domestic economic performance, was leading rapidly to what O'Connor (1973) has referred to as the 'fiscal crisis of the state', necessitating the restructuring of the state's revenue and expenditure patterns. Local government, as a major spender, was clearly to play a key role here. Hence, for example, the transfers of population which resulted from local government reorganization were very favourable to financial retrenchment in key services such as education and social welfare. Control of these functions passed from high-spending, urban and potentially Labour local authorities, to low-spending, quasi-rural and pretty solidly Conservative authorities (Dunleavy, 1980).

Moreover, Cockburn (1977) has developed related arguments in terms of the changes in the *internal* functioning of local government, which, in general terms at least, involved the quite widespread adoption of the methods of scientific management and, in particular, corporate planning. She argues that these were '. . . a response to these two problems. On the one hand the growing need to keep down costs, to manage scarce resources as fears grew about the level of public spending. On the other the apparently undiminishing problem of deprivation, the shame of urban poverty in what was supposed to be a thriving and exemplary capitalist society.' (1977:65)

Clearly, this latter point is especially important for our purposes. It serves to underline the fact that the reforms which we have described – both specifically and more generally – were ostensibly formulated to ameliorate the problems which were becoming increasingly apparent as Britain's economic decline worsened. In particular, as we saw in Chapter 2, this decline and the attempts by capital to counter it, were having especially severe consequences for the cities. As we shall see later, however, the constraints imposed by the need to limit public expenditure served to incapacitate urban and regional reforms.

All this is not to suggest, however, that it is sensible to conceive of the reorganization of local government simply in terms of responses to external pressures. Again Dearlove (1979) is especially clear in his arguments that such pressures were only part of the complex structure of determinants. For example, he reports that the *Written Evidence of HM Treasury to the Royal Commission on Local Government in England* (1969:4–5), whilst anxious to impose constraint on local authority expenditure by means of greater central government control, recognized the contradiction between such control and the need to maintain the supposed independence and responsiveness of local government. Similarly, he argues that whatever the influence exerted by private industry and commerce over the structure of local government reform, it remains the case that local authorities, more than other parts of the state, are accessible to working-class control. And we shall return to the implications of these arguments later.

Nevertheless, despite these *caveats,* it is clear that the influence exerted by external industrial and commercial interests on the reorganization of local government was very powerful. Indeed, the same general conclusion holds for all of the attempts at reform which we have considered here. So much may, of course, be unsurprising, given the arguments of earlier chapters. However, the circumstances of the 1960s were important in that not only did they produce a context in which the reformulation or urban and regional policy was essential, but also they imposed severe constraints upon what new forms of state intervention could achieve. Accordingly, we need to understand more about the interrelationships between this context, class interests and the effects of the restructured urban and regional policies.

Economic decline, class interests and urban and regional policy

The newly returned Labour administration after 1964 was almost immediately confronted with massive economic problems, which were defined conventionally, in terms of balance-of-payments deficits and the need to maintain the parity of sterling. Initially, the government was able to resist the considerable pressures to resort to the traditional, deflationary measures – especially from the Bank of England – and pressed ahead with its 'growth through planning' strategy. However, certainly by 1965, there was beginning to be a retreat from this innovative position, back to the orthodoxies of economic restraint. For instance, Crossman (1975) shows that there was a clear recognition by at least some members of the Cabinet that the *National Plan* would have to be revised even before it was published!

By the following year, the external pressures on the government were even heavier. As Shanks (1977), then working for the administration, recalls:

> During the summer of 1966 renewed pressure on the pound developed, and partly due to inattention by Ministers in the euphoria and exhaustion following the election victory in March, things were allowed to deteriorate to the point in July when the economy faced a massive crisis of confidence.

> In this crisis, the Cabinet was divided. George Brown and a small group of ministers argued for devaluation as the only alternative to deflation. They were over-ruled, largely due to the insistence of the Prime Minister and the Chancellor. Instead, a massive series of deflationary measures was announced, including heavy cuts in public investment, tighter building controls, increased taxes on consumption, and higher bank rate. (1977:44–5)

However, even these measures were inadequate and by 1967, the Six-Day War between Israel and the Arab states was precipitating yet another sterling crisis, which led to the devaluation of the pound anyway (Beckerman, 1972).

These events, in turn, implied the abandonment of the economic strategy which had borne Labour into government in 1964 and again – much more convincingly – in 1966. The *National Plan* was formally scrapped in July 1966. Certainly, during the period after 1966, not only did the Labour government resort to 'stop–go' policies, but also introduced compulsory wage restraint through the National Board for Prices and Incomes (NBPI), to combat rising inflation (which was, in fact, endemic to the Keynesian-Welfare State) (Tarling and Wilkinson, 1977). Moreover, legislation was proposed to restrict strikes, in face of increasing concern over Britain's supposed 'strike proneness' (Crouch, 1977). All, of course, policies which were arguably more appropriate to a Conservative than a Labour government.

Industrial restructuring and regional strategy

It is important to recognize, however, that the significance of these events extends beyond their immediate context. The point here is that the mid-1960s Labour programme was a major attempt to resolve what – as we have seen – was a *chronic* weakness in the British economy. This was so despite the very real doubts as to the effectiveness of the 'growth through planning' strategy, even if it had been allowed to operate fully (for example, Budd, 1978). Hence, Labour's attempt to modernize and restructure the economy was, in effect, an attempt to reverse the long-term decline in the domestic manufacturing base, on terms which preserved the essential elements of the post-war settlement, but which extended Keynesian strategy into the direct organization of production (at least in intent). Accordingly, its ultimate failure marked the beginning of the demise of the post-war settlement and the ending of the ideological dominance of social democratic consensus in British politics. Moreover, the circumstances of the abandonment of the strategy in its strong form serve to highlight some of the realities of the distribution of power in post-war Britain.

Most importantly, these circumstances demonstrate the important distinctions to be drawn between different fractions of capital in terms of the kinds of economic policies which best serve their interests. Thus, as we suggested in Chapter 2, the resilience of 'stop–go' policies – reflected in their reassertion after 1966 – should be understood in the context of the pre-eminence of British financial capital over other forms. The dependence of the City on *international* operations meant that a priority was attached to the maintenance of the stability of sterling against the US dollar and of other symbols of the reliability of British finance. This effectively ruled out a whole range of *alternative* policy options, such as the control of international capital flows or devaluation, to provide a breathing-space for further industrial reorganization. Similarly, the *international* activities of British multinational companies also had a limiting effect upon the choice of economic strategy. And certainly, the relevance of this sector in the preclusion of import controls (in general, at least) is clear. Moreover, of course, the actual effects of the deflationary part of the 'stop–go' cycles were felt most acutely by those directly dependent upon the home economy: domestic manufacturing industry and the working class.

Hence, the economic orthodoxies which were pushed so strongly during the late 1960s (and, indeed, at other crisis periods) by the Treasury and the Bank of England *within* the state apparatus (for example, Shanks, 1977), in reality reflected the structure of interests which existed *externally*. In addition, the conflict at the level of economic strategy was matched by a wholly institutional one between the DEA and the Treasury over the control of economic policy. The Treasury's victory in the latter was recognized beyond doubt with the abolition of the DEA in October 1969. More generally, this outcome exemplified the established subservience of the economic *planning* apparatus (whether in the form of the DEA, the NEDC, the IRC or whatever) to the central axis of the Treasury and the Bank of England (Jessop, 1980).

These general propositions about the determinants of economic policy are by no means remote from our immediate concerns with urban and regional development. For example, we suggested earlier that an important part of the ineffectuality of Labour's land policies during the 1960s may be explained by the power and influence of very often precisely the same financial interests which were exerting a determining influence upon more general economic policies. More specifically, again as we showed earlier, even at the height of the property boom of the late 1960s and early 1970s, when genuine fears were being expressed that manufacturing industry was being starved of investment because of the vast profits to be made out of speculative property development, successive governments (of both parties, in fact) failed to restrict such activity either by controling commercial rents, or by limiting bank lending to property companies or by increased taxation of profits from speculation (Cox, 1984).

There were also clear implications for the pattern of regional policy. Most immediately, the failure of the 'growth through planning' strategy and the resumption of 'stop–go' meant that economic growth in the depressed regions was made much more difficult than it could otherwise have been. In effect, then, what was implied here was a choice of political priorities between the interests of British international capital and those of the regions; and, of course, of domestic capital and the labour movement more generally. The clear devaluation of the latter was further emphasized with the virtual demise of the administrative machinery of regional planning, which went hand-in-hand with the abolition of the DEA (Sharpe, 1975).

However, it is clearly *not* the case that there was any straightforward abandonment of regional policy after 1966. On the contrary, as we have already seen, there was a considerable *increase* in the expenditure on regional policy, right up until the last year of Labour's tenure of office. Furthermore, many commentators have argued that regional policy was very effective in restructuring the economies of the regions during these years, generating many thousands of new jobs, irrespective of the difficulties occasioned by 'stop–go' policies for the national economy (for example, Moore and Rhodes, 1973).

Morgan (1980) has argued most emphatically, however, that to consider regional policies after 1966 as self-contained and autonomous is only very partial. Rather, they should be seen as one part of a much more general attempt to carry through the reorganization and modernization of the British economy which had been at the centre of Labour's original programme, and which continued to be necessary to facilitate industrial capital's attempts to counter falling rates of profit, now that the long boom had ended (as we saw in Chapter 2).

Hence, it is significant that the investment grants introduced by the Industrial Development Act of 1966 were in fact available over the *whole* of the country and only differentially in the Development Areas. Moreover, they were not tied to the provision of extra employment; and assistance was to be focused on those industries with a key contribution to make to the balance of payments. In addition, the grants were more advantageous to industries retaining a large share of profits and undertaking large *capital* investments, and they were used to support major import-substitution investments in sectors such as aluminium and pulp and paper (Dunford, Geddes and Perrons, 1981).

Furthermore, these investment grants were part of a much wider programme of subsidy, aimed at the restructuring of British industry, which was introduced at more or less the same time. Most notable here was the creation of the IRC, to push through the rationalization of key industrial sectors by direct intervention, using its own money capital (set initially at £150,000,000). It was a major force behind the reorganization of the nuclear industry, the electronics and electrical engineering industries and the indigenous motor-car industry; it also intervened in other areas to encourage centralization and concentration of industrial capital. In addition, the Ministry of Technology encouraged scientific and technical innovations and their application in industry; for example, in modernizing the machine-tool industry and promoting the British computer industry (Young with Lowe, 1974).

This kind of analysis has led some commentators to dismiss the 'regional' element in regional policy altogether. For example, Pickvance (1981) argues that '. . . state regional policy has become, since 1966 if not before, a means by which accumulation by industrial capitalists is bolstered in a period of falling profitability. In other words the 'regional' element of the policy is completely subsidiary, and is an example of the way that thinking in terms of spatial units can conceal the real social processes involved . . .' (1981:241) He also claims that subsidies have been given to many firms which would have located in the Development Areas *irrespective* of the grants available; an obvious example here is the oil installations in the north of Scotland and west Wales. In short, then, the post-1966 regional policies were aimed at facilitating the restructuring of British industry; a restructuring which, moreover, was carried out on capital's terms, in response to the immanent problems of the accumulation process.

There would appear to be some considerable force in this argument. As we have seen, there is ample evidence of the profitability problems being experienced by many industries during this period (for example, Glyn and Sutcliffe, 1972). In addition, the responses to such problems by some of the more advanced sectors of industrial capital did involve the substantial restructuring of the technology of production and of the labour process, which could only have been made easier by the kinds of policy we have described. More specifically, the analysis by Massey and Meegan (1979) of the reorganization of the electrical engineering and electronics industries, under the aegis of the IRC, demonstrates the disastrous effects of such reorganization on the inner areas of the cities, as the trend towards the decentralization of manufacturing to the more rural areas and to the peripheral industrial regions proceeded. In this sense, then, state policies (including regional development strategies) served to facilitate a process of industrial change which was already underway, with the severest consequences for many inner-city residents.

However, in its stronger forms, the analysis with respect to regional policy understates the complexities of the processes involved.[3] Hence, for example, it does not satisfactorily explain why *any* element of discrimination in favour of the less prosperous parts of the country was retained in the post-1966 legislation. Whilst Pickvance's (1981) argument that there was a need to ensure that investment was actually carried out in Britain explains the advantages of the grant system over other forms of subsidy, it does not have much bearing on the issue of the *differential* rates available in the different types of region.

Similar arguments can be made more powerfully if we turn to the Regional Employment Premium, which was introduced in 1967. Clearly, Selective Employment Tax, through which the Regional Employment Premium was administered, was intended to subsidize employment in manufacturing, rather than in the services, and may

[3]Pickvance has himself recognized this subsequently; see Pickvance, (1985).

therefore be considered a part of the general programme aimed at industrial restructuring. However, the extra premium paid for workers in the Development Areas is difficult to comprehend except in terms of an intention to reduce regional unemployment, by means of – in reality – increasing the competitiveness of manufacturing in the depressed regions. Admittedly, however, as a subsidy paid on employees already in employment, its precise effects are rather difficult to determine.

What is left out of the sort of analysis presented by Pickvance (1981) is the pressure exerted upon the state by the labour movement – in terms of the need to generate more jobs – and, more specifically, regionalist and, by the later 1960s, nationalist groupings (often including local industrial capital) – in terms of the specific problems of their area (Rees and Lambert, 1981). Moreover, it seems likely that during periods of Labour administration, the state may be especially susceptible to such pressures, given the Party's traditional constituency (for example, Crossman, 1975). It is considerations such as these which perhaps explain the continued emphasis upon regional policy during these years, in spite of the manifest deterioration of the economies of the cities, irrespective of their regional location.

What, then, are the general conclusions to be drawn from this rather diffuse discussion? Firstly, we would argue that the policy shifts of the later 1960s and early 1970s which we have outlined, should be understood in terms of the pressures exerted by powerful external interests. In particular, the abandonment of the 'growth through planning' strategy owed a great deal to the priority attached to the aims and objectives of an internationally orientated sector of capital, centred upon the financial interests of the City and the multinational companies.

Nevertheless, the fundamental problems of the British economy – underlying those of the balance of payments and sterling parity – remained those of the lack of competitiveness of the domestic industrial sector; and, indeed, these problems were accentuated by the policy context. However, the attempt at modernization continued, albeit in an attenuated and modified form. In particular, policies aimed at the restructuring of sectors of industrial capital (and regional policy may be included here) should be interpreted in the light of the mobilization of tendencies to counter the fall in profit rates, consequent upon the end of the long boom. And the decentralizing trends in manufacturing industry, away from the major urban areas, which were the major spatial expression of these countertendencies, were thereby facilitated.

Furthermore, the *form* which these modernization policies took after 1966 – one aspect of which was the enduring regional dimension – should be interpreted in the context of the complex of influences exerted by particular sectors of industrial capital, as well as sections of the labour movement and, indeed, regionalist/nationalist groups. Finally, it is clear that these diverse determinants did not act upon a wholly compliant state. Rather, the nature of the state, both in terms of the political complexion of the administration, as well as the character of the bureaucracy, was a significant mediating factor, contributing in full to the eventual policy outcomes and their effects.

The emergent 'fiscal crisis', urban policy and the cities

The latter point is more clearly illustrated by reference to another aspect of the reforms which we sketched earlier: the reorganization of local government. It is worth quoting at length from Dearlove's (1979) authoritative account:

> At the most general level, the problem of local government can be seen as an aspect of the overall problem of the public sector in a capitalist economy. This is the problem that centres on the sources of state revenue and the scale of public expenditure, and on the scope and direction of state intervention . . . . More fundamentally, however, the problem of local government goes beyond this. It derives from the fact that local government is neither an instrument of business nor a mere agent of the central state. This does not mean that it is completely autonomous and neutral as some might maintain. But the *particular and enduring* problem of local government in all of this century has been one that transcends the immediate moment of any economic crisis . . . . In my view the particular problem of local government centres on its relative autonomy from both the concerns of the central state and the impact of the dominant classes. Related to this, local government is especially vulnerable to working-class demands, pressures, and even control . . . . The study of the reorganization of local government has to be undertaken as a study of the struggle to counter its relative autonomy from dominant interests and the state in order that closer links might be asserted between economic and governmental power. (1979:244–5)

A number of extremely important points are made here. Firstly, the reorganization of local government cannot be disassociated from the wider crisis of the Welfare State, which was beginning to become urgent by the 1960s. An emergent 'fiscal crisis' necessitated the attempt to restructure state spending, although in ways which did the least damage to the dominant interests of capital. What was implied, then, was the need to subordinate the local state to centralized control, thereby ensuring local state activities in accordance with the interests of industrial and financial capital.

However, secondly, the very form of the state itself, the very relative autonomy of local government which was under attack, set an important constraint on the form of reorganization which could be carried out. On this view, for example, traditional and deeply embedded ideas with respect to the necessity of maintaining a legitimate local democracy, responsive to the immediate constituency, conflicted with and restrained any movements in the direction of either redefinitions of that constituency to reflect more closely business interests, or of vastly increased central state control. What this, in turn, implied was that the effects of the reorganization which did take place, though real enough, were very much less significant than they might have been. Certainly, as we shall see in subsequent chapters, the deepening problems of both the national economy and of the cities more particularly, have prompted the continued attempt at redefining the nature of local government and its relationships with the central state.

As we suggested earlier, some form of local government reorganization was likely to have been carried out irrespective of the particular political party in control of the state administration. We do not believe, however, that this gives any general indication of the salience of the political ideology of the governing party. Hence, we have argued throughout that the specific complexion of the Labour administrations of the 1960s was an essential ingredient in the determination of the sort of policy options which were adopted. We have already shown, for example, that whilst the reformulated system of land-use planning introduced after 1968 may be considered as a product of a professionals' debate, the general context set by Labour's aim of revitalizing and 'technicizing' government and administration as a whole was also significant.

However, it is possible to be more precise than this. The scope of change implied by such a programme was itself extremely limited, even if it had been possible to see it through to its fullest implementation. In the case of land-use planning, for instance, the new system failed to achieve even its own objectives. Accordingly, the Layfield Report (1973) on the Greater London Development Plan, was totally scathing in its criticisms of the pretensions of the Greater London planners to have any real effect on the development of the economic, social or even demographic fabric of the capital. And, indeed, subsequent government circulars, setting out guidelines on the proper approach to be adopted in the new Structure Plans, made it quite clear that there was no intention of moving very far beyond the old tradition of limited land-use designations. Certainly, there was no hint of making a reality of the 30-years-old vision of the Barlow Committee to integrate land-use planning and the shaping of the urban environment with control of the national and regional economies (despite the obvious links between the two, which we sketched in the previous section).

In a more thoroughgoing way, however, Pickvance (1977) has argued that even if a more innovative style of planning *had* been adopted effectively, it would not have gone beyond what he dubs 'trend' planning: that is, the facilitation of what market forces in any case dictated. Thus, he concludes his analysis of the development of high-rise housing and of the decline of employment in London with the comment that '. . . it is the largely unrestricted operation of market forces (in land, finance, and so on), which has been the prime determinant of urban development and that if the latter is deemed a 'failure' then there is a *prima facie* case for interventive planning on a much larger scale than has been tried in the past 25 years.' (1977:49)

His conclusion, of course, accords with the arguments which we have presented in this and earlier chapters. Certainly, there was nothing in the new approaches to urban planning which were formulated during the later 1960s which suggested a form of state intervention which would tackle effectively the deepening problems of Britain's urban areas. Indeed, it must be remembered that the general approach adopted by the Labour administrations of this period was consistent with the 'Whig' emphasis of the planning professionals on narrowly defined technical competences. The need for a genuinely interventionist system of urban planning, which would shape the distributive consequences of urban and regional change explicitly, was simply not recognized; as we saw earlier, Crossman, for example, was quite unable to see the *political* relevance of urban planning at all.

All this is the more remarkable in that during these years, in which the debates about the planning system were being conducted, there was mounting evidence of an incipient 'urban crisis'. The property boom reached its height; housing problems became more and more severe; urban poverty was being 'rediscovered'; and the inexorable decline of the British economy was reflected in the state of the cities in an increasingly intense fashion.

In fact, however, it is not simply that state policies failed to confront these problems adequately; they also contributed to their emergence. We have already discussed some of the effects of regional policies on the cities. In addition, however, throughout the 1960s, public expenditure on the built environment (excluding public house-building) continued to rise steeply, peaking at some £3,200,000,000 (in constant 1975 prices) in the early 1970s (Ball, 1983).[4] Therefore, the state system of urban planning could at least lay claim to the orchestration of this spending, which, of course, was a necessary condition of the patterns of urban development which we have described. However, in line with the general responses to the crisis of the Keynesian-Welfare State, this expenditure began to fall in the early 1970s and has continued to do so ever since. This, in turn,

[4]See Note 4 of Chapter 3 for an explanation of these data.

has posed the severest problems for urban planning, as well as for major sections of capital. In these ways, it has been symptomatic of the wider conditions which have determined the emergence of the contemporary 'inner-city crisis'.

5

Corporatism, the New Right and the urban crisis

Our purpose in this chapter is to try to make sense of the most recent phase of urban and regional strategy, when the British economy has plummeted to new depths of crisis and, of course, the 'inner-city crisis' has become a predominant focus of policy-making (for example, Loney and Allen, 1979). To do so, we shall have to draw together many of the themes and issues which have concerned us in earlier chapters. What follows, then, is the culmination of our general arguments, although formal conclusions are reserved for the next chapter.

We shall examine what appear to be two distinct phases of policy formulation; although we shall argue that there are, in fact, crucial continuities between the two. The first, whilst originating in developments during the later 1960s, is identified most closely with the high point of corporatist government in peace-time Britain, during the middle years of the 1970s (for example, Jessop, 1980). In terms of our present concerns with the cities, its most distinctive feature was a plethora of so-called 'urban experiments', which have been exhaustively described by earlier writers (for example, Lawless, 1979; 1981a). Its final statement is to be found in the analysis presented in the 1977 White Paper, *Policy for the Inner Cities* (Cmnd. 6845), subsequently embodied in the Inner Urban Areas Act of 1978.

The second phase is most readily associated with the period after the General Election of 1979, at which the New Right Conservative administration of Mrs Margaret Thatcher was returned. Indeed, much of what we have to say about this phase will be concerned with the implications of what has come to be called the 'politics of Thatcherism' (Hall and Jacques, 1983) for urban and regional change. Nevertheless, we should reiterate that there are important continuities between these Thatcherite policies and those of the previous administration, especially after 1976.

This latter point serves to remind us that the development of state policies generally was conducted *throughout* the 1970s – and particularly during the later part of the decade – within constraints set by an unremitting and persistently deepening economic decline. In these terms, then, both corporatist forms of state policy and the New Right alternative constituted attempts to resolve this economic crisis, in ways favourable to distinct combinations of class and other social interests. They both represent attempts to come to terms with the failures of the Keynesian-Welfare State and the breaking-up of the social democratic consensus and settlement on which it was based.

Hence, the central argument here (as in earlier chapters) is that urban and regional policies during these years are best understood as a part of these wider trends and developments: in marked contrast to the 'Whig' accounts sketched earlier. More precisely, we shall show how these policies were beset by the same contradictions as the wider state strategies which contain them. These contradictions, in turn, open up important possibilities for the future of Britain's cities.

'Gilding the ghetto' and the rediscovery of urban poverty

When six years of Labour government ended in 1970, an important factor in the defeat was the failure to combat effectively poverty and social inequality. Mr Wilson's outgoing administration proved vulnerable to revelations that during the years since 1964, family poverty had increased and, far from ensuring rising living standards, things had actually got worse under Labour (for example, Field, 1969). Earlier, the activities of campaigning pressure groups, allied with the discoveries of numerous official inquiries into diverse aspects of Britain's social condition, revealed circumstances which cried out for drastic policy action.

What had actually emerged, however, was a style of anti-poverty policy which focused aid and, perhaps more importantly, attention, on small *areas* of supposedly greatest need. Hence, for example, the Educational Priority Areas (or rather the schools within them) could provide a target for extra resources in the form of, for example, enhanced teachers' salaries; General Improvement Areas in the form of higher levels of housing improvement subsidies; and so on.

Such initiatives held an appeal for those whose notion of welfare benefits was that they should be reserved for the particularly needy; whilst at the same time, they avoided the embarrassment of means-testing, which was the normal way in which *selective* benefits were administered. Means-testing *areas* is something quite different from means-testing *people* of special need. In addition, they were an indication of the increasingly obvious failure of the post-1945 Welfare State to tackle the *causes* of the contingencies affecting individual citizens, as opposed to treating their symptoms through an essentially redistributive system of financial support (Jessop, 1980).

The influence of contemporary experience in the United States was also of some significance; not only in offering the policy model of area-based positive discrimination, but also in the significance of racial problems. As we mentioned in Chapter 1, the scale and intensity of the riots in American cities during the late 1960s inevitably gave rise to forebodings over their repetition on this side of the Atlantic. More generally, political controversies surrounding the settlement in Britain of Commonwealth citizens from the Caribbean and the Indian subcontinent were a continuous feature of the 1960s, which were scarred by the growth of racialist political activity (Miles and Phizacklea, 1979). Notoriously, these two trends came together in the speech given by Mr Enoch Powell, then the Member of Parliament for Wolverhampton South-West in the West Midlands and a contender for the leadership of the Conservative Party, to an audience in Birmingham in April 1968.

The furore which the speech provoked was remarkable: it spurred the Prime Minister – also in a speech made at Birmingham – to promise resolute and urgent action, not of the kind which Mr Powell hoped for, but to strike at the conditions of poverty and deprivation which were seen to fuel the fears and hostilities which Mr Powell had done so much to legitimize. In effect, Mr Wilson's response launched what seemed a significant vehicle of urban policy, which survives to the present day, although in modified form: the Urban Programme (Edwards and Batley, 1978).

In many respects, the Urban Programme exemplifies rather well the essential features of the policies of this period. What it actually involved was the direction of extra resources to areas of supposed 'special need', many of which would contain concentrations of coloured residents, by means of the subsidization of projects in the fields of education, housing, health and welfare. Hence, under the 1969 Local Government Grants (Social Needs) Act, the Home Secretary was empowered to invite local authorities to bid for 75 per cent of the cost of the projects which they themselves or voluntary organizations in their areas wished to undertake.

It may be argued that the reasons for the creation of the Urban Programme in this form reflected nothing more than the predominant ideas about urban poverty. Certainly, the areal basis of discrimination corresponded to notions of 'scattered pockets' of residual social need; a point reinforced by the manifest spatial concentrations of the coloured ethnic minorities. Equally, the concern with particular spheres of policy – and especially children – may be indicative of contemporary thinking about the origins of poverty in individual or family weaknesses and handicaps (for example, Townsend, 1979). On the other hand, Higgins *et al.* (1983) point out that, in the absence of a clearly worked-out formula before it was announced, the form which the Programme eventually assumed was shaped as much by administrative considerations, as anything else.

What is clear, however, is that the sorts of projects which have been made possible under the Urban Programme can have had little impact upon the issues of economic structure and change which we showed in Chapter 2 to constitute the most fundamental conditions of the 'inner-city crisis'.[1] Higgins *et al.* (1983) conclude even more harshly that the Programme was never *intended* to tackle basic issues:

> That the Programme was in essence a money-dispensing mechanism is one reason why it could remain relatively untouched by changing orthodoxies, but a more important reason is that the *implicit* purpose of the Programme, as the means by which successive governments have been able to give tangible expression to their social conscience, has always been more important than its explicit purpose of alleviating urban deprivation. (1983:85)

Certainly, in spite of the very public furore which provoked it, the Urban Programme – justifiably – has attracted very little attention subsequently.

It is ironic, therefore, that the Urban Programme provided the funds for a further initiative intended to combat urban poverty – the Community Development Project (CDP) – whose career concluded (somewhat abruptly) in the presentation of analyses very similar to those presented in the earlier chapters of this book. The CDP, although separate in its administrative origin, shared many of the characteristics of the Urban Programme. Again, it was intended to focus upon local areas (only 12 of them) which were presumed to be afflicted by severe social deprivation. Moreover, there can be little doubt that, at least initially, such deprivation was officially viewed as the product of individual and family malfunctioning. The task of the CDP was to develop new means of eradicating these problems by the careful implementation and evaluation of experimental projects within the selected areas; the idea was that those which were deemed successes could be adopted into the general armoury of anti-poverty policies (Loney, 1983).

In fact, these plans for a technocratic 'action-research' programme never approached fulfilment. Rather, the significance of the CDP lay in the contribution which it made to the debate about

---

[1]The breakdown of the types of projects which have been funded (between 1968 and 1982) is as follows: 40 per cent have made provision for children (nursery classes, day-care and so forth); 14.5 per cent for community projects (community centres, etc.); 14 per cent for social work and health projects; 11 per cent for special education; 8.5 per cent for advice and information centres; 7 per cent for teenagers and the elderly; and 5 per cent for miscellaneous projects (Higgins *et al.*, 1983: 74).

the origins and nature of urban poverty and the role played by the state in these. As is by now well known, what emerged most distinctively from the Project was an analysis of the deprived local areas which attributed the problems of their residents to the *normal* functioning of an economy structured by the imperatives of capitalism (see, for example, Community Development Project, 1977a). Hence, what was required from the state was a thorough-going form of intervention which would secure, at the minimum, control over the movement of capital investment from one area to another.

Given this analysis, it is not surprising that the CDP regarded what was actually being done by the state to combat the problems of the inner-urban areas with a highly critical eye. Indeed, it was argued that the multiplicity of projects and programmes which had been conjured up by the state by the later 1970s represented nothing more than an attempt to secure the compliance of working people in the face of the major economic changes which were blighting their lives (Community Development Project, 1977b). Hence, it could be claimed, the state was in reality in the business of 'Gilding the Ghetto'; of keeping the lid on potential working-class unrest.

Most crucial to the force of the CDP's analysis was the use of evidence drawn from the selected local areas to demonstrate that the roots of these areas' problems lay in wide-reaching processes of industrial reorganization and other economic change. If even the *general outline* of this conclusion was accepted, the clear implication was the irrelevance of small-area positive discrimination, especially if directed at individual or family conceptions of social deprivation.

Higgins *et al.* (1983) have argued that within central government itself there was an increasing recognition through the early years of the 1970s of this primacy of economic determinants of urban problems; the consequent futility of small-area approaches; and of the consequent necessity of new kinds of policy initiative. However, this sort of transition bears little relationship to the orderly learning process, so beloved of the 'Whig' account which we described in Chapter 1.

During this period, there were two major ministries with an involvement in urban problems: the Home Office and the newly created Department of the Environment. Indeed, there was frequently rivalry and duplication between the two. At the former, following the creation of an Urban Deprivation Unit in 1973 to oversee policies in this field, a major internal review of current initiatives was undertaken (a Policy Analysis and Review (PAR)) at the instigation of Mr Robert Carr, the Home Secretary.[2] The eventual

---

[2]The PAR system had been introduced, along with the Public Expenditure Survey Committee (PESC) to coordinate strategy across the whole range of government activities involving significant use of public resources, to evaluate departmental aims

report was never published, but according to Higgins *et al.* (1983), it advocated '. . . a strategy to "forge a new partnership" between residents, local authorities, regional authorities and central government. This could be achieved through a comprehensive community programme.' (1983:96)

What was in fact envisaged was the preparation by special teams, in close collaboration with the interests identified as part of the 'new partnership', of programmes of policies for selected areas (of some 10,000 population) of severe deprivation. Such programmes would be submitted to central government for ratification and, if accepted, would be funded to the extent of £100 per head of population. After trials, some 100 such programmes were to be set up throughout Britain.

Such proposals reflected, of course, the context in which they were produced. One the one hand, in a Home Office largely responsible for its pioneering in the British context, the small-area approach was retained. On the other, there appeared to be a growing realization of the need for *central* government policies to be redirected to alleviate the problems of low income, unemployment, poor physical and environmental conditions, which, it was argued, were as much the cause of urban deprivation as individual or family handicaps. In the light of subsequent developments, the emphasis upon the idea of 'partnership' is particularly significant here. What was required was not simply a collaboration between different *levels* of government, but also one *between* the departments of central government itself.

In the event, following the appointment of Mr Roy Jenkins to the Home Office after the election of a Labour administration at the General Election of February 1974, whatever was innovative about the Comprehensive Community Programme proposals evaporated. Only two (in Gateshead and in Motherwell) were ever operational and even these were more concerned with the coordination of local authority policies with respect to deprivation than anything that had been suggested in the original proposals. Moreover, it is not clear what was achieved even in this redefined role.

Nevertheless, this emphasis upon the coordination of policies clearly echoed developments at the Department of the Environment, the second of the ministries to concern itself with urban deprivation during the earlier 1970s. Mr Peter Walker, the Department's first Secretary of State, had been greatly influenced during the late 1960s by the experience of the Shelter Neighbourhood Action Project (SNAP) in inner Liverpool. SNAP had concluded that the barriers to urban renewal and regeneration were as much the result of the

and objectives, and to control public expenditure more effectively. In addition, it was intended that the PESC-PAR system should serve to coordinate the expenditure programmes of central and local government (Spiers, 1975).

ineffectiveness and intransigence of local government departments as anything to do with the residents of the inner areas. What was therefore implied in terms of policy was the *coordination* of the key agencies of central and local government in a concerted programme of reinvestment (Shelter, 1972).

Such a 'total approach' appealed greatly to Mr Walker, who was closely associated with the diverse administrative modernizations carried out during the Heath Government. Accordingly, a whole series of studies was instigated which were intended to explore both the nature of inner-city problems (the Inner Area Studies), as well as the potentialities for the development of new, improved policy responses (the Inner Area Studies; the Urban Guidelines studies; the Area Management trials; etc.)

It may be argued, of course, that there is nothing very tangible here. Nevertheless, it is noteworthy that the most important of the studies – the Inner Area Studies – conducted by private planning consultants in Lambeth in London, inner Liverpool and inner Birmingham – stressed in their Final Reports (Department of the Environment, 1977a, b and c) accounts or urban problems which were entirely compatible with the policy directions adopted in the 1977 White Paper on the inner cities. Indeed, the White Paper acknowledged quite explicitly the contribution that they made to the formulation of its strategy. It is perhaps surprising, therefore, that the avalanche of *interim* materials generated by these Studies should have had such little apparent effect upon policy.

Indeed, the larger question of the failure to develop effective policies – at both the Home Office and the Department of the Environment – during the earlier 1970s is one which merits close attention. Higgins *et al.* (1983) quote with approval the verdict of Mr Alex Lyon, himself a Minister at the Home Office after 1974, but with no direct responsibilities for urban initiatives: '[d]espite two years of valiant work by experts recruited to the [Urban Deprivation] Unit, nothing has been achieved because bureaucratic ineptitude has been compounded by ministerial indifference.' (*Sunday Times,* 26 May 1976; quoted in Higgins *et al.,* 1983: 110)

Mr Lyon's remarks obviously refer to only one specific period of the Home Office's activities. However, there is a sense in which they apply much more widely to the whole of the attempt to combat urban poverty and deprivation during the period we have considered. Certainly, there is abundant evidence of an unwillingness on the part of the major spending departments of central government – such as the Departments of the Environment, of Education and Science, of Health and Social Security, and, most importantly, of Industry and of Employment – to make substantial alterations in their spending priorities to take account of the special problems being experienced by the inner areas of the cities. In this unwillingness, they were, of course, wholeheartedly supported by the Treasury (Higgins *et al.,* 1983). In turn, in spite of Mr Walker's enthusiasms, there is indeed little indication of major political pressures being brought to bear to alter this situation. However, to understand these circumstances, it is necessary to extend our discussion to the wider context within which urban deprivation policies were being made.

The Heath government and the problems of the cities

At the 1970 General Election, a Conservative government under Mr Edward Heath was elected, dedicated to turning round the British economy and achieving a sustained economic growth. The essential context for this attempted redirection was the determination to make Britain a member of the European Economic Community (EEC), thereby, of course, acknowledging her reduced world-role. As Gamble (1981) has pointed out, entry to the EEC required not only convincing the existing membership (and, in particular, France) of Britain's conversion to a European outlook, but also creating a strong national economy, able to compete on equal terms with West Germany and France.

Initially, and in response to intense pressures from its own supporters to distance Conservative policies from those of the previous Labour administrations, this economic transformation was to be achieved by relaxing the constraints of economic management. Hence, the subsidies and incentives which had accumulated under Labour were eliminated and all the agencies of detailed intervention were axed; public expenditure and taxation were reduced. The intention was to force industry to resolve its own problems by increasing efficiency and competitiveness, thereby restoring profitability, boosting investment and preparing the way for expansion of output and increased productivity. To this end, the Industrial Relations Act of 1971 attempted to restrict the powers of the trades unions, thereby removing obstacles to the modernization programme. Formal incomes policy was renounced, however, with the restraint of wage costs being entrusted to the new competitive climate of industrial relations. Finally, any constraints on expansion imposed by balance-of-payments considerations were removed by the floating of the exchange rate of sterling, in the aftermath of the collapse of the Bretton Woods monetary system in 1971 (Gamble, 1981).

This generalized withdrawal of the state from key areas of economy and society inevitably had direct consequences for urban and regional development. For example, the emphasis of regional policy was switched from investment grants to tax allowances; a shift which focused state support on those firms which were *profitable* (and hence liable to taxation). Moreover, many of the so-called 'lame-ducks', which were denied special state assistance, and, as a result went out of business or undertook substantial reorganizations and redundancy programmes, tended to be concentrated in the older industrial regions and/or the inner areas of the conurbations.

Likewise, we have already noted the effects of the Conservatives' withdrawal from the regulation of the land and property markets, in the boom of the early 1970s. Whilst in terms of housing policy, the 1971 Housing Act reinforced the trend established under the previous Labour government, away from large-scale clearance and redevelopment toward the rehabilitation of the existing housing stock through a revamped system of improvement grants. More contentiously, the Housing Finance Act of the following year sought to redirect resources from the public sector into private housing; housing subsidies were replaced by a means-tested rebate for the needy; local authority rents were pushed up to 'fair' levels; the building of council houses was limited; and, thereby, every encouragement was given to council tenants to do the decent thing and become owner-occupiers. Clearly, then, the intention was to relegate public housing to an even more marginal and residual category; those who were not poor were expected to enter the property-owning democracy; and if this meant picking up more Conservative votes from working-class families, so much the better (Merrett, 1982).

Now, in the context of these rather abrupt changes in the direction of major urban and regional policies, the *continuities* which we have noted in the urban deprivation policies may appear somewhat surprising. One element of the explanation lies in the latter's sheer insignificance; they were, after all, small-scale, confined to particular local areas and the resources committed to them were very limited. Certainly, it is clear that the effects of the changes which we have described in the mainstream of urban policies were enormously greater for the inner cities and their residents; whatever benefits resulted from the anti-deprivation policies, they were undoubtedly swamped by the exacerbation of the cities' problems as a result of the other policy changes. In addition, moreover, there was a consistency between the highly *selectivist* nature of the anti-poverty policies and the brand of Conservatism which was in the ascendancy after 1970; as in the case of housing, *special* provision was required for the small sections of the population in exceptional circumstances.

It also should be borne in mind that the developing emphasis on an administrative solution to problems of urban deprivation was entirely consistent with a much more general orientation of the Heath government. If Britain was to be modernized out of its preoccupations with its past Imperial world-role, not only would the economy need overhauling, but the machinery of government and administration would too. And, of course, in this concern with administrative reform, there are strong echoes of the previous Labour government's programme. Hence, for example, central government departments were reorganized into huge super-ministries, overseeing wide areas of policy; for example, the Department of the Environment with responsibility for the infrastructural provision of the economy and the Department of Trade and Industry for industrial and commercial policies. Meanwhile, as we have seen, local government was restructured to deliver a more strategic and effective service. Indeed, as Cockburn (1977) has pointed out, there was a more pervasive move toward the introduction of management techniques from the private into the public sector. Hence, perhaps the world's most prestigious management consultants, McKinsey and Company, were responsible for plans for the armed services, the National Health Service, the gas and electricity authorities, British Airways and the BBC, as well as central and local government. Indeed, they became something of specialists in the latter and, in particular, the problems of the cities.

Such continuities between the Wilson administrations of the 1960s and that of Mr Heath became much more marked, however, in the later years of the latter, when it had become clear that the return to the disciplines of the market would not have the desired effect upon economic performance. By 1972, all the 'free market' policies were in disarray. The attempt to reform industrial relations not only provoked intense opposition from the trade union movement, but also had little effect on the level of pay increases. Attempts to reduce public expenditure proved singularly unsuccessful, whilst there was little indication of the creation of a more efficient and competitive industry; indeed, although aid was cut off to some well publicized firms such as Upper Clyde Shipbuilders (thereby causing still more industrial unrest), the large part of state funding continued and, in spectacular instances like the bankruptcy of Rolls-Royce in 1971, was actually extended.

By 1971, then, the Conservative government faced persistently high wage settlements, rising inflation, high unemployment, an absence of proper investment in industry, as well as considerable industrial unrest and growing electoral unpopularity. Not surprisingly, in 1972, there was an abrupt change in the policies underpinning the attempt to achieve economic growth: the famous 'U-turn'.

In effect, what was involved here was a return to more or less the orthodoxies of Keynesian demand-management; in this case, with a view to expanding demand on such a scale that investment and productivity in industry would be bound to grow. However, inflation was to be limited by prices and incomes policy; and any balance-of-payments deficits would be covered in the short term by overseas borrowing. Hence, during 1972–73, public spending was greatly increased, as was the money supply. Industrial policy was reversed and the Industry Act of 1972 presaged state intervention on a very major scale. Finally, the most comprehensive statutory prices and incomes policy since the war was introduced at the end of 1972 (Gamble, 1981).

Again, it should be clear that the implications of all this for urban and regional policy were considerable. Accordingly, the prices and incomes policy had dramatic effects on the land and property markets. Business rents were completely frozen, thereby removing the principal source of profit from property speculation and precipitating the collapse of property shares. At the same time, incomes policy caused the supply of finance for home-buyers to decline, limiting their ability to pay inflated property prices; whilst controls were imposed on building society lending, restricting mortgage finance. The result was a rapid decline in the prices of houses and land. What this meant, in turn, was that property companies, developers, landlords and building companies holding land and property, experienced a massive decline in the value of their previously inflated property assets. This occasioned a major crisis for those financial institutions which, directly or indirectly, had lent money for land and property speculative investment.

All this, of course, created a severe problem for the government. On the one hand, substantial industrial interests and the labour movement pressed for the extension of controls over land and property speculation. On the other, it was clear that such policies would induce a substantial financial collapse, at a time when the City's capacity to finance industrial investment and to assist the balance of payments through invisible earnings was crucial. It is therefore instructive that it was the latter considerations which won out in this conflict: commercial rents were allowed to rise, eventually to full market rates. Nevertheless, fiscal controls over speculative gains in land and property were proposed (and were eventually implemented after 1974 by the new Labour Government) (Cox, 1984).

These conflicts over land and property were made even more acute because the government clearly needed to secure the cooperation of the CBI and the TUC – and the industrial and labour movement interests they represented – in other aspects of its economic strategy, especially the central one of industrial relations. Thus, for instance, Grant (1983) quotes the comment of Viscount Watkinson, a CBI activist at the time and later its president, that '[n]o prime minister has ever devoted as much care and patience as Edward Heath did to seeking to bring about tripartite agreement between the CBI, the TUC and the government on the cure to Britain's economic ills. Had the Industrial Relations Act not soured relationships, the initiative might well have succeeded' (1983:70).

Certainly it is clear that the expansionary industrial policy embodied in the 1972 Industry Act was a response to pressures from both the TUC *and* the CBI (Dunford *et al.*, 1981). Its adoption, moreover, had major consequences for the character of regional strategy. Hence, two kinds of regional incentive were introduced: Regional Development Grants of 20 to 22 per cent on buildings, plant and machinery, available to manufacturing firms in the designated areas automatically and irrespective of job-creation; and Selective Assistance to firms in the Assisted Areas, whether in manufacturing or services, of up to 20 per cent on a discretionary basis. This usually took the form of interest relief grants and was available either for employment creation or, more often, modernization. Accordingly, the scale of regional policy expenditure was enormously increased; indeed, by 1973–74, it had reached levels in excess of those current in 1969–70.

In this way, then, regional policy reverted to the kind of facilitation of industrial restructuring which we saw in the previous chapter was characteristic of the preceding administration. Moreover, as previously, it seems likely that the effects of this expenditure on the economic resources of the residents of the inner urban areas far outweighed those of anti-deprivation policies, as the decentralization of manufacturing industry from the cities continued.

What we find during these later years of the Heath government, therefore, is an attempt to implement a particular form of corporatist strategy, involving a 'tripartism' of the CBI, the TUC and the government in policy formulation (for example, Jessop, 1980). And, in this sense, there was a clear progression from the Labour administrations of the 1960s. However, as Viscount Watkinson pointed out, ultimately Mr Heath (like Mr Wilson before him) *failed* to achieve what he desired in the face of trades union opposition. In fact, it was this opposition – in the shape of the miners – allied to the escalation of world oil prices after 1973, which precipitated the fall of the Heath administration at the General Election of February 1974. Ironically, the administrations which followed, up until 1979, were both an expression of the high-point of this corporatism and of its ultimate failure.

A policy for the inner cities

The Labour government was elected in February 1974 only on the basis of its being the largest Party in parliament; it was dependent for its majority on the tolerance of the Liberals and the other minority parties. At the second election of 1974 – in October – although Labour did achieve an overall majority, it was effectively only three. And even this slender advantage whittled away in Scottish Party schisms and by-election defeats, so that once more after April 1977, the Labour government was dependent on the minority parties. Clearly, then, this electoral weakness limited the government's capacity to deal with both the immediate economic problems which confronted it and more fundamental reform (Coates, 1980).

However, there was one area in which a plausible case has been made out that 'fundamental reform' *did* take place. This was, of course, in the field of urban and regional policy, where the explicit recognition of an 'urban crisis' led to the apparent rejection of the supposed orthodoxies of the post-war period and the reformulation of state intervention in urban and regional development.

As the *Diaries* of Mrs Barbara Castle (1980) – then a leading member of the government – show, as early as August 1975, priority treatment for the inner urban areas was recognized as a major issue, even at Cabinet level. She recalls that at a Cabinet meeting held to discuss major cuts in public expenditure, Mr Peter Shore, the Secretary of State for the Environment, successfully argued that the inner-city areas should be spared. 'The priorities emerging for safe-guarding were housing (but not housing subsidies), industrial retraining, and inner cities. The lowest priorities were transport and higher education.' (Castle, 1980: 485)

What is not clear, however, is exactly how such a priority for the inner cities was to be implemented. Hence, the task of formulating actual policy measures was given first of all to an inter-departmental group of officials under the chairmanship of the Department of the Environment's Chief Planner, Mr Wilfred Burns; and subsequently (in August 1976) to a working party of junior ministers, under the leadership of Peter Shore himself. This political committee introduced a new sharpness into the debate and, within a matter of months, Mr Shore was able to set out the framework for future policy.

Firstly, the problems confronting the cities were identified as unequivocally economic in their character. As Shore put it in a speech at Manchester, '. . . the causes of the decline of the inner city . . . lie primarily in their relative economic decline, in a major migration of people, often the most skilled, and in a major reduction in the number of jobs which are left' (26 September 1976, Manchester).

What was perhaps more novel was the second major strand of argument, that the causes of this economic decline were in large part attributable to the effects of what he described as the 'general consensus' over urban and regional policy and planning. Hence, planned decentralization and decongestion of inner-city residents had been accompanied by a voluntary out-migration far larger than had been anticipated. As a result, policies with respect to industrial location should be modified to give greater assistance to the inner areas (without, of course, damaging regional policy). Similarly, however valuable the New Towns had been in the past, in these changed

changed circumstances, their future role should be reassessed. Whilst, within the urban area themselves, rigorous land-use zoning, comprehensive redevelopment schemes and so forth, had all had a deleterious effect on industry, especially on the medium and smaller firms, and consequently upon job opportunities.

What was required to deal with this situation, then, was a substantial redirection of resources into the inner cities. This, in turn, would necessitate the creation of an appropriate administrative machinery to ensure that the spending programmes of both central and local government were directed in this way. In addition, of course, wholly new resources should be made available; but, given the general economic stringency, these could inevitably be on only a small scale.

What was involved here was certainly a major reformulation of the urban and regional issue so far as the state was concerned. It had undoubtedly been presaged by earlier events; for example, as early as 1976, the Greater London Council had been forced to reassess one of the key objectives of post-war planning in the South East – the encouragement of population movement out of London to the New and Expanded Towns – because of the pace of industrial decline and population loss in the capital. However, this initiative by Mr Shore was an authoritative statement of a new central state perspective.

It recognized that the problems of the cities could not be relegated to the policy margins of experimental anti-poverty policies; they were integral to broader processes of urban and regional change and accordingly required the weight of mainstream urban and regional policies to combat them. Indeed, the designation of the Department of the Environment as the responsible ministry was, in part, a recognition of this. Furthermore, it implied that these urban problems were not simply problems for the state to deal with, but also that they *derived from* past state intervention. And clearly, this latter point was highly significant, even if – as may be judged from the arguments of earlier chapters – the nature of the relationships between past policies and current problems was mis-specified.

What actually emerged as new policies was somewhat less spectacular than had been expected. Nevertheless, their impact was not inconsiderable. On the one hand, decentralization of population through the New and Expanded Towns programmes was to be curtailed. In his parliamentary statement of April 1977, Mr Shore announced reductions in the proposed growth rates of many of the New Towns. In the case of those designated during the 1960s, these cuts were to reduce original targets by about 400,000 people. No new designations were announced, of course, and the existing New Towns were urged to take a larger number of the urban poor. Within 18 months, discussions were also under way to reduce some of the 29 Expanded Town schemes in which the Greater London Council was involved.

On the other hand, and more significantly, there were to be *positive* attempts to revitalize the economies of the inner areas themselves. Two elements were involved here: resources and administrative machinery. On the first, the initial response was actually given by the Chancellor of the Exchequer in his Budget statement of March 1977, when he announced a £100,000,000 package of construction works in selected inner cities. In addition, the Secretary of State for the Environment announced a month later that the Urban Programme was to be expanded from £30,000,000 to £125,000,000 per annum, with a continuing commitment of £1,000,000,000 over the subsequent decade. Given these increased resources, its scope was to be expanded to cover industrial, environmental and recreational provision, in addition to the traditional social projects. Most significantly, the bulk of the money was to be concentrated into designated Partnership and Programme local authorities, which were obviously intended to comprise those areas with the most severe inner-city problems.

The most important element, however, in the direction of resources to the inner areas was to be by the 'bending' of the *normal* expenditure programmes of central and local government in their favour. Hence, great emphasis was placed upon the use of the needs element of the Rate Support Grant to favour those local authorities with pressing urban problems, at the expense of the rural areas, principally the shire counties. It was also made clear that *all* spending programmes would be '. . . given an inner-area dimension and priority in order to assist the regeneration of these areas.' (Department of the Environment, 1977: paragraph 45) To achieve this, however, a new administrative machinery was required.

This was to take the form, in the first instance, of Partnerships involving central government, designated local authorities, other statutory bodies (such as the Area Health Authorities) and local voluntary organizations, including representatives of local capital (but not, apparently, labour organizations). Their task was to prepare coordinated plans for the regeneration of industry in their areas; and, of course, a major element in this was to implement the 'bending' of expenditure programmes to which we have referred. In addition, a larger number of Programme local authorities were designated, whose special powers were set at a lesser level.

Partnerships were established in Liverpool, Manchester and Salford, Birmingham, Newcastle–Gateshead and in Hackney–Islington, Lambeth and Docklands in London. Programme arrangements were offered to a further 15 local authorities. In 1978, the Inner Urban Areas Act gave to all these authorities (together with 14 additional areas) powers to permit the direct encouragement of industrial and other economic improvement and development: including the provision of loans for land acquisition and development; the designation of industrial and commercial improvement areas; and, in the Partnership areas only, grant assistance in the payment of industrial and commercial rents and for the relief of loan interest for smaller firms, as well as for site preparation and infrastructural provision. All this, Mr Shore emphasized, was not intended to weaken the effects of conventional regional policy, but simply to supplement it.

Since the inception of this policy approach, in addition to the inevitable administrative changes (most notably, the designation of 14 further Programme areas in February 1983), there has been the major upheaval occasioned by the change of government at the 1979 General Election. We shall, of course, return to this later. However, at this stage, we shall present a preliminary evaluation of the effectiveness of inner cities policy.

As the 1977 White Paper made clear, the key to the economic revival of the inner-urban areas was thought to lie in the extent to which the new administrative machinery would effect genuine innovation. In the event, it seems that such innovation has simply not been achieved. As Stewart (1983) puts it:

> the potentially innovatory partnership arrangements for developing and managing Inner Cities policy have lapsed into a more traditional form of central/local relationship. The task of maintaining the administration of the programme has become more important than the task of reviewing policies and practice and encouraging innovation and change and there is considerable disillusionment with the idea of joint working between central and local government and between government and other organizations. (1983:212)

This is clearly reflected in the crucial area of economic development initiatives, where the emphasis has been placed predominantly upon traditional practices, such as site preparation, the provision of nursery factory units and small workshops, and the refurbishment of older industrial buildings (often in Industrial Improvement Areas). What this implies is the influence of past local authority experience in this field, originating in the early local Acts of the 1930s, through the estate development of the 1960s and earlier 1970s (often in association with regional policies), to the wider range of initiatives attempted in the second half of the 1970s (Stewart and Underwood, 1983). Moreover, with the severe limitation of the funds which have traditionally been used to support such economic activities at least since the mid-1970s, it is not surprising that inner-city money should have come to be regarded as a useful alternative source.

This latter point raises the whole issue of the resources which have actually been made available to inner-city initiatives. As we saw earlier, the critical element here is the extent to which the routine spending of central and local government could accord inner-urban areas priority. Lawless (1981b) provides an extremely useful analysis of the extent to which the expenditure of three key agencies of economic policy – the Department of Industry, the National Enterprise Board (NEB) and the Manpower Services Commission (MSC) – operated in favour of inner-city areas up until the end of the 1970s. We shall return to the roles played by these agencies more generally in a later section; however, it should be noted here that together they comprised by far the most important sources of *potential* support for the cities from the central state.

In fact, it is clear that there was almost no 'bending' of these major spending programmes. Indeed, it is more likely that the activities of these agencies have acted *against* the regeneration of the inner cities. Hence, the Department of Industry remained much more interested in the promotion of regional economic growth than inner-city expansion. Moreover, with an increasing emphasis upon the encouragement of *profitable* industrial expansion, priority was given to the locational preferences of private capital and these, of course, were mostly for greenfield sites. Similarly, the NEB's support for high-technology industry, in line with the increasingly *selective* industrial strategy, meant that a considerable proportion of its investment was directed to the 'sun-belt' of the South of England. Whilst even the MSC followed the national strategy of assisting high-technology sectors and of facilitating the relocation of individuals away from areas of poor job prospects, such as the cities (Lawless, 1981b). In addition, from 1975 onwards, there was persistent pressure to reduce the level of public expenditure generally, in response to the mounting problems of the British economy. And, in these circumstances, it was extremely difficult to put very much extra into the cities.

In conception, then, inner-cities policy certainly represented a major break from the kinds of urban policies which had preceded it. However, its impact on the problems of the inner-urban areas was far less radical. Equally, it should be apparent that we cannot legitimately separate out the fate of the cities from what was happening in the wider economy or from the state's responses to these wider changes. It is to a consideration of some of these issues that we turn in the next section.

The Labour Party, tripartism and the economic crisis

We noted earlier the political weakness of the Labour government, even after the second General Election of 1974. It is unfortunate, then, that this partially crippled administration was confronted with some of the most serious economic problems to afflict Britain during the post-war period. The world economy was, of course, still reeling from the effects of the 1973 oil price rises; and in Britain, these were compounded by the aftermath of the 'Barber boom'. Moreover, the fundamental weaknesses of the British economy continued to impede economic growth and the achievement of anything like general prosperity.

In consequence, by early 1975, the government was faced with a combination of high and rising price inflation; a succession of very large wage and salary increases; a persistent lack of industrial investment at home and resulting lack of competitiveness; and, not surprisingly, massive balance-of-payments deficits and recurring sterling crises. We cannot deal in detail with the responses which were made to these problems (see, for example, Coates, 1980). However, three of the central strands of Labour's response are highly germane to our more general arguments.

Firstly, there was the attempt to capitalize upon the supposed special relationship between the Labour Party and the trades union movement, by the negotiation of voluntary wage restraint from the latter, in return for concessions to trades union opinion in a wide range of policy areas. This 'Social Contract' was at least partly successful. The average annual increases in wage rates did moderate from their 1975 level over the period up until 1979; certainly, real wages fell during this period, without significant retaliation from the labour movement. In return, the legislative programme of the Labour government included substantial concessions to trades union demands. The Heath Industrial Relations Act was repealed; as was the Housing Finance Act; a new Trade Union Act and Employment Protection Act followed; so did Acts on equal pay and sexual equality. Intervention in the labour market was strengthened by the creation of the MSC and the Advisory Conciliation and Arbitration Service (for example, Warde, 1982). In addition, there were elements of Labour's industrial strategy which favoured the trades unions, such as the treatment of the British Steel Corporation (a number of whose older plants were kept open to avoid high unemployment in steel-making areas).

However, the success was only partial and, eventually, the Social Contract simply disintegrated. In the arena of social welfare policies – intended to be a crucial element in the 'social wage' of workers – there were major difficulties in responding to union demands, given that the levels of expenditure on such services were consistently and drastically reduced after 1975. This contributed, in turn, to the problems experienced by the leadership of the trades union movement, both the TUC and in the individual unions, in delivering their constituencies; in ensuring the continued cooperation of the rank-and-file memberships in the pursuit of these policies. Indeed, it was the failure to achieve this cooperation which manifested in the rash of strikes – particularly concentrated in the public sector – during the winter of 1978–79, which led ultimately to the fall of the Labour administration.

The extent of the cuts in public expenditure instituted by this government should not be understated: by 1978–79, non-defence spending was some 8.5 per cent below its level in 1975–76. Indeed, the restriction of the Public Sector Borrowing Requirement (PSBR) and the cuts in public expenditure which this required became the second major strand in the government's overall strategy and a principal weapon in the attempt to combat rising inflation. Hence, state spending was cut initially in 1975 and then, much more stringently in 1976: by some £3,600,000,000 for 1977–78 and a further £4,500,000,000 for 1978–79. In addition, the system of 'cash limits' was introduced, which restricted the amounts of *money* available to spend, so that if prices and wages rose above a certain level, services and jobs would have to be cut.

The effects of these measures on the actual delivery of services may perhaps be judged by reference to one particular policy area – housing. State housing completions fell from 129,000 in 1976 to only 76,000 in 1979. And this was the lowest peace-time figure since 1935, irrespective of the 1974 General Election promises. Moreover, local authority mortgage finance – intended to assist the least well-off house-buyers – was cut back; as were funds for the rehabilitation of older housing stock, much of which, of course, was concentrated into the inner areas of the cities (Merrett, 1982).

The reasons for the resort to this kind of policy on public expenditure were complex. Recurrent sterling crises had forced the government to negotiate a massive loan from the IMF in 1975; in return for which, the IMF had *required* extensive cuts in state spending, especially in the field of social welfare. However, the first cuts actually pre-dated this; and we can only conclude that the Labour administration was persuaded by the professional advice from the Treasury and the Bank of England to an acceptance of a form of monetarism, involving the radical rejection of the orthodoxies of the Keynesian-Welfare State. And certainly, by this time, this was the kind of approach which was being widely canvassed amongst City interests. In addition, the CBI had also been converted to the virtues of strict monetary policy as *the* anti-inflation strategy, in spite of the effects of the resulting high interest rates on industrial investment (Grant, 1983).

It is also significant that the impact of the cuts was felt particularly acutely in local government, for the simple reason that many of the services which have been affected are actually delivered by this part of the state. And there have been corresponding losses of local authority jobs. In short, then, the extent of autonomy enjoyed by local government was clearly reduced as a result of the cuts; a trend which was reinforced by the introduction of specific budgeting systems, such as the Housing Investment Programmes.

Indeed, the relationship between the central and local parts of the state came to be a preoccupation in much the same way that local government reorganization had been during the later 1960s. Rather than the *effectiveness* of local government in carrying out new tasks, however, the major issue had become how to limit the local authorities' supposed extravagance, in face of Britain's reduced economic circumstances. What nevertheless remained constant was the priority which was attached to the interests of industrial and commercial capital in determining policies for the local state; what changed was the perception of what these interests comprised. Hence, for example, the CBI concerned itself with a wide range of local government issues, including opposing Private Bills sponsored by local authorities and, most importantly, resisting the further encroachment of rates on diminishing profits (Grant, 1983). And, of course, as we have seen, the favouring of capital's interests by these means had directly adverse effects on the inner cities and their residents.

In similar ways, the third major strand in Labour's strategy – industrial policy – had the effect of restricting the autonomy of the local state. Boddy (1983), for example, has argued that the restriction of public sector funds for industrial development purposes throughout the 1970s has driven local authorities to the private sector for finance. In consequence, they have become increasingly constrained by the commercial criteria of private development and financial interests; and correspondingly less able to pursue wider employment or other non-market objectives. More specifically the circular from the Department of the Environment in 1977, *Local Government and the Industrial Strategy* (71/77), which set out the contribution which the local authorities should be making to the resolution of Britain's industrial problems, whilst emphasizing the significance of local government's role, also *specified* that role in terms of the national strategy; namely, achieving an efficient and competitive – that is, profitable – industry.

In more general terms, the development of the national strategy itself casts a great deal of light on the 1970s Labour administrations. Thus, during the period of Opposition between 1970 and 1974, the Labour Party had reacted against the manifest failures of 'indicative planning' by formulating a much more radical programme of intervention in industrial affairs, aimed particularly at curbing the activities of the large, multinational corporations. By 1973, then, the Labour Party Programme promised: the extension of public ownership, both through the *nationalization* of industries such as North Sea oil, docks, aircraft production, ship-building and – selectively – the financial institutions and the pharmaceutical industry, and through the activities of the NEB; effective state direction of the investment and development programmes of the remaining major private firms, by means of a system of *planning agreements*; and an Industry Act which would give the appropriate Ministers extensive powers to obtain information from private companies, to invest in them and to issue directives to them on matters such as prices, profits, investment and industrial relations practices (Coates, 1980). Even here, of course, the commitment to making British industry more efficient and competitive remained. However, there appeared to be an equal intention to achieve this on terms which would be more acceptable to the mass of the people: economic power was to be made more democratically accessible.

Budd (1978) – amongst many others – has traced the progressive retreat from these highly interventionist proposals, through the promise of the General Election Manifesto of 1974, to the 1974 White Paper, *The Regeneration of British Industry* (Cmnd. 5710), and, eventually, to the adoption during 1975 of an industrial strategy which was, in all essentials, indistinguishable from those purused by the 1960s Labour administrations or that of Mr Heath's government after 1972. As Coates (1980) comments, '. . . the strategy came to amount to little more than an attempt at tripartite indicative planning and the creation of conditions for successful private capital accumulation . . . .' (1980:99).

In particular, the major effort became concentrated on the attempt to increase productivity in those sectors of British industry which appeared to offer the best prospects of future growth; and the main part of the planning which was involved here was carried out at the NEDC, between the representatives of the CBI, the TUC and the government. For the remainder, little of the 1973 Programme remained. Only very limited nationalization was carried out. Planning agreements were voluntary and therefore, not surprisingly, only one was ever signed; and that, in effect, was to bail out the Chrysler Motor Company with a massive injection of state funds. The NEB became a vehicle for providing finance for industrial investment, on terms which were scarcely distinguishable from those of a merchant bank. Although it did hold shares in private companies, these were for the most part 'lame ducks' requiring state assistance, such as British Leyland, Rolls-Royce 1971 and Ferranti. Moreover, its industrial restructuring activities were small-scale and again confined to particular sectors.

Whether or not the radical strategy outlined in 1973 would have worked if it had been implemented properly remains a hotly disputed issue; although the Left in the Labour Party has remained convinced of its potential. However, what is entirely clear is that the policies which were actually implemented were catastrophically unsuccessful in securing any turn-around in the British economy. Thus, between 1973 and 1978, British manufacturing output actually fell by an average of 1 per cent per year. Between the autumn of 1973 and that of 1977, male unemployment rose nearly two and a half times; female unemployment rose more than fivefold. Total unemployment was still well in excess of 1,300,000 by the time of the 1979 General Election, having fallen slightly from its 1977 peak of 1,300,700. It is perhaps not surprising, then, that Labour's strategy failed to attract popular support! However, as Warde (1982) comments:

> That the Industrial Strategy would not succeed might have been anticipated. The underlying principle that capital should not be forced into doing anything it would not wish to do meant that it was unlikely that private investment in industry would rise since there were more lucrative ways of employing capital, abroad and in non-industrial spheres. So, as is often the case in recession, many companies made substantial profits but refrained from reinvesting them in ways which would increase the productive sector of British industry. The government had neither the will nor the means to make them do otherwise. (1982: 151–2)

The effects of all this on the inner cities were, of course, considerable, as we have already seen in Chapter 2. Certainly, with the general rise in levels of unemployment and the reassertion of regional unemployment differentials during the later 1970s, arguments that regional policies should be directed towards the cities were weakened. Initially, the Labour government had anyway attached major significance to regional strategy; the Regional Employment Premium expenditure was doubled and the Assisted Areas were extended to include almost the whole of Britain west of Exeter and the Welsh border and north of Nottingham. It also established the Scottish and Welsh Development Agencies, with specific responsibilities for the restructuring of industry in their respective areas, by means of commercial loans and equity finance, promotional activities and environmental improvement schemes.

However, as the industrial strategy was transformed, the ambiguities of state policy for the regions became clearer. Public expenditure cuts had inevitable consequences for regional policy spending: the Regional Employment Premium was first reduced and then withdrawn altogether at the end of 1976, and in the following year the status of some areas was down-graded. As a result, actual expenditure declined dramatically between 1975–76 and 1978–79 by some £400,000,000. Moreover, the growing emphasis upon sectoral planning and the encouragement of efficiency and competitiveness in growth industries, obviously cut across attempts to revive the fortunes of ailing firms and, to some extent, depressed regions. Most striking here was the move away from *automatic* subsidies towards *selective* assistance linked to rationalization programmes.

In this way, then, the consequences of wider changes in Labour's strategy had the effect of diverting policies concerned with urban and regional development. Often this produced the most intense contradictions. For example, in the inner cities, the impact of the specially devised inner cities policy was cut across by both regional policy and, in rather different ways, wider industrial and public expenditure policies.

In other policy areas too, the contradictions of the government's strategy were manifest. For instance, the 1975 Community Land Act and the associated Development Land Tax of 1976 arose out of the context of the general economic strategy which was being attempted. As we have already seen, concern was expressed during the earlier 1970s over the intrusion of the financial institutions into speculative development in land and property, by both industrial capital and the labour movement. Hence, what was feared was not simply the effects upon working-class housing in the cities, but also the diversion of investment funds from industry during a period of severe crisis (Massey and Catalano, 1978).

However, as with all previous initiatives, the legislation which emerged could in its very nature only provide a partial response to the problem. Initially, for example, at the end of 1974, it was decided to lift the freeze on business rents entirely by February 1975, some 14 months earlier than the date which had been set in the Heath administration's proposals. Once again, it proved impossible for even a Labour government to break the power of financial capital and to threaten its dependence on land and property investment. As Tony Crosland, then Secretary of State for the Environment, remarked, ' . . . a healthy market in commercial property is necessary for the achievement of the government's social and economic objectives . . . . [because] much savings and pension money depends on income from commercial property, which also constitutes an important credit base for industry' (quoted in Cox 1984: 181).

In addition, rather than wholesale land nationalization, what was embodied in the Community Land Act was the nationalization of *development* land, through the agency of the local authorities.[3] Whilst this went further than any of the earlier attempts to deal with the land question, it stopped short of tackling the institution of private landownership itself. Moreover, on the way to legal enactment, the Act's powers were whittled away by the increasingly narrow definition of what should constitute 'development land'. Similarly, the Development Land Tax, intended to recoup to the state some of the increase in value resulting from development, was hedged about with exemptions.

Furthermore, in its actual operation, the Community Land

[3] In Wales, the centralized Land Authority for Wales was created.

scheme was severely constrained. As it was permissive, Conservative local authorities were loath to make use of it. Whilst given the cuts in local authority finance, most councils simply could not afford to deal in land, even on the favourable terms embodied in the Act. All in all, then, it contributed little to the creation of more rational patterns of urban development or, indeed, to the resolution of the problems of inner-city residents. In fact, it is instructive that by the run-up to the 1979 General Election, numerous *property* interests were arguing the need to retain a modified Community Land Scheme if the Conservatives were elected, to facilitate land and property dealing (Cox, 1984).

What emerges from this discussion, then, is that very little was achieved during these years to combat the effects of the processes which we described in Chapter 2. On the contrary, it would appear that many aspects of state policy actually had the effect of facilitating these trends. And, in consequence, the inner cities (as well as other economically depressed areas) continued on their downward spiral of decay.

The limits of corporatism

We mentioned earlier the constraints imposed upon the Labour government by their political weakness and the economic crisis of the later 1970s. Hence, political expediency clearly played its part in shaping the administration's programme. Certainly, for example, the publicly expressed concern over the plight of the inner cities owed something to the traditional geographical distribution of Labour's electoral support; the decline of the inner-urban areas meant the decline of Labour voting strongholds too. Likewise, the definition of inner-city problems in terms of economic circumstances cannot have required too much imagination in the midst of the rapid de-industrialization and imminent collapse of the British economy as a whole.

Nevertheless, there is a great deal more to be said about the manner in which the Labour government responded to the circumstances of this period. Accordingly, it has frequently been argued that there was a radical disjuncture between what the Labour Cabinet was prepared to do in government and what the Labour Party as a whole wished it to do (for example, Coates, 1980). It is not surprising, for instance, that the industrial strategy should have reverted after 1975 to a form very similar to the strategy of the later 1960s, when key Cabinet posts were held by individuals who had been closely involved in those earlier policies.

Other accounts have emphasized the extent to which the state bureaucracy was able to thwart the initial intentions of the administration. In a lively analysis of the demise of the industrial strategy, Forester (1978) claims that on Mr Tony Benn's first day as Secretary of State for Industry in 1974, he was greeted by Sir Antony Part, his Permanent Secretary, with the words 'I presume, Secretary of State, that you don't intend to implement the industrial strategy in Labour's Programme' (1978: 10). Whether this is apocryphal or not, it is revealing that in the same article, Sir Antony himself is reported as arguing that the Civil Service *had* to oppose the industrial strategy because it was so strongly opposed by private industry. Moreover, we referred earlier to the influence exerted by the Treasury and the Bank of England in advancing strictly orthodox monetary policy to the forefront of the battle against inflation. These arguments, however, lead us to a much more fundamental consideration of the nature of the state which was responsible for the policies we have described.

The 1970s were marked by the attempt to construct a corporatist solution to Britain's chronic economic problems. Hence, both the Heath administration after 1972 and the Labour ones between 1974 and 1979 were engaged in a project to generate forms of 'tripartism' which would imply both the representation of the interests of the CBI and the TUC in policy-formulation, and the active participation of these institutions in policy implementation. For example, we noted earlier the basis of the post-1975 industrial strategy in the sectoral planning of the NEDC and the activities of QUANGOs such as the NEB and the Development Agencies in Scotland and Wales. As Jessop (1979) puts it:

> Corporatism involves the fusion of political representation mediated through a system of public 'corporations' which are constituted on the basis of their members' functions within the division of labour and state intervention through these same corporations and/or administrative agencies formally accountable to them. (1979: 195)

It should be stressed, however, that such liberal corporatism did not imply the kind of accommodation between labour and capital which, as we have seen, characterized the post-war settlement. Rather, it represented the explicit recognition of the antagonistic interests of capital and labour, but equally the need for their regulation, if national development out of economic crisis were to be possible (Warde, 1982). Moreover, the attempt to create this form of corporatist strategy was not based upon an equality between the partners to the various tripartite arrangements. As Panitch (1980) has argued more generally:

> this . . . approach to corporatism in advanced capitalist liberal democracies does not assume equivalence of power or influence between the classes or the groups based on them, nor the neutrality of the state

vis-à-vis them. . . . . On the contrary, by situating corporatism explicitly within the parameters of advanced capitalist society, it invites investigation of the manner in which corporatist structures reflect, mediate or modify the domination of capital and the way they are themselves subject to the contradictions of capitalist society, not least as they are concretely embodied in continuing class struggle. (1980: 174)

Hence, in the most general terms, the principal effect of the Social Contract was to hold down real wages and to ensure the acquiescence of workers (at least until 1978–79), in the face of rising unemployment, expenditure cuts and restrictions on wage increases. This is not to suggest, however, that trades unions were simply duped into this highly disadvantageous arrangement; because – at least at the leadership levels – there was a genuinely shared perspective between the unions and the government on the appropriate strategy to adopt (Coates, 1980).

At the same time, there is abundant evidence that this corporatist attempt to resolve Britain's economic ills was conducted on terms which overwhelmingly reflected capital's interests. For example, industrial reorganization was pushed ahead, almost irrespective of the consequences in terms of redundancies and rising unemployment; consequences which, as we have seen, exerted especially severe effects on the cities. Government strategy once again worked to reinforce the attempts by sectors of industrial capital to modernize and, thereby, to escape from the effects of the deepening economic crisis of the later 1970s. Moreover, this was deemed to necessitate the redirection of state expenditure away from social welfare programmes (such as in our example of housing provision) toward what Miller (1978) has referred to as the 're-capitalization of capitalism'.

If these years, then, represented something of a high-point of corporatist tendencies for the British state, they also represented a dramatic expression of their failure. The problems confronting the British economy were very far from being resolved, as there was certainly no sign of the emergence of the kind of efficient and effective national economy which was being sought. Even from the perspective of industrial capital itself, although restructuring and increased productivity were facilitated, this was clearly not widespread, but confined to particular industrial sectors. In addition, it must not be forgotten that, as in the 1960s, financial capital, largely *outside* of any corporatist planning arrangements and working through its influence in the Treasury and the Bank of England, exerted the central impetus upon economic strategy.

Finally, for labour, the policies of these years can only be described as a catastrophe: not only was there a significant worsening of the conditions generally experienced by working people, but also the institutions of organized labour were unable to hold the loyalty of their rank-and-file in the face of the manifest inadequacies of the leaderships' preferred course of action. What this underlines, in turn, is the fragility of the *social basis* of the corporatist strategy. Furthermore, this fragility paved the way for the election of Mrs Margaret Thatcher's administration at the General Election of 1979 and the much more radical break with the political orthodoxies of the post-war settlement.

The emergence of the New Right

In the aftermath of the debacle of the fall of the Heath government in 1974, there had been a major regrouping and strategic rethinking on the Right of British politics. As we have mentioned, the CBI's conversion to monetarist economic strategy was one part of these changes. Of even greater significance, however, was the transformation of the Conservative Party, which was marked at the level of personalities in the ousting of Mr Heath from the leadership and his replacement by Mrs Margaret Thatcher in 1975 (Behrens, 1980). However, it is the much more fundamental *ideological* shift which will concern us here. What was involved was the establishment of the dominance of *New Right* thinking within the Conservative Party.

The emergence of such an ideological dominance was by no means a bolt from the blue. Indeed, as Gamble (1981) has shown most clearly, the influence of liberal political economy within the Conservative Party may be traced back at least until the 1920s and the demise of the Liberal Party as a major force. We ourselves, in earlier chapters, have referred to some of the precursors of Thatcherism: the anti-interventionists of the 1950s; Powellism during the 1960s; the 'Selsdon' period of the Heath administration. However, the mid-1970s did witness a significant upsurge in the influence of this ideological tendency and, equally important, its successful combination with what Hall (1983) has referred to as 'authoritarian populism'.

Hence, what emerged in terms of political strategy, vigorously promulgated by the Conservatives in the run-up to the 1979 Election, was a complex mixture of social market strategy and traditional Conservative values. For example, the public sector could be depicted as an unproductive burden on the wealth-creating sector in general and on tax-payers in particular. There was thus a need to reduce public expenditure by returning as many state services to the market and/or the family as possible. By these means, the real costs of such services would be prevented from rising at a time when output and productivity were stagnant or falling. In addition, it would be possible to make the kind of tax cuts necessary to encourage the revival of private enterprise and to restore family and individual responsibility.

In economic policy, the principal aim was to maintain price stability by the firm control of the money supply. This implied the steady reduction of government borrowing, so removing the temptation to print money to increase revenue, and the setting of monetary targets and controls on the volume of private credit in line with them. Hence, there was no need to engage with the trades unions in attempts to moderate wage demands or, indeed, to discuss with them matters of general economic policy.

However, the trades unions *were* responsible for the creation of unemployment, insofar as they demanded wages higher than firms could afford. They were also guilty of holding back Britain's industrial development by their entrenched opposition to the rationalization of the labour process, aimed at raising productivity. Accordingly, there was a need to restrict the activities of the unions both by the removal of many of their traditional legal rights, as well as by the effects of unemployment (although this was argued to reach a 'natural' level, irrespective of the level of demand in the economy).

The role of the state in the economy was therefore confined to maintaining the conditions for markets to function properly. Clearly, the stability of money was one such condition. Equally, the maintenance of the security of property was another. Indeed, for wider social reasons too, there was an urgent need to pursue strict standards of law and order and morality more generally. Certainly, however, there was no place for extensive state subsidization of industry, in that this was wasteful of public funds and hindered the restructuring of the economy by forcing individuals to respond to the rigours of the market.

In short, then, what was involved *at the ideological level* was the radical rejection of the principles which had underpinned the social democratic consensus of the Keynesian-Welfare State. By the massive re-direction of the state's activities, the British economy could be turned around, on terms which necessarily implied the regeneration of capitalism and the reassertion of the social power of the class groupings whose interests it supported.

We certainly do not wish to understate the significance of this ideological shift; however, in terms of practical policies, the break was not quite as radical as one was led to believe. In part, of course, this was because the policies adopted by the new Conservative government were, in a number of respects, little more than intensifications of those which had been pursued by the previous Labour one. Hence, for example, as we have seen, the case for monetarist approaches on public expenditure had been conceded as early as 1975. In addition, short-term political realities and narrow electoral considerations also exerted a restraining influence on the cutting-edge of policy implementation. The government found itself quite unable to cut off subsidies to ailing giants of British industry, such as British Leyland and the British Steel Corporation, for the simple reason that the unemployment consequences would have been too horrific and potentially damaging electorally. Nevertheless, in both of the instances cited, major restructuring and redundancy programmes were forced through at the government's behest. Similarly, perhaps with the memories of Mr Heath's difficulties with trades union reform still fresh, the administration proceeded much more cautiously against the trades unions than some of the New Right ideologues would have wished.

Nevertheless, bearing these qualifications in mind, it remains the case that the impact of the New Right has been very substantial. Certainly, this impact has been significant in respect of policies for urban and regional development; and it is to an examination of these issues that we now turn.

Thatcherism and the cities

Paradoxically in view of the claim we have just made, after an initial period of review, the new Secretary of State for the Environment, Mr Michael Heseltine, made it clear that he intended to continue the essential elements of the Partnership and Programme arrangements. In this sense, then, Mr Shore's original appeal for bipartisan support for his policy was successful; in fact, Mr Heseltine's objectives appeared to differ hardly at all from those of his predecessor.

However, this surface impression belies an underlying reality of major change. Two related issues are significant here. Firstly, since 1979, there has been a much greater emphasis placed upon the role of the private sector within the Partnerships and Programmes; much more so than previously, the harnessing of private-sector initiative to inner-city development has been the centrepiece of the policy. Secondly, this shift of emphasis has been made necessary (quite apart from ideological considerations) by the reduction of public funds being made available to the major urban local authorities, in line with the general directives of state policy. Thus, between 1978–79 and 1982–83, although central government expenditure *increased* by 10.7 per cent in real terms, local authority spending *fell* by 3.6 per cent.

This reduction had direct effects on the Partnership and Programme authorities, in that their specific budgets were cut back, although not severely. What was much more significant was the effect of changes in the allocation of *general* central government funds to local authorities through the Rate Support Grant. Accordingly, Mr Heseltine's decision to reverse the priority which had previously been accorded to those authorities with major inner-city problems, actually reduced the Partnership areas' grants in 1981–82 by some £166,000,000 compared with 1980–81, which amounted to a reduction of 17 per cent, compared with the national average of 9.7 per cent (Lansley, 1982).

These changes, in turn, have meant that, not surprisingly, capital's interests have come to play a much greater part in the determination of policy direction. And, as Hambleton (1980) has indicated, the predominant view within the private sector has been that until inner-city areas offer opportunities for *profitable* operation, there is little that the private sector can or should do. There is no reason to believe that this view has changed through the operation of the Partnerships (Stewart and Underwood, 1983), or, indeed, by other private-sector initiatives introduced in the aftermath of the 1981 urban riots, such as the Urban Development Grant, the Financial Institutions Group and the Merseyside Taskforce (for example, Parkinson and Duffy, 1984).

Furthermore, the reduction in Rate Support Grant payments to the inner-urban authorities was bound up with much more far-reaching changes in the relationships between central and local government. For example, in its controversial Local Government, Planning and Land Act of 1980, the Conservative government broke with previous practice, which had linked central government payments to measures of local resources available to local authorities and the levels of expenditure necessary to cope with the problems they faced, and substituted the 'block grant' system. Here, central government would allocate monies on the basis of *its* estimate of what was required to provide a reasonable level of local services (the Grant Related Expenditure Assessment). Where local authorities exceeded prescribed expenditure levels, they would be penalized (Jackman, 1982).

Since then, the control of the central state over local government spending has become tighter and tighter, and the penalties for exceeding targets ever more severe. Hence, the Local Government Finance Act of 1982 banned the raising of a supplementary rate and introduced retrospective rate support penalties – if a local authority spends excessively in one year, it will receive proportionately less grant in the following year. By 1984–85, the Rate Support Grant settlement provided that an authority spending only 9 per cent above target would lose grant equivalent in value to a 68p rate or in some cases all of their grant (Stewart, 1984).

Clearly, despite the government's vociferous claims to the contrary, these changes imply a considerable reduction in the extent of autonomy enjoyed by the local state. And, in this respect, they represent a major step in what, as we have seen, has been a much longer process of development in the form of the British state. Moreover, the 1984 Rates Act extends even further the limits of central state control by, in effect, removing the rights of local authorities to determine their expenditure patterns within the bounds of their budgets (Stewart, 1984).

Predictably, the effects of all this on the Partnerships have been profoundly unhelpful. As Stewart and Underwood (1983) argue:

> it is clear that the concept of 'partnership' over inner cities is almost an irrelevance at a time when it is felt (correctly or incorrectly) that one of the partners is doing its best to reduce the general status of the other to, at best, an agent and, at worse, a corpse. The ambiguity inherent at present in the central – local relation is clear, particularly for those metropolitan authorities threatened with penalties for overspending. How is it possible for 'partners' to develop a constructive, positive, joint relationship over extra spending for the special needs of the inner area while at the same time conducting a wider battle over the general question of expenditure targets? (1983: 147)

Again, it would appear, the interests of the inner cities and their residents have been traded-off against the pursuit of a wider state strategy to resolve Britain's economic ills.

Much the same sorts of general arguments may be made in respect of the Urban Development Corporations introduced in the London Docklands and that part of the Liverpool Partnership area within the old Merseyside Docks. These bodies, modelled on the New Town Development Corporations, were granted extensive powers to acquire and assemble land, to grant planning permission on land they own or sell, manage and build housing, and allow public and private residential development on their land, and to construct the necessary roads. In addition, certain powers are allowed to provide infrastructure for and financial assistance to industry.

What is crucial, however, is that they were appointed directly by central government; thereby, local authority powers in the areas concerned were effectively removed. It is not immediately clear, however, why such initiatives should be restricted to only two areas; except insofar as their creation appeared to contradict the more general opposition of the Thatcher administration to QUANGOs (Cawson, 1982).

Of rather more general significance is what was arguably the most innovative of the inner-city initiatives introduced by the new Conservative government: enterprise zones (EZs). Again, however, one of their effects was to reduce the powers of local authorities; although, in this case, this was associated with the wider concern to restrict the activities of the state, so as to remove the supposed constraints upon entrepreneurship.

Hence, some 12 EZs were designated between June 1981 and April 1982. They comprised quite small localities (not exceeding 600 acres) in areas afflicted by severe physical and economic decay, many of them in the inner parts of the major urban centres.[4] Within these areas, there was to be a reduction in the extent of government regulation of economic activity. Exemption was to be granted from development land tax and from rates on commercial and industrial buildings; 100 per cent capital allowances were to be allowed for corporation and income tax purposes on commercial and industrial buildings; planning regulations were to be applied less stringently, in that developers were not required to obtain permission in many instances; local authorities were to ensure that speedy responses were given to planning and building regulations matters and issues of health, safety, fire and pollution control; and the statistical information required by government was to be kept to a minimum.

As was pointed out at the time of their announcement, the EZs were based upon an analysis of economic development which bears little apparent relationship to reality. Certainly, there is little reason to believe that economic initiative is being significantly restricted by the kinds of controls which were removed within the zones; nor that such controls contributed in major ways to the economic decline of inner-city areas (Anderson, 1983).

In the event, the experience of the first few years of their operation seems to have confirmed the pessimism which greeted their introduction. An officially commissioned evaluation found that the EZs' main effect has been to encourage the *transfer* of business activity over short distances, particularly where difficulties were being encountered at the old locations. Similarly, many firms *already intending* to open new branches or to start up from scratch, have been attracted to the EZs. Hence, economic activity has been attracted into run-down areas, but, for the most part, at the expense of other localities. There is little indication that the EZs have been responsible for substantial *net* employment increases (Roger Tym and Partners, 1981; 1982).

It seems improbable that much of this was not foreseen by the government even before the EZs were introduced. Certainly, by 1982, when some 12 further EZ designations were announced, it was well known. In reality, then, their purpose was to provide an important practical dimension to the essentially ideological resort to the supposed benefits of the market; they were an expression in policy of the loudly proclaimed benefits of free enterprise. And what is interesting here is that whilst Mr Shore could attribute certain urban problems to the effects of *particular* planning policies, it was the very notion of planning itself which was being decried by the New Right Conservatives.

In fact, of course, whatever the rhetoric of state withdrawal, the development of the EZs has occasioned substantial public expendi-

[4]The complete list and location of all EZs is given in Shutt, 1984, Table 3.

ture, especially in removing the costs of land reclamation and assembly and infrastructural provision; as well as in the rate and tax incentives. This has led one recent commentator to conclude:

> the evidence suggests that [the EZs] are not performing functions which differ significantly from traditional regional policy. They are based on the assumption that 'bribing capital' to shift location and subsidizing development costs for construction and finance capital can actually halt the processes of industrial restructuring which is creating chaos in our conurbations and contribute to new job creation. (Shutt, 1984: 38)

The New Right perspective has been reflected in other areas of urban and regional policy too. The Community Land Act was deemed to be simply unnecessary and far too expensive, and was repealed; whilst the Secretary of State was constantly exhorting local authorities to sell off their land-holdings to the private sector. Likewise the 1980 Housing Act introduced for tenants of municipal housing and housing associations the statutory right to buy. This, accompanied by the increased subsidization of mortgage-payers, the sharp increase in council-house rents and the dramatic fall in council-house building, clearly indicated the administration's conviction of the superiority of owner-occupation (Merrett, 1982).

However, as Ball (1983) shows, the combination of low levels of public expenditure on the built environment with an emphasis upon owner-occupation has created severe problems for planning. The point here is that the locational priorities of the planners (in favour of, say, the inner cities) cannot be implemented, as there are such drastically reduced incentives (in the form of state subsidy of the built environment) for builders and developers to abide by them. In effect, urban planning has retreated almost wholly to a passive role of merely facilitating the pursuit of private-sector objectives.

Hence, Mr Heseltine made it clear that in plan-making and implementation, much greater emphasis should be placed on the encouragement of private initiatives and development. Planning controls were to be made more flexible and speedier in their operation, by placing them wholly in the responsibility of the district councils. Plan-making was similarly to be made quicker and more realistic in its proposals, with less attention being paid to the strict zoning of land-uses. More surprisingly, the planning professionals appear to have embraced this role with some enthusiasm. For instance, the chief adviser to the House of Commons Expenditure Committee's investigations of development control, has commented:

> The early 1970s was a period of resistance to change: motorway protest groups, community action against slum clearance, opponents of town centre redevelopment. Strategic and entrepreneurial interests were

sacrificed to local community pressures. Conceivably, however, we are moving into a different period in which the entrepreneurial role becomes dominant. . . . . We need the entrepreneurial approach to planning. (Davies, 1980: 23; quoted in Ball, 1983: 270–1)

As for regional policy, it has also been transformed in its scope. IDC and ODP controls have been effectively abolished; whilst the Assisted Areas have been reduced from covering some 40 per cent of the employed population to only about 20 per cent. The rate of Regional Development Grant has been reduced and there has been an intensification of the trend toward the use of selective rather than automatic aid (Regional Studies Association, 1983). In particular, there has been a growing emphasis upon the use of such funds as a means of attracting foreign investment into Britain, especially in the high-technology sectors (Cooke, Morgan and Jackson, 1983). In general, then, there has been a much closer alignment of aid with the market's criteria; a trend which is particularly marked in the new directives to the NEB and the Development Agencies. Moreover, this trend is confirmed in the most recent White Paper on regional policy. Insofar as there has been any continued use of regional policy for unemployment relief, it has been concentrated into those areas with the very highest levels of unemployment (Townsend, 1980); thereby directing attention away from the extent of *general* unemployment increases.

The consequences of urban policy for the New Right

It is, of course, extremely difficult to disentangle the consequences of these particular changes in urban policy from those of the wider strategy which has been pursued by the Conservatives since 1979. With respect to the latter, there has been remarkably little indication that its central objective of reviving British industrial capital has been fulfilled. Some commentators would, of course, attribute this to the international economic crisis (for a discussion of this issue, see Coutts *et al.*, 1981); others to the government's failure to stick to the strategy which it mapped out in opposition – a failure which is marked most dramatically in the apparent inability to control the central state's own expenditure in line with the targets deemed necessary.

Nevertheless, inflation has moderated as a result of the intensification of the recession which has resulted from Conservative policies. But equally, de-industrialization has proceeded apace, with only an imperfect distinction between 'efficient' and 'inefficient' firms. At the same time, as we have suggested, *some* sectors of industry have continued to prosper; whilst financial capital and the multinational companies have flourished under a regime which has removed foreign exchange and capital export controls.

The most pressing consequence of this pattern of economic change, however, has been the rapid and enormous increase in unemployment, which was *officially* recorded as having topped 3,000,000 by the time of the 1983 General Election. Moreover, the uneven distribution of this unemployment has been intensified, exacerbating the crisis confronting those areas which are least attractive as locations for economic activity, such as the cities.

Given all this, it is remarkable that Mrs Thatcher was able to win such an emphatic endorsement from the electorate at the 1983 General Election. In part, of course, pure good luck played its part here: the British electoral system operated in her Party's favour; the Falklands crisis re-established her popularity at a critical period (Barnett, 1982); and, perhaps most critically of all, the Labour opposition was weak and divided.

This latter circumstance, however, was indicative of something more far-reaching. The divisions within the Labour Party reflected its inability to develop a new strategy after the manifest failures of 1974 to 1979 and, for that matter, 1964 to 1970 too. Indeed, it was the profound disaffection with the policies of these years which contributed so much to the Conservatives' initial victory in 1979; a disaffection which was reflected in the widespread attitudes towards the bureaucracies of the welfare state, the nationalized industries and, perhaps above all, the trades unions themselves, especially in their corporatist guise as policy-makers. More fundamentally still, Hall (1983) has argued that this disaffection derives from the essential contradiction which beset the Labour Party in office: on the one hand, it had to present itself as the vehicle through which Britain's problems could be resolved in a way which protected the interests of ordinary people; on the other hand, the constraints exerted by capital prevented its achieving very much more than the easing of capitalist development.

However, in terms of voting at least, it must be borne in mind that support for the Thatcherite solution is by no means spread evenly across the population as a whole. In the same way that, for example, one of the clearest symbols of Mrs Thatcher's victory in 1979 was the support which she attracted from skilled male trades unionists in the West Midlands, so the 1983 General Election revealed its own patterns of differentiation. Hence, as Massey (1983b) has demonstrated so perceptively, what remains of Labour support is concentrated into population *groups* such as public-sector workers and council tenants, and into *areas* like the inner cities and the declining industrial regions of the North East, Scotland and South Wales. Moreover, the kinds of urban and regional policies which we have described in this and earlier chapters are likely to have made the coincidence of such groups and areas more likely. It is precisely these areas which have been most extensively deserted by private capital and which remain as the residual *foci* of state intervention.

It is equally the case, of course, that support for Mrs Thatcher's regime remains concentrated most strongly in the southern parts of Britain. Again, as we have seen, the operation of urban and regional policies has facilitated the concentration into these areas of particular types of economic activity and, correspondingly, certain types of occupational position. McEnery (1981), for example, points out that the South East increased its proportion of service workers from 56 per cent to 67 per cent between 1965 and 1977. Similarly, Buck (1979) has drawn attention to the concentration of 'higher-order' occupations in regions such as the South East of England. However, the most striking expression of these processes has been the creation of what we referred to in Chapter 2 as the 'sun-belt'; and it is here, as Massey (1983b) argues, that Mrs Thatcher scored some of her most spectacular victories in 1983.

Ironically, then, it may be argued that a major effect of urban and regional policies since 1945 has been to contribute to the generation of those conditions which have allowed political forces to flourish which are avowedly opposed to such state intervention. And, we would suggest, this seeming paradox is only resolvable by reference to the wider context of class relations out of which these urban and regional policies have been forged. Moreover, it is a context which makes much more difficult and complex the task of developing effective strategies for the cities in the future.

6

Social conflict, the local state and the future of the cities

The inner-city crisis: the historical process

The origins of the current 'inner-city crisis' lie in the working-out of two historical processes, both of which have concerned us in this book. On the one hand, there are the changes taking place in the material conditions of the cities: in economic structure, demographic composition, environmental quality and so forth. On the other, there are the shifts in the intensity of concern which is expressed over these material conditions. Here, a number of social institutions play their part. However, by far the most significant role is played by the state. In Britain, as in other advanced capitalist societies, it is the state which has assumed a progressively greater responsibility for shaping urban development, irrespective of the crisis of the Keynesian-Welfare State and the cuts in public expenditure since the mid-1970s. For this reason, the response of the state to urban conditions has achieved paramount importance.

The essential point to grasp, however, is that there is no straight-forward relationship between these two broad processes. For example, contrary to what we are led to believe by certain versions of what we have termed the 'Whig' perspective, conditions of deprivation and disadvantage do not *automatically* call forth policy responses. There is a *social and political* process through which such responses are produced.

At one level, this is determined by the ways in which material conditions are themselves conceptualized – 'socially constructed' in ·the language of some sociologists. This sort of argument is made very clearly, for example, by Edwards and Batley (1978) in respect of the development of the Urban Programme and anti-poverty policies more generally. Hence, they are able to document in some detail the parallel develoments of theoretical perspectives on poverty and of policy initiatives; developments which we ourselves sketched in earlier chapters.

Crucially, however, the effects of these conceptualizations are dependent upon the *power* of the groups which hold them to translate them into actual responses. And this is precisely the point which, as we have seen, Stedman Jones (1971) makes about the treatment of the poor in nineteenth-century London. It was not simply that the nature of poverty was viewed in particular ways by predominantly middle-class groups; but also that these groups were in a position to *act* on the basis of their ideas. It is thus no coincidence that the conceptualizations of the poor themselves are largely unknown.

Where we are concerned with state responses – as we must be in the context of the arguments we have presented earlier – our attention must correspondingly focus upon the influences exerted in the process of policy-formulation. This, in turn, involves the explicit theorization of the nature and operation of the state in Britain. All too often, attempts to explain the development of policy have been based upon a kind of *instinctive* and *unstated* pluralism. This is simply inadequate (for example, Cawson, 1982). Accordingly, in what follows in this section of the chapter, we seek to draw together our ideas about the two historical processes which we have identified, and the relationships between them.

The anatomy of urban decline

It is impossible to disassociate the current state of Britain's cities from the long-term trajectory of British society as a whole. In the same way that many of the great urban centres were the product of Britain's nineteenth-century Imperial expansion and economic pre-eminence, so the dramatic decline of the cities in recent decades is rooted in the collapse of Britain's domestic economy. The explanations for this decline must be sought in the local manifestations of much wider, societal processes.

In this way, then, the problems of the inner cities are fundamentally economic in character; they derive from changes in economic structure. The direct effects of these changes are to be measured in terms of the new patterns of employment, the high levels of unemployment, the recomposition of population and the physical dereliction, all of which we have seen to be characteristic of the older areas at the heart of Britain's cities. However, we have also shown the *indirect* effects of such changes on state policies. Hence, for example, economic problems have prompted successive administrations to curtail severely their expenditure on social welfare programmes. This, in turn, has worked its way through to the provision of the facilities of what Castells (1977) has called 'collective consumption': public housing, education, health services, the built environment and so on. The impoverishment of this provision has, of course, accentuated and exacerbated the urban crisis, especially as many of the inner areas are populated by citizens acutely dependent upon such state services.

We can identify a number of distinct processes which together have contributed most to the economic decline of the inner cities. Firstly, there has been the massive reorganization of British manufacturing industry, which has been especially significant over the past two decades or so. At the most general level, British manufacturing has failed to maintain its international competitiveness; a failure which was masked by the special conditions of the long boom of the 1950s. In consequence, there has been a *general* decline in employment in manufacturing firms, which has exerted a disproportionate effect upon the cities, as these tended to be the centres of such activity. Moreover, superimposed upon this general decline, there has been a spatially differentiated pattern of growth, reflecting the attempts of certain sectors of industrial capital to counter falling rates of profit. Hence, those sectors of manufacturing which *have* been expanding have not, for the most part, been locating their new enterprises in the major urban areas; rather, they have been attracted to rural locations and to the peripheral industrial regions of Britain. In employment terms, these changes are reflected in the shifts between manual and non-manual jobs, between male and female employment and in the frequently sharp differentiation between local rates of unemployment.

Secondly, the cities have been severely affected by the changes which have taken place in the tertiary sector of the economy. At the aggregate level, of course, there has been a dramatic increase in employment in this heterogeneous sector, at least until recently. However, in the inner cities, there has been an actual decline in jobs in the private services. Accordingly, whilst there has been a marked trend toward the location of higher-level administrative and management functions in the major urban centres and, above all, in London and the South East, the more routine tasks have been more widely distributed to outer suburban locations and even the peripheral regions. In the public services, there have been parallel trends, such as the relocation of certain central government functions to regions such as South Wales. More generally, however, public services are distributed according to non-market criteria and, therefore, there have been small increases in employment in the inner-urban areas; these have, nevertheless, been insufficient to compensate for the decline in the private sector.

These developments in both manufacturing and in services have set the context for the third major economic process to have a significant impact upon the cities: the development and redevelopment of land and the built environment. On the one hand, the decline of manufacturing industry in many inner-urban areas has been manifested in the closure of large numbers of plants and the consequent release of land formerly in industrial use. On the other, there has been a growth in demand for land for building of commercial property, such as offices, retail stores and so forth, often for purely speculative gains. In addition, considerable inner-area housing has been cleared for redevelopment in retailing and offices. These processes – operating, of course, in the context of an essentially unregulated market – have together produced the apparent paradox of extensive derelict and vacant land in many city areas, allied to persistently high land prices. Equally, traditional jobs and established communities have vanished; whilst some new employment opportunities have been created in the tertiary sector, although these tend not to have been taken by inner-city residents.

As we have already suggested, these local changes are most convincingly explained in terms of the long-term trajectory of British society as a whole. At one level, then, they may be identified as the product of the operation of the capitalist mode of production. Individual capitals compete to ensure their profitability, irrespective of the social consequences of this competition (except insofar as these consequences provoke organized opposition from labour). Thus, the reorganization and restructuring of manufacturing industry which we have described is a manifestation of this competitive imperative. Similarly, capital's quest for profitability is not limited to industrial production; and we have noted the attractiveness of property and land speculation as investment outlets.

However, this is obviously to specify highly complex social relations in an extremely crude and oversimplified fashion. Certainly, for example, the general characteristics of the capitalist mode find expression in a form thoroughly mediated by the specificities and peculiarities of British society. Therefore, Britain's twentieth-century development has been profoundly shaped by the legacy of its Imperial past. Of major importance here is the enduring international orientation of significant sectors of British capital. This is most marked, of course, in the activities of finance capital; the City has persistently sought out overseas investment where this has been most profitable, irrespective of the consequences domestically. Equally, however, many of the largest British manufactuing companies are similarly multinational in their operations, holding what are massive overseas investments, even by world-wide standards. And, of course, these multinationals, along with those from overseas operating within Britain, have been at the forefront of the reorganization of manufacturing which we have sketched.

What is significant, however, is not simply the fact of this international orientation, but also the political dominance of the interests which pursue it. Therefore, British domestic manufacturing industry has not only been denied those investment funds which have been directed elsewhere (not exclusively abroad, of course); but has also been incapacitated by the effects of the economic policies which

British governments have, for the most part, pursued. And this has contrasted with the generally favourable treatment received by the international sectors of British capital. In consequence, the domestic economy has been especially vulnerable; particularly in the context of the general crises which have periodically afflicted the advanced capitalist economies as a whole.

One of the principal groups to suffer as a result of this vulnerability is British labour. Unemployment rates in Britain have generally been rather higher than in competitor economies; whilst over large sections of industry, pay and working conditions have been inferior. However, it is a further feature of these specifically British class relations that the labour movement's energies have been more successfully directed at alleviating the symptoms of Britain's economic malaise (through, for example, often militant wage-bargaining) than at developing effective strategies to eradicate its causes.

The compromise of state intervention

Those analyses of the nature of urban decline which seek its causes somewhere in the cities themselves are paralleled by accounts of policy which ignore the wider context of politics and the state-form. As we have argued, however, these 'Whig' accounts are the staple form of analysis of urban and regional policy.

In contrast, therefore, we have sought to argue a radically different analysis. A preliminary step here is to recognize that the role of the state in the inner-urban areas comprises much more than just those policies which have been publicly designated with an inner-city label. At the very least, we must be concerned with the whole panoply of urban and regional policies; so much is clearly implied by even the most restricted of contemporary definitions of the nature of the cities' problems.

If we do focus upon this wider range of state intervention, then it is clear that these policies have been largely unsuccessful in negating those trends in economic and social development which have led to the present sorry state of Britain's inner-urban areas. Indeed, we have argued that they have actually operated to *facilitate* those trends. For example, the combined effect of land policy and the operation of the land-use planning system has been promotive of the kind of property speculation whose results we have catalogued. Similarly, regional policy has contributed significant resources which have assisted in the restructuring of certain sectors of manufacturing industry, with adverse effects upon the employment prospects of many inner-urban areas. Or again, the distribution of subsidies between different categories of housing tenure has, in the main, supported a pattern of housing development inimical to the regeneration of the inner areas as thriving residential communities. And, of course, this sort of list could be extended with many further examples.

However, we should be clear as to precisely what is being argued here. Certainly, it is not to impugn the *intentions* of those individuals and groups who were involved in the creation of post-war urban policy or in its subsequent implementation. There appears to have been genuine concern during these years of post-war reconstruction to use the resources of the state as a means of eradicating the problems which had been so manifest during the period between the wars and to create towns and cities which would cater in an equitable fashion for people's needs for employment, housing, recreation and so forth.

The explanation for the failure to achieve such an out-come – even, it should be noted, in the comparatively favourable conditions of the 1950s – lies in the nature of the system of urban and regional policy itself. As we have seen, state intervention was quite simply insufficient to the task. And this, in turn, results from the constraints exerted by the balance of class interests, as these were expressed in the politics of the process of policy-formulation. Powerful interests within capital were wholly antipathetic to the pursuit of strongly interventionist policies, especially in the conditions of the 1950s. Organized labour, on the other hand, was neither sufficiently powerful nor sufficiently convinced of the policies to press hard for such intervention.

With the deepening economic crisis through the 1960s, urban and regional policies came to be increasingly subservient to the demands of general state strategies with regard to this economic crisis. Hence, the attempts to reorganize planning during the 1960s were very much part and parcel of the wider attempt to resolve Britain's economic problems by transcending the Keynesian orthodoxies through a national planning strategy. The significant point here is that this national strategy constituted an attempt to resolve the crisis on terms which were essentially favourable to large sections of the dominant class groupings.

Similarly, during the 1970s, the character of urban and regional policies was shaped by the exigencies of the attempt to implement a corporatist solution to Britain's economic decline. Here, however, the most pressing problems for successive administrations was that of constructing a sufficient basis of popular support for a strategy which was so asymmetrical in the demands which it imposed upon capital and labour respectively.

Moreover, as we have seen, it was the antagonisms internal to capital which were largely responsible for the ultimate failures of the state strategies of the 1960s and 1970s. The same pre-eminent power of the international sectors of British capital which has contributed so much to the genesis of the economic crisis, also exerted a major constraining influence on the strategies adopted to combat it.

Most recently, this influence has been significantly bolstered by the growth of a widespread ideological commitment – in political circles and more widely – to strict monetary policy and the reduction of state expenditure over wide areas of policy. Again, the effects of the adoption of a general state strategy based, more or less, upon such an ideology have been profound upon the operation of urban and regional policy. Even more clearly than before, the boundaries of this policy are drawn so as to be consistent with the wider political context. Accordingly, urban and regional development reflects much more markedly than hitherto the exigencies of market forces. Whilst public expenditure cuts have exerted an especially severe impact upon the major urban areas. Certainly, it is difficult to be other than pessimistic about the future of the inner cities given the continuation of such trends.

The state and class relations

As should be clear from these summary arguments, our central concern has been to explain the origins of *particular* state policies in order to understand better their impact upon the cities. Certainly, we have not attempted to contribute formally to the debates about the nature of the 'capitalist state' (see Jessop, 1982). Nevertheless, our analysis has certainly implied a particular view of the character of the British state and of the process of policy-formulation which this embodies.

Block (1980) has recently presented a general account of state policy-making which expresses with considerable clarity what we take to be the key features of the British context. Hence, his central proposition is that there are limits upon the state policies *which are possible*, as a result of the exigencies of class relations. More specifically, ' . . . state managers will tend to maximize [their interests] within particular political "rules of the game". Beyond these rules lie particular patterns of class relations that reinforce the limits on state managers' pursuit of their collective self-interest. Yet it must be stressed that all of these limits are contingent and not absolute.' (1980: 229–30) Those directly responsible for the direction and management of state policy are thus active agents in the genesis of that policy. But furthermore, they are constrained in what they are able to do by the external reality of the balance of power between class interests; and this is reflected in common expectations and understandings about the legitimate scope of state action.

In British society, dominated by the capitalist mode of production, there are certain types of policy which the state cannot – and will not attempt to – implement, given the class relations defined by this mode of production. For instance, the social and political dominance of capitalist class groupings ensures – as we have shown in earlier chapters – the *virtual* inviolability of property rights; whilst, on the whole, state policies have operated to support the process of accumulation and, what is more important to the present argument, have certainly not acted to redirect it in any ·calculated fashion towards more socially responsive ends. All this is not to suggest, however, that such limits to state policy are immutable; but rather that they are inherent in the class relationships characteristic of the capitalist mode. To change the former requires the transformation of the latter.

Equally, it is not to suggest that the *specific form* of state policy which is implemented is necessarily the most favourable possible to capital's interests. The reason for this (amongst others) is that *within the limits* specified by fundamental class relations, there exists a considerable latitude for *different* forms of state action. To appreciate this point, all we have to do is to compare the actions of, say, the Labour administrations of 1945–51 with those of the Conservative governments after 1979.

Moreover, as we have emphasized, the specific form of state policy is the outcome of the struggles of a wide variety of class and other social groupings. As we have seen, it is the influence of *financial* capital which has been generally dominant in the determination of state economic strategy; and only on occasion has this influence been consonant with that of domestic industrial capital. Similarly, the nationalization programmes of 1945–51 owed a great deal to the influence of the trades unions and the labour movement more generally. Whilst in other areas of policy, it may well be the ethnic minorities, women's organizations or nationalist and regionalist alliances which have played a crucial role.

What this implies, of course, is a highly complex political process; for it is through the political system that these struggles are generally worked out. On the one hand, the diversity of social groupings to which we have referred attempts to influence the state managers, whether through the representative institutions or by other means. On the other, the state managers themselves engage in the organization and orchestration of support in order to push state policy in the direction which they desire.

And here there is by no means an equivalence between social groupings. As we have argued repeatedly in the previous chapters, it has been a central priority of all post-war administrations up until 1979 to secure some form of accommodation with industrial capital *and* the labour movement. Since 1979, however, a much lesser priority has been attached to the latter. Equally, financial capital has been pervasively influential through its direct relationship with the Bank of England and the Treasury. In addition, these priorities are mirrored in the very structures of what have been the major political parties in Britain during this century; and, in rather a different way, in the extent to which *general* state strategy for *economic* development has been dominant over other aspects of state activity (see also Walker, 1984).

Clearly, in *analyzing* the intricacies of historical reality, it is extremely difficult to distinguish any separate effects on state intervention of fundamental class constraints and the political processes by which specific policy forms are determined. Indeed, it may well be that in terms of *political practice* there are close interconnections too. The possibilities of *changing* fundamental class relations may be made more or less likely by the specific form of state policies adopted. Block (1980) is rather more categorical:

> in late capitalism [n]either the state nor capital are willing or able to carry out the forms of reorganization needed to release new productive forms that could overcome the economy's weaknesses. Instead, the contradictions and conflicts between capitalists and state managers grow deeper as neither statist nor 'free market' solutions are capable of solving the underlying problems. The result is likely to be political paralysis and an accelerating erosion of bourgeois ideological hegemony. In the context of deepening state–capital conflicts, new opportunities would exist for oppositional social forces determined to eliminate the oppressive power of both capital and the state. (1980: 240)

In short, then, for Block, it is precisely the *failures* of specific state policies which will create the space for wider transformations in the nature of late capitalist society. Whilst there is ample evidence of such failures in the British post-war experience, we confess ourselves to be less sanguine as to the potentialities thus implied. Nevertheless, in the next part of the chapter, we extend upon this analysis by considering some particular 'oppositional social forces', which have a special relevance to the future of the cities.

The political economy of inner-city revival

The specific question which we wish to address here is that of the implications of the analysis which we have presented for future policies with respect to the inner cities and urban and regional development more widely. Hence, we have stressed that it is not possible to separate out issues of *policy* from those of *politics*: policy-formulation and implementation necessarily express the interplay of class and other social interests, in the ways which we have described. To this extent, then, any resolution of the 'inner-city crisis' must involve the development of a politically informed strategy, which clearly recognizes the class relationships involved.

Moreover, given our account of the basic economic processes under-pinning this crisis, it is clear that such a strategy would require to penetrate beyond what we have specified as the limits of state policy in a context of capitalist class relations, especially with regard to interference with property rights and state control of the accumula-tion process.

Now, it must be clear to everyone that the preconditions for the development of such a full-blooded strategy are simply unfulfilled. Accordingly, we have argued that the British social formation is thoroughly permeated by capitalist class relations. More immedi-ately, the political arena is currently dominated by a New Right Conservative administration, following the collapse of the social democratic consensus, expressed most clearly in the failures of the Labour governments of the 1960s and 1970s. And, as we have seen, this administration is dedicated to the pursuit of strategies wholly inimical to those which our analysis tells us are necessary.

Are we to conclude, therefore, that the space for the development of a strategy sufficient to tackle the cities' problems (as we have defined them) does not exist? Certainly, the logic of our arguments suggests that this space is highly constrained. However, it is not the case that there is a total absence of 'oppositional social forces', prepared to undertake struggles against the predominant direction of current state policies and the interests which they serve. Further-more, it is clear from the analysis which we have presented that to tackle the problems of the inner cities *implies* organizing around such oppositional forces; and this does no more than express the necessary link which we have identified between *policy* and *politics*.

This, in turn, implies a radically different role for the urban professionals from the one which they have traditionally fulfilled. In these terms, they become social agents facilitating the development of strategies which themselves constitute part of a process of testing the limits of change, of politicizing the context (Walker, 1984).

Social Conflict and Urban Development

Consideration of 'oppositional social forces' clearly brings us back to the extraordinarily dramatic expression of such forces in the 1981 urban riots. As we argued in Chapter 1, whatever the immediate context of these outbursts, the more general context of the inner-urban areas undoubtedly exerted a significant influence too. More specifically, some commentators have suggested that the riots served to impose limits upon what even a New Right administration such as Mrs Thatcher's could do. For instance, Rex (1982) argues:

> Clearly riots have placed limits on the extent to which a capitalist govern-ment can pursue its policies of restructuring industry and altering the

class balance of the society. Before the riots the government could assume that it had not reached the limits of hardship which it could impose on the population without resistance, and it could argue that there was broad consent to the notion of accepting that hardship. That argument is no longer possible. (1982: 107)

It seems probable that the force of this analysis seemed greater in 1981–82 than it does some years later. As we have indicated, there has certainly been little indication of substantial state investment in the cities since the riots and, in many respects, conditions have got worse. Moreover, as Harloe and Paris (1984) suggest, one reason why these outbreaks of violent disorder have not led to radical reversals of policy is that they represented the response of one particular group of inner-city residents – the young, predominantly unemployed – to their immediate circumstances, rather than a more directed and broadly based 'urban social movement'. It is also significant that this group of young unemployed occupies one of the least advantaged and most marginalized of locations within the working class.

Neither is it at all clear that the continuing impoverishment of the inner cities is likely to generate forms of social protest which *are* more widely representative. In fact, such a context is as likely to reinforce *divisions* within the urban working class as to create alliances. Hence, for example, Miles and Phizacklea (1981) demonstrate that a very high proportion of working-class whites blame blacks for the deterioration of inner-urban areas. Likewise, there appear to have been substantial increases in the recruitment to and activities of extreme racialist organizations in recent years (Husbands, 1983).

Nevertheless, in spite of these arguments, there is some evidence that changes in the social structure of the cities and the potentialities which are thereby opened up for resistance to current trends *are* important. As we mentioned earlier, Massey (1983b), for example, emphasizes the emerging possibilities of social change in the inner cities, on the basis of her analysis of Labour Party voting at the 1983 General Election.

It is very much the electoral patterns of the inner cities which stand out from the rest, especially as you come South. In part this must be a reflection of demographic change, and possibly too the first fruits of the attempts to build new alliances in some inner urban areas.

In London, Labour certainly did relatively well in those constituencies (Islington North, Hampstead, Hornsey, Peckham, Tooting, Southall . . .) with high proportions of Irish, blacks and progressive middle classes. . . . . ITN's poll captured the character of some of these constituencies perfectly: it found a high correlation of Labour voting with high proportions of unemployed people, high proportions of blacks, and what it called a strong polytechnic and university presence. Such areas also have, in increasing numbers of cases, active and left-wing local parties. (1983b: 19)

What is perhaps most significant here is that the creation of such *new* alliances is *necessary* precisely because of the decline in these areas of the more traditional forms of labour organization. Hence, at the most general level, Urry (1981b) has argued that one of the general consequences of the reorganization of economic activity characteristic of Britain during much of the post-war period – and, paradoxically, of the centralization of control functions associated with the growth in the size and scope of the major firms, in particular – has been the increasing diversity of *local* class structures. Certainly, it has been central to our own analysis that such economic processes have had especially severe impacts upon the inner-urban areas, with the collapse of manufacturing in such localities and the associated growth in unemployment, drift of population, etc. In addition, of course, the undermining of the social fabric of these places has been assisted by the direct effects of certain state policies, such as the large-scale clearance and redevelopment schemes of the 1950s and 1960s.

What concerns us here is the relationship between these trends and the potential for regeneration through the kind of politically based strategy which we described earlier. Most significantly, one of the consequences of this pattern of urban decline has been the erosion of what, in other circumstances, may provide the foundation of such a strategy, the trades union movement. Hence, it is manufacturing industry which has been the traditional bastion of union organization in the cities; whilst in the services sector, union growth has been patchy, with a heavy concentration of strength in the public sector (Massey and Miles, 1984).

What this implies, then, is that if the emergent new alliances are to grow stronger, then alternative focuses of organization to the historically rooted trades unions ones (overwhelmingly, of course, wages and working conditions) need to be developed. We wish to suggest that the local state may have an especially important role to play in this context.

The local state and oppositional planning

Initially, this sort of claim with respect to the local state may appear little short of fantastic, in view of the functions which it has traditionally performed. For example, in the key area of economic development, local authorities have conventionally done little more than *respond* to events and initiatives orginating in the market itself; hoping to gain for their localities a larger share of the development which was taking place quite irrespective of their activities. Whilst even well-intentioned, socialist authorities have often produced outcomes which have not worked to the best advantage of those least privileged residents whom they have been trying to benefit; and high-rise flats provide an obvious example here.

However, as Miliband (1973) recognizes, there is an essential duality in the functioning of the local state.

> In one of its aspects, sub-central government constitutes an extension of central government and administration, the latter's antennae or tentacles . . . . [O]n the other hand, sub-central government is rather more than an administrative device. In addition to being agents of the state these units of government have also traditionally performed another function. They have not only been the channels of communication and administration from the centre to the periphery, but also the voice of the periphery, or of particular interests at the periphery; they have been a means of over-coming local particularities, but also platforms for their expression, instruments of central control and obstacles to it. For all the centraliza-tion of power which is a major feature of government . . . sub-central organs of government . . . have remained power structures in their own right, and therefore able to affect very markedly the lives of the popula-tions they have governed. (1973: 49)

In short, then, what may be termed the 'relative autonomy' of local government from central state control offers the *possibility* at least of opposing the dominant direction of state strategy at the local level. As Dearlove (1979) argues, moreover, this possibility is at least partly dependent on the capacity of *dominated* social groupings to gain control at this local level.

In fact, in the light of the arguments made by Urry (1981b), it may well be that the significance of local-level strategy is actually increasing. However, it must be borne in mind that the 'relative autonomy' to which we have referred is *contingent*. As we have seen in earlier chapters, one of the persistent trends in the evolving form of the British state has been the progressive extension and intensification of control over its local elements: the 1970s reorganization of local government; the introduction of 'scientific management' techniques; and the severe constraints upon local authorities' expenditure have all contributed significantly here. Nevertheless, again as we have seen, there are real limits to this erosion of what are regarded as the traditional prerogatives of the local state. And there cannot be an indefinite extension of cuts in local authorities' expenditure, given the *electoral* significance of the services which are provided locally, especially in the sphere of consumption (Cawson, 1982; Harloe and Paris, 1984).

These points are well illustrated by recent events. Hence, for example, even though Mrs Thatcher's administration has sought radically to extend central-state control, every step has been highly controversial. Perhaps most dramatically, the government's proposals to abolish the Greater London Council and the Metropolitan County Councils have been vigorously and widely opposed. Indeed, the attempt to cancel the 1985 elections for the threatened local authorities was actually defeated by a vote in the *House of Lords*. Irrespective of the eventual outcome, this issue has served to raise questions of local democracy and accountability in such public and prominent ways that, in the longer term, it is likely to redound *against* the process of ever greater state centralization.

Equally important, however, has been the agreement between Labour local authorities to oppose controls on council expenditure by refusing both to enter the procedure of negotiation created by the 1984 Rates Act and to set a rate for 1985–86. At the same time, expenditure plans are to be prepared as normal, and widely publicized in the localities. Again, irrespective of the eventual outcome, the question of the legitimate boundaries of local state autonomy will be even further politicized.

Moreover, it is clear that the pursuit of an oppositional strategy by the local state is more than an abstract possibility. Currently, many of Britain's major conurbations – including, for example, London, Manchester, the West Midlands, Sheffield and Leeds – have local councils, controlled by left Labour Party groups, which, to a greater or lesser degree, are in the process of implementing strategies to combat the economic decline of their localities on what may be described as a socialist basis. Perhaps the most developed (and certainly the best documented) of these employment strategies is that of the Greater London Council (GLC). Accordingly, we shall use the GLC as an example of what is possible, bearing in mind, of course, the peculiarities of the capital's situation.[1]

The GLC employment initiatives
Robin Murray (1983), the Chief Economic Adviser to the GLC, has summarized the general aim of London's strategy as follows:

> The main issue in the UK (and in London) at the moment is restructuring. Capital through monetarism is carrying through their version of restructuring at the expense of labour, with enormous waste, and with fearful consequences so far as the state of the world economy is concerned. The task of socialists is to resist this version, and instead to work through alternative versions which we have called restructuring for labour. This involves workers, and socialist controlled authorities, developing projects which can hold their own in the long run, but which produce outputs which are directly related to working people's needs, in

---

[1] We shall not attempt to analyse any of the initiatives undertaken by the GLC in other policy areas, such as housing, race relations, the police, etc.

ways which build on the skills of labour rather than deskilling them. (1983: 101–2)

What is striking here is the similarity between Murray's 'official GLC' position and the one which we have presented in earlier chapters of this book. How, then, do policy initiatives develop from it?

Firstly, in the face of the severe effects of capitalist restructuring on London's economy, there have been attempts to defend labour: to maintain employment levels and, thereby, to preserve what remains of trades union organizational strength. At one level, this has involved direct participation in the struggles of particular groups of workers against management proposals to close plants and declare redundancies. In particular, the financial resources of the GLC have been used to mount rescue operations on firms or individual plants, where these could be justified in terms of future employment and greater worker control over development strategy.

Secondly, there has been a move to establish new initiatives which demonstrate the viability of alternative forms of economic organization to those currently pursued by management and supported by the central state. Three working principles have been identified here:

1 The principle of bringing wasted assets – human potential, land, finance, technological expertise and resources – into production for socially useful ends.
2 The principle of extending social control of investment through social and cooperative ownership and increased trade union powers.
3 The principle of development of new techniques which increase productivity while keeping human judgement and skills in control. (*Capital and Class* Editorial Collective, 1982: 125)

Of particular significance here has been the adoption of what has been termed 'popular planning', based upon the model of the Lucas Aerospace workers' plan for *socially useful* production (Wainwright and Elliott, 1982). Thus, the GLC has involved itself with trades unions and community-based organizations in identifying the needs which it would be 'socially useful' to fulfil; defining the otherwise wasted resources which could be used; and choosing the appropriate technologies.

At the centre of the industrial strategy is the Greater London Enterprise Board (GLEB), which, in cooperation with the councillors and officers of the GLC itself, plans and implements the investment programme. Of central significance to the latter, of course, is the finance available. Two principal sources have been used: firstly, under Section 137 of the 1972 Local Government Act, it has been permissable to raise up to a 2p rate, which in London would yield £40,000,000; the future of this source, however, remains uncertain. Secondly, increasing use has been made of the investment possibilities of local authority pension funds, which in fact have greater potential resources, but are restricted to some degree by the legal constraints on their use (Murray, 1983; Minns, 1983). What is clear, however, is that, at least in London, major finance has been available to undertake investment according to criteria which are radically different from those of the private market (for example, merchant banks) and, indeed, of other parts of the public sector too (for example, the Development Agencies in Scotland and Wales).

Hence, in line with the principles set out earlier, guidelines have been established for GLEB's investments which provide for higher financial support according to whether the enterprise is based upon some form of social ownership and control, on how many employees are blacks or women, how many apprenticeships are created, how high the wages are, and how long the jobs are maintained. In addition, whilst GLEB legally has to charge commercial rates of interest for its loans, where it calculates that the social benefits will justify it, it will provide a grant to wipe out or reduce these interest charges. In these ways, therefore, the principles of *social* accounting have at least partially shaped patterns of economic development in London; thereby, attempting to break with those criteria of economic organization which lie at the root of its decline.

Now, we need to be clear as to precisely what is being claimed for strategies such as the GLC's. Firstly, as we have already noted in passing, there are certain features of the capital's situation which have been especially favourable to the implementation of this kind of programme. Most obviously, the scale of financial resources available to the GLC has been far in excess of that available to most other local authorities. As Minns (1983) points out, the product of a 2p rate in London is some £40,000,000; in the West Midlands it is only £9,000,000; whilst in Mid Glamorgan it is only hundreds of thousands. Nevertheless, even sums such as these latter are not wholly negligible; and the full potential of the much larger pension funds remains to be fully exploited. However, as we have seen, of course, the vulnerability of these sources of finance to politically directed opposition from the central state remains to be completely exposed.

In addition, the political circumstances in London are such as to enable the creation not simply of a Labour controlled administration, but also one which is internally committed to the local strategy which we have sketched; hence, for example, Ward (1983) has described the struggles to gain control over the London Labour Party by those committed to current strategies, which obviously had to precede the latter's implementation. However, it seems likely that the possibilities of creating such political conditions are greater at the *local* than the national level, given the much looser control over the selection of candidates for local elections by the more conservative elements within the Labour Party, such as the trades unions. Nevertheless, whilst a large number of conurbations are currently left Labour controlled, there are other major urban areas where such a political structure is simply non-existent. Moreover, it remains to be seen the extent to which the present dominance of this type of Labour group in the cities is the product of genuinely forged support networks, or simply coincidence (*pace* Massey, 1983b). On the other hand, it should be remembered that Sheffield's programme of oppositional planning is based upon a very different kind of Labour politics. As Alcock and Lee (1981–82) put it, '[t]he Labour Party is truly integrated – incorporated – into the running of the local state. The "Socialist Republic" slogan is as much a proud proclamation of this record of the Sheffield labour movement in running the affairs of local government, as it is of anything else.' (1981–82: 80)[2]

An oppositional programme for the inner cities

Quite apart from these peculiarities of the situation in the capital, there are other, more fundamental isues to be raised with regard to the GLC-type programme. Thus, Urry (1983) has recently argued that there are dangers inherent in what he sees as the growing significance of locally based political organization and struggle. In particular, the emphasis on the locality may become translated into an opposition against *other localities*. Indeed, there are already examples of trades union organizations in the South East and the West Midlands complaining over the preferential treatment of regions in the North of England, and in Scotland and Wales, in terms of state subsidies. Equally, of course, such tendencies are even more absurdly expressed in the current promotional activities of local authorities (see Massey and Meegan, 1982).

As our earlier discussion showed, this sort of danger has been avoided in the case of the GLC as a result of the very clear identification of *capitalist restructuring* as the root cause of London's problems, rather than the economic growth of some other place. Indeed, the latter is as much a product of this restructuring as the capital's decline. Nevertheless, there remains the problem of how to *combine* the different, locally conceived strategies into a coherent whole. This operates at a number of different levels. *Within* a given local area, there are the difficulties of deciding which projects are to be undertaken, as presumably not all proposals can be funded from

[2]Sheffield has been Labour controlled since 1926, with only two short breaks.

finite resources; even for those which are pursued, there remains the issue of where they are to be located.

More generally, there is the question of the potential conflicts between the strategies of different areas; between that of the GLC and, say, the West Midlands. This may be posed especially acutely in the case of defensive action to preserve existing plants and jobs; successful opposition in London *may* imply the opposite in Birmingham. But even in the more innovative aspects of the employment strategy, the potential for clashes exists.

This discussion, in turn, raises the much more general issue of the relationships between locally devised initiatives and national-level, macro-economic development. As we showed earlier, the growth of local government initiatives in the economic field was positively encouraged by successive central administrations during the 1970s and, of course, continue to be so, at least nominally. However, the whole point about such initiatives was that they were intended to *complement* and *contribute* to the fulfilment of central state objectives.

Ironically, it was the experience of such earlier initiatives that provided part of the foundation of the much more radical strategies which we have been discussing here (Young and Mason, 1983). More importantly, what has shaped the development of these 'oppositional strategies' is the debate within the Labour Party itself, following the retreat from the interventionist industrial strategy of 1973, which we described in Chapter 5. Hence, the widespread reaction within the Party to the disasters of the administrations of 1974 to 1979 has been the reaffirmation of the necessity of that interventionist strategy, now frequently referred to as the Alternative Economic Strategy (AES).

We cannot undertake an extended discussion of the AES (in its many varieties) here (the best analysis is that of the London CSE Group, 1980). It must suffice to say that it embodies an extension and development of the 1973 strategy, which we have described in some detail. What we do wish to emphasize, however, is that the success or otherwise of programmes such as the GLC's is obviously crucially dependent upon the implementation of a complementary strategy at the level of the central state. Given the latter, then what is being attempted in London (and elsewhere) becomes an essential input into a broader, more comprehensive framework.

Given these arguments, therefore, it becomes possible to specify a set of minimum criteria which an effective strategy for the inner cities should fulfil.[3]

1 Local strategies for particular areas must be coordinated with wider, national ones. Different macro-economic strategies have

[3]There is no claim to originality in what follows; see, for example, Massey, 1982.

profoundly different implications for diverse types of locality. This should be built into the development of policy at *both* levels.

2 Any strategy must be based upon public-sector investment. Only in this way will it be possible to break away from the facilitation of private-sector initiative and development, which we have seen to be the standard post-war pattern.

3 Such public-sector investment would provide the opportunities for integrating inner-city strategy with wider policy aims. Hence, it would provide possibilities of encouraging new forms of ownership and control (for example, cooperatives), as well as improved working conditions, equitable recruitment and training practices, etc. In addition, where finance capital *is* made available to private industry, real returns should be demanded and implemented through compulsory planning agreements.

4 In particular, the right of capital to locate investment where it chooses must be challenged. Thus, rather than the current system of overlapping and wasteful incentives, there should be some form of direct, socially responsive control, possibly again operating through planning agreements.

5 Bearing in mind criterion 1, policies should be rooted in a strong local base, with numerous initiatives at the locality level being undertaken by a wide variety of community-based groups – trades councils, tenants groups, workers in particular plants, consumer organizations, etc. Clearly, it is most important to avoid an overly statist and centralized strategy by retaining a thoroughly democratic structure.

6 The latter implies – even more ambitiously – that strategy should be shaped around *social needs*, rather than simple profitability. It is in defining such needs – which can only be done by groups of potential *consumers* of the planned goods and services – and planning their fulfilment – which requires technical expertise – that the barriers between workers and consumers will be broken down.

7 There must clearly be close coordination of the employment elements of a strategy with broader social ones. Certainly, for example, urban land markets should be directly controlled through land nationalization. Moreover, socially responsible housing programmes must be promoted, at least in part, by rebuilding the local authorities' capacity to provide houses through the direct labour organizations. In addition, the allocation and management of public housing (as with all state services) must be democratized and more closely attuned to social needs.

8 All this clearly necessitates financial commitments to the cities on a scale hitherto unapproached. And this, in turn, will require the use of funds presently controlled by the financial institutions.

Measured against these sorts of criteria (and they are no more than suggestive), it should be clear that the kinds of initiative currently being undertaken by the GLC and the other socialist local authorities cannot provide the means of any thoroughgoing *resolution* of the problems of the cities. Of themselves and as oppositional strategies only, they are unlikely to make a substantial contribution to the alleviation of the immediate problems confronting inner-city residents; and any contributions that they make are likely to be swamped by the contrary tendencies originating from the central state and from capital itself.

Rather, we wish to argue that their major significance lies in their educative and ideological functions. Crucially, then, they have a major role to play in demonstrating that there *are* alternatives to the dominant, New Right strategies. A similar conclusion is drawn by the *Capital and Class* Editorial Collective (1982) on the basis of their evaluation of the early operation of the GLC strategy.

> Socialists working within the GLC have to work at two levels at once. They have to do their best to make some real material gains, to save or create as many secure and fulfilling jobs as possible. For this they need a determined optimism, otherwise they will not test all the options. On the other hand, they have to prepare for the defeat of many of their policies in the short term. They have to be able to use that defeat politically to learn the lessons for new advances rather than allow it to demoralize the labour movement in London. This requires a degree of pessimism whose basis is constantly explained in order that the obstacles which their experience reveals can be identified and in the future overcome. (1982: 133)

Given the strict limitations on what is possible, it may well be that the most valuable product of local strategies of this type is as a test-bed for future actions. This is true, firstly, in a technical sense; particular policies can be tried out and evaluated. Secondly, however, the experience of such strategies should have the effect of transforming the perspective of those workers, residents, community groups and so forth who are affected by them; of demonstrating the possibility of alternatives to the present, crisis-ridden patterns of economic organization and state provision, whose shortcomings are nowhere more clearly exposed than in the cities.

A pertinent illustration of the possibilities in this respect is provided by the decentralization of housing services undertaken in Walsall, where a left Labour council was elected in 1980. Thirty-three neighbourhood offices were set up, thereby making the housing department and repairs teams more accessible and localized than ever before. Indeed, the scheme proved so popular that it has survived the election of an anti-Labour coalition in Spring 1982. However, what is most important here is not simply increasing accessibility, but rather demystifying and democratizing local services. Seabrook (1984) summarizes the effects of the Walsall initiative.

> People have been given fresh confidence that they can work for their own neighbourhood to get things done – help the unemployed, get a community centre, petition over bus services or road safety. Many of the myths of the council and its power have been dispelled. The people who staff the offices do not wrap themselves in a cloak of professional jargon and mystery. The limits of the council's power are visible; the cuts and limits imposed by central government become plainer.
>
> The real innovation in Walsall has been the imagination and inventiveness that have been brought to politics; the fact that political discussion involves our whole lives, our relationships, our feelings for one another, is a living expression of our deepest hopes and fears; is something far more than the two-dimensional preoccupation with mere administrative convenience; and is something far richer and more complex than the cardboard cut-out of a working-class that figures in the rhetoric of the far left. (1984: 128)

In short, then, these kinds of attempts to resolve problems which manifest at the local level may contribute to the liklihood of the adoption of equivalent strategies (in the form, say, of the AES) at a broader scale. The latter would clearly begin the task of pushing at the boundaries imposed upon societal development by capitalist class relations.

Our claims, therefore, are necessarily very limited. Contrary to the orthodoxies of the 'Whig' perspective (and, indeed, some brands of Marxism), there is nothing *inevitable* about the development of solutions to the problems confronting the cities and their residents. However, we have shown in earlier chapters that urban development and policies in post-war Britain, as well as being shaped by a particular form of politics, has contributed in a small way to the latter's creation. Similarly, an urban policy founded upon an alternative basis may make its contribution to the growth of an alternative politics. And, as we have tried to show, it is the growth of such an alternative politics which is the essential precondition of resolving the problems of Britain's cities.

Postscript

From the vantage point of July 1985, the growth of an alternative politics focused upon the issues with which this book has been concerned remains more of a possibility than a reality. The themes relating to the local state which we stressed in the final chapter – the innovatory development policies pursued by the Greater London Council (GLC) and the metropolitan county councils, the concerted opposition to central government's rate capping and the promotion of decentralized services – would now appear less significant than more general political changes.

The vociferous opposition to the abolition of the GLC and the metropolitan counties undoubtedly raised public consciousness of the issues involved; but the Royal Assent to their abolition (in April 1986) was nevertheless granted in July 1985. By then, the organized resistance to rate capping had collapsed as legal rates were set: Labour councillors (pressed by the Labour Party centrally) opted to 'fight, fight and fight again' *within* the system, rather than risk exclusion from office (and worse). The decentralizing process has raised many difficult problems for Labour-controlled local authorities and public-sector trade unions and has been hindered by the general context of severe restrictions on public employment and service development.

At the same time, however, there has been precious little indication that the policies of the New Right are doing anything but intensify the economic and social crisis afflicting the cities. Indeed, the Thatcher government's increasingly strident attempts to effect a stubbornly unattainable 'turn around' in Britain's economic fortunes by means of further cuts in welfare services and payments and the general depression of wages seem destined most severely to penalize precisely those groups which are concentrated in the poor inner-city areas – 'unqualified' school-leavers, 'unskilled' workers, the under- and unemployed, the ethnic minorities and so on.

However, the past year has also demonstrated that it is by no means *only* such groups in such areas which are experiencing the brunt of Thatcherism and the wider economic crisis. The 1984–5 miners' strike originated in the most traditional of Britain's industrial regions, for the most part far removed from the inner areas of the conurbations. Nevertheless – as in the cities – the essential issue of the strike was whether or not there could be a secure economic base which could support jobs and decent living conditions. Moreover, the resolution of this issue was shown to be *contingent*; economic and social changes in the coalfields are not the result of some 'logic' of economic development, but rather the outcome of irreducibly political conflicts. And this, of course, is precisely what we have argued for the apparently very different case of the inner cities.

What this implies, in turn, is that the form which economic and social change will take in the future both in the coalfields and the inner cities will depend upon the forces which can be mobilized against the strategy and policies currently being implemented by the New Right and the interests which are thus represented. At a minimum, the campaigns which have been organized in support of both the major urban local authorities and the miners are suggestive of what is possible, as well as the oppositional power of the state. If, as we have argued, there is nothing inevitable about the recovery of the inner cities (or the mining communities), there is nothing inevitable about their demise either.

Bibliography

Abercrombie, P. 1945: *The Greater London Plan 1944*. London: HMSO.

Abrams, M. and Rose, R. 1960: *Must Labour Lose?* Harmondsworth: Penguin.

Addison, P. 1975: *The Road to 1945: British politics and the Second World War*. London: Cape.

Alcock, P. and Lee, P. 1981–82: The Socialist Republic of South Yorkshire. *Critical Social Policy* 1, 72–93.

Aldridge, M. 1979: *The British New Towns: a programme without a policy*. London: RKP.

Ambrose, P. and Colenutt, B. 1975: *The Property Machine*. Harmondsworth: Penguin.

Anderson, J. 1983: Geography as Ideology and the Politics of Crisis – the Enterprise Zone experiment. In Anderson, J., Duncan, S. and Hudson, R. (eds.), *Redundant Spaces? Industrial Decline and Social Change in Cities and Regions* (London: Academic Press), 313–50.

Backwell, J. and Dickens, P. 1979: Town planning, mass loyalty and the restructuring of capital: the origins of the 1947 planning legislation revisited. *Urban and Regional Studies Working Paper No. 11*. Brighton: University of Sussex.

Ball, M. 1983: *Housing Policy and Economic Power: the political economy of owner occupation*. London: Methuen.

Barlow Report 1940: *Report of the Royal Commission on the Distribution of the Industrial Population*. Cmnd. 6153. London: HMSO.

Barnett, A. 1982: *Iron Britannia: why parliament waged its Falklands war*. London: Alison & Busby.

Beckerman, W. 1972: *The Labour Government's Economic Record 1964–70*. London: Duckworth.

Behrens, R. 1981: *The Conservative Party from Heath to Thatcher*. London: Saxon House.

Best, R. 1981: *Land Use and Living Space*. London: Methuen.

Beveridge Report 1942: *A Report on Social Insurance and Allied Services*. Cmnd. 6404. London: HMSO.

Blackaby, F. (ed.) 1979: *Deindustrialisation*. London: Heinemann.

Blackburn, R. 1971: The Heath government – a new course for British capitalism. *New Left Review* 70, 3–26.

Blank, S. 1973: *Government and Industry in Britain*. London: Saxon House.

Block, F. 1980: Beyond relative autonomy: state managers as historical subjects. In Miliband, R. and Saville, J. (eds.), *The Socialist Register 1980* (London: Merlin Press), 227–42.

Boddy, M. 1983: Changing public-private sector relationships in the industrial development process. In Young and Mason 1983, 34–52.

Booth, A. 1982: The Second World War and the origins of modern regional policy. *Economy and Society* 11, 1–21.

Brand, J. 1974: *Local Government Reform in England: 1888–1974*. London: Croom Helm.

Briggs, A. 1968: *Victorian Cities*. Harmondsworth: Penguin.

Brittan, S. 1971: *Steering the Economy*. Revised edition. Harmondsworth: Penguin.

Buchanan, C. 1963: *Traffic in Towns*. London: HMSO.

Buck, T. 1979: Regional class differences. *International Journal of Urban and Regional Research* 3, 516–26.

Budd, A. 1978: *The Politics of Economic Planning*. London: Fontana.

Butler, D. and King, A. 1965: *The British General Election of 1964*. London: Macmillan.

Butterfield, H. 1931: *The Whig interpretation of history*. London: Bell.

Cambridge Economic Policy Group 1977: *Cambridge Economic Policy Review No. 3*. Aldershot: Gower.

—— 1982: *Cambridge Economic Policy Review No. 8*. Aldershot: Gower.

Cameron, G. 1973: Intraurban location and the new plant. *Papers of the Regional Science Association* 31, 125–43.

Capital and Class Editorial Collective 1982: A socialist GLC in a capitalist Britain? *Capital and Class* 18, 117–34.

Castells, M. 1977: *The Urban Question: a marxist approach*. London: Edward Arnold.

Castle, B. 1980: *The Castle Diaries 1974–1976* London: Weidenfeld & Nicolson.

Castles, S. with Booth, H. and Wallace, T. 1984: *Here For Good: Western Europe's new ethnic minorities*. London: Pluto.

Caves, R. and Krause, L. (eds.) 1980: *Britain's Economic Performace*. Washington, DC: Brookings Institution.

Cawson, A. 1982: *Corporatism and Welfare: social policy and state intervention in Britain*. London: Heinemann.

Chadwick, G. 1971: *A Systems View of Planning*. Oxford: Pergamon.

Cherry, G. 1974: *The Evolution of British Town Planning*. Leighton Buzzard: Leonard Hill.

Coates, D. 1980: *Labour in Power? A study of the Labour Government 1974–1979*. London: Longman.

Cockburn, C. 1977: *The Local State: management of cities and people*. London: Pluto.

Commission for Racial Equality 1982: *Youns People and the Job Market: a survey*. London: Commission for Racial Equality.

Community Development Project 1977a: *The Costs of Industrial Change*. London: CDP Inter-Project Editorial Team.

—— 1977b: *Gilding the Ghetto: the state and the poverty experiments*. London: CDP Inter-Project Editorial Team.

Cooke, P., Morgan, K. and Jackson, D. 1983: New technology and regional development in austerity Britain: the case of the semi-conductor industry. Paper presented to the Fourth Urban Change and Conflict Conference, University of Essex.

Coutts, K., Tarling, R., Ward, T. and Wilkinson, F. 1981: The economic consequences of Mrs Thatcher. *Cambridge Journal of Economics* **5**, 81–93.

Cox, A. 1984: *Adversary Politics and Land: the conflict over land and property policy in post-war Britain*. Cambridge: CUP.

Crosland, C. 1956: *The Future of Socialism*. London: Cape.

Crossman, R. 1975: *The Diaries of a Cabinet Minister. Volume One: Minister of Housing 1964–1966*. London: Hamilton/Cape.

Crouch, C. 1977: *Class Conflict and the Industrial Relations Crisis*. London: Heinemann.

Cullingworth, J. 1975: *Environmental Planning 1939–1969. Volume One: Reconstruction and Land-Use Planning 1939–1947*. London: HMSO.

—— 1979: *Town and Country Planning in Britain*. Seventh edition. London: George Allen & Unwin.

—— 1980: *Environmental Planning 1939–1969. Volume Four: Land Values, Compensation and Betterment*. London: HMSO.

Davies, H. 1980: The relevance of development control. *Town Planning Review* **51**, 7–24.

Deakin, N. and Ungerson, C. 1977: *Leaving London: planned mobility and the inner city*. London: Heinemann.

Dearlove, J. 1979: *The Reorganisation of British Local Government: old orthodoxies and a political perspective*. Cambridge: CUP.

Dennis, N. 1968: The popularity of the neighbourhood community idea. In Pahl, R. (ed.), *Readings in Urban Sociology* (Oxford: Pergamon), 74–94.

—— 1972: *Public Participation and Planners' Blight*. London: Faber & Faber.

Dennis, R. 1978: The decline of manufacturing employment in Greater London. *Urban Studies* **15**, 63–73.

Department of the Environment 1977: *Policy for the Inner Cities*. Cmnd. 6845. London: HMSO.

—— 1977a: *Inner London: Policies for Dispersal and Balance*. London: HMSO.

—— 1977b: *Change and Decay*. London: HMSO.

—— 1977c: *Unequal City*. London: HMSO.

—— 1977d: *Local Government and the Industrial Strategy*. Circular 71/77. London: Department of the Environment.

Department of Industry 1974: *The Regeneration of British Industry*. Cmnd. 5710. London: HMSO.

Donnison, D. with Soto, P. 1980: *The Good City: a study of urban development and policy in Britain*. London: Heinemann.

Duncan, S. 1982: Inner City Critique. *Area* **14**, 193–197.

Dunford, M. 1977: Regional Policy and the Restructuring of Capital. *Urban and Regional Studies Working Paper No. 4*. Brighton: University of Sussex.

Dunford, M., Geddes, M. and Perrons, D. 1981: Regional policy and the crisis in the UK: a long-run perspective. *International Journal of Urban and Regional Research* **5**, 377–410.

Dunford, M. and Perrons, D. 1983: *The Arena of Capital*. London: Macmillan.

Dunleavy, P. 1979: The urban basis of political alignment: social class, domestic property ownership, and state intervention in consumption processes. *British Journal of Political Science* **9**, 409–43.

—— 1980: *Urban Political Analysis*. London: Macmillan.

—— 1981: *The Politics of Mass Housing in Britain 1945–1975: a study of corporate power and professional influence in the Welfare State*. Oxford: Clarendon Press.

Edwards, J. and Batley, R. 1978: *The Politics of Positive Discrimination: an evaluation of the Urban Programme 1967–1977*. London: Tavistock.

Engels, F. 1973: *The Condition of the Working Class in England: from personal observation and authentic sources*. First published in German in 1845. London: Lawrence & Wishart.

English, J., Madigan, R. and Norman, P. 1976: *Slum Clearance: the social and administrative context in England and Wales*. London: Croom Helm.

Federation of British Industries 1963: *The Regional Problem*. London: FBI.

Field, F. 1969: *Poverty and the Labour Government*. London: Child Poverty Action Group.

Fishman, R. 1977: *Urban Utopias in the Twentieth Century: Ebenezer Howard, Frank Lloyd Wright and Le Corbusier*. New York: Basic Books.

Foot, M. 1975: *Aneurin Bevan*. Two Volumes. St Albans: Paladin.

Forester, T. 1978: How Labour's industrial strategy got the chop. *New Society* 6 July, 7–10.

Fothergill, S. and Gudgin, G. 1982: *Unequal Growth: urban and regional employment change in the UK*. London: Heinemann.

Francis, H. and Smith, D. 1980: *The Fed: a history of the South Wales miners in the twentieth century*. London: Lawrence & Wishart.

Fraser, D. 1979: *Power and Authority in the Victorian City*. Oxford: Basil Blackwell.

Friedman, A. 1977: *Industry and Labour: class struggle at work and monopoly capitalism*. London: Macmillan.

Friend, A. and Metcalfe, A. 1981: *Slump City: the politics of mass unemployment*. London: Pluto.

Gamble, A. 1981: *Britain in Decline: economic policy, political strategy and the British state*. London: Macmillan.

Glyn, A. and Harrison, J. 1980: *The British Economic Disaster*. London: Pluto.

Glyn, A. and Sutcliffe, B. 1972: *British Capitalism, Workers and the Profits Squeeze*. Harmondsworth: Penguin.

Gower Davies, J. 1972: *The Evangelistic Bureaucrat: a study of a planning exercise in Newcastle-upon-Tyne*. London: Tavistock.

Grant, W. 1983: Representing Capital. In King, R.(ed.), *Capital and Politics* (London: RKP), 69–84.

Hall, P. (ed.) 1981: *The Inner City in Context: the final report of the Social Science Research Council Inner Cities Working Party*. London: Heinemann.

Hall, P., Thomas, R., Gracey, H. and Drewett, R. 1973: *The Containment of Urban England. Volume Two: The Planning System: objectives, operations, impacts*. London: George Allen & Unwin.

Hall, S. 1983: The great moving right show. In Hall and Jacques 1983, 19–39.

Hall, S. and Jacques, M. (eds.) 1983: *The Politics of Thatcherism*. London: Lawrence & Wishart.

Hambleton, R. 1980: Inner cities: engaging the private sector. *School for Advanced Urban Studies Working Paper No. 10*. Bristol: University of Bristol.

Hamnett, C. 1983: The Conditions in England's Inner Cities on the Eve of the 1981 Riots. *Area* **15**, 7–13.

Harloe, M. and Paris, C. 1984: The Decollectivization of Consumption: housing and local government finance in England and Wales 1979–81. In Szelenyi, I. (ed.), *Cities in Recession: critical responses to the urban policies of the New Right*. (London: Sage), 70–99.

Harris, N. 1972: *Competition and the Corporate Society: British Conservatives, the State and Industry 1945–1964*. London: Methuen.

Higgins, J., Deakin, N., Edwards, J. and Wicks, M. 1983: *Government and Urban Poverty: inside the policy-making process*. Oxford: Basil Blackwell.

Hobsbawm, E. 1968: *Industry and Empire: an economic history of Britain since 1750*. London: Weidenfeld & Nicolson.

Howell, D. 1976: *British Social Democracy: a study in development and decay*. London: Croom Helm.

Hudson, R. 1983: Capital accumulation and regional problems: a study of North East England, 1945–80. In Hamilton, F. and Linge, G. (eds.), *Spatial Analysis, Industry and the Industrial Environment* (Chichester: John Wiley), 75–101.

Husbands, C. 1983: *Racial Exclusionism and the City: the urban support of the National Front*. London: George Allen & Unwin.

Jackman, R. 1982: Does central government need to control the total of local government spending? *Local Government Studies* **8**, 75–90.

Jenkins, R. 1984: Divisions over the international division of labour. *Capital and Class* **22**, 28–57.

Jessop, B. 1979: Corporatism, parliamentarism and social democracy. In Schmitter, P. and Lehmbruch, G. (eds.), *Trends Toward Corporatist Intermediation* (London: Sage).

—— 1980: The transformation of the state in post-war Britain. In Scase, R. (ed.), *The State in Western Europe* (London: Croom Helm), 23–93.

—— 1982: *The Capitalist State: marxist theories and methods*. Oxford: Martin Robertson.

Jones, C. 1979: Population Decline in Cities. In Jones, C. (ed.), *Urban Deprivation and the Inner City* (London: Croom Helm), 191–214.

Joshua, H. and Wallace, T. with Booth, H. 1983: *To Ride the Storm: the 1980 Bristol 'riot' and the state*. London: Heinemann.

Karn, V. 1981: Public sector demolition can seriously damage your wealth. *Roof* January–February 1981, 13–23.

Keeble, D. 1976: *Industrial Location and Planning in the UK*. London: Methuen.

—— 1977: Spatial policy in Britain: regional or urban? *Area* **9**, 3–8.

Kellett, J. 1969: *The Impact of Railways on Victorian Cities*. London: RKP.

Kennett, S. and Spence, N. 1979: British Population Trends in the 1970s. *Town and Country Planning* **48**, 7.

Kettle, M. and Hodges, L. 1982: *Uprising! the police, the people and the riots in Britain's cities*. London: Pan.

Kilbrandon Report 1973: *Report of the Royal Commission on the Constitution*. Cmnd. 5460. London: HMSO.

Labour Party 1961: *Signposts for the Sixties*. London: Labour Party.

Laclau, E. 1979: *Politics and Ideology in Marxist Theory*. London: New Left Books.

Lansley, S. 1982: The Road to Toxteth. *New Society* 22 April, 133.

Lawless, P. 1979: *Urban Deprivation and Government Initiative*. London: Faber & Faber.

—— 1981a: *Britain's Inner Cities: problems and policies*. London: Harper & Row.

—— 1981b: The role of some central government agencies in urban economic regeneration. *Regional Studies* 15, 1–14.

Layfield Report 1973: *The Report of the Panel of Inquiry on the Greater London Development Plan*. London: Department of the Environment.

Lebas, E. 1982: Urban and regional sociology in advanced industrial societies: a decade of marxist and critical perspectives. *Current Sociology* 30, 1–271.

Lipietz, A. 1977: *Le Capital et Son Espace*. Paris: Maspero.

London CSE Group 1980: *The Alternative Economic Strategy*. London: CSE Books.

Loney, M. 1983: *Community Against Government: the British Community Development Project 1968–78*. London: Heinemann.

Loney, M. and Allen, M. (eds.) 1979: *The Crisis of the Inner City*. London: Macmillan.

Lukes, S. 1977: *Power: a radical view*. London: Macmillan.

McCallum, J. 1979: The development of regional policy. In Maclennan, D. and Parr, J. (eds.), *Regional Policy: past experience and new directions* (Oxford: Martin Robertson), 3–41.

McCrone, G. 1969: *Regional Policy in Britain*. London: George Allen & Unwin.

McDougall, G. 1979: The state, capital and land: the history of town planning revisited. *International Journal of Urban and Regional Research* 3, 361–80.

McEnery, J. 1981: Manufacturing two nations. *Institute of Economic Affairs Research Monograph No. 36*. London: IEA.

McKay, D. and Cox, A. 1979: *The Politics of Urban Change*. London: Croom Helm.

McLoughlin, J. 1969: *Urban and Regional Planning: a systems approach*. London: Faber & Faber.

Maddison, A. 1979: The long run dynamics of productivity growth. In Beckerman, W. (ed.), *Slow Growth in Britain* (Oxford: OUP).

Mandel, E. 1975: *Late Capitalism*. London: Verso.

—— 1978: *The Second Slump: a marxist analysis of recession in the seventies*. London: New Left Books.

Marriott, O. 1967: *The Property Boom*. London: Hamish Hamilton.

Massey, D. 1978: Regionalism: some current issues. *Capital and Class* 6, 106–25.

—— 1982: Going to town on the jobs crisis. *New Socialist* 4, 38–41.

—— 1983a: The shape of things to come. *Marxism Today* 27, 18–27.

—— 1983b: The contours of victory. *Marxism Today* **27**, 16–19.

Massey, D. and Catalano, A. 1978: *Capital and Land*. London: Edward Arnold.

Massey, D. and Meegan, R. 1978: Restructuring versus the cities. *Urban Studies* **15**, 273–88.

—— 1979: The geography of industrial reorganisation: the spatial effects of the restructuring of the electrical engineering sector under the Industrial Reorganisation Corporation. *Progress in Planning* **10**, 155–237.

—— 1982: *The Anatomy of Job Loss: the how, why and where of employment decline*. London: Methuen.

Massey, D. and Miles, N. 1984: Mapping out the unions. *Marxism Today* **28**, 19–23.

Merrett, S. 1979: *State Housing in Britain*. London: RKP.

Merrett, S. with Gray, F. 1982: *Owner Occupation in Britain*. London: RKP.

Middlemas, K. 1979: *Politics in Industrial Society: the experience of the British system since 1911*. London: Andre Deutsch.

Miles, R. and Phizacklea, A. (eds.) 1979: *Racism and Political Action in Britain*. London: RKP.

—— 1981: Racism and capitalist decline. In Harloe, M. (ed.), *New Perspectives in Urban Change and Conflict* (London: Heinemann), 80–100.

Miliband, R. 1973: *The State in Capitalist Society: the analysis of the Western system of power*. London: Quartet.

Miller, S. 1978: The recapitalization of capitalism: *International Journal of Urban and Regional Research* **2**, 202–12.

Minns, R. 1983: Pension Funds – an alternative view. *Capital and Class* **20**, 104–16.

Moore, B. and Rhodes, J. 1973: Evaluating the effects of British regional economic policy. *Economic Journal* **83**, 87–110.

Morgan, K. 1980: The reformulation of the regional question, regional policy and the British state. *Urban and Regional Studies Working Paper No. 18*. Brighton: University of Sussex.

—— 1982: *State Policy and Regional Development in Britain: the case of Wales*. Unpublished D.Phil. thesis, University of Sussex.

—— 1983: Restructuring steel: the crises of labour and locality in Britain. *International Journal of Urban and Regional Research* **7**, 175—201.

Mumford, L. and Osborn, F. (ed. Hughes, M.) 1971: *The Letters of Lewis Mumford and Frederic J. Osborn: a transatlantic dialogue*. Bath: Adams & Dart.

Murie, A., Niner, P. and Watson, C. 1976: *Housing Policy and the Housing System*. London: George Allen & Unwin.

Murray, R. 1983: Pension funds and local authority investments. *Capital and Class* **20**, 89–103.

NEDC 1963: *Conditions Favourable to Faster Growth*. London: HMSO.

New Society 1971: The carve up. *New Society* 18 February, 259.

O'Connor, J. 1973: *The Fiscal Crisis of the State*. New York: St Martin's Press.

Pahl, R. 1975: *Whose City? and other essays on urban society*. Second edition. Harmondsworth: Penguin.

Panitch, L. 1980: Recent theorizations of corporatism: reflections on a growth industry. *British Journal of Sociology* **31**, 159–87.

Parkinson, M. and Duffy, J. 1984: Government's response to inner-city riots: the Minister for Merseyside and the Task Force. *Parliamentary Affairs* **37**, 76–96.

Pavitt, K. (ed.) 1979: *Technical Innovation and British Economic Performance*. London: Heinemann.

Pickvance, C. 1977: Physical planning and market forces in urban development. *National Westminster Bank Quarterly Review* August, 41–50.

—— 1981: Policies as chameleons: an interpretation of regional policy and office policy in Britain. In Dear, M. and Scott, A. (eds.), *Urbanization and Urban Planning in Capitalist Society* (London: Methuen), 231–66.

—— 1985: Spatial Policy as Territorial Politics. In Rees, G. (ed.), *Political Action and Social Identity* (London: Macmillan), 117–142.

Planning Advisory Group 1965: *The Future of Development Plans*. London: HMSO.

Pollard, S. 1962: *The Development of the British Economy 1914–1950*. London: Edward Arnold.

Prais, S. 1976: *The Evolution of Giant Firms in Britain*. Cambridge: CUP.

Ravetz, A. 1980: *Remaking Cities: contradictions of the recent urban environment*. London: Croom Helm.

Redcliffe-Maud Report 1969: *Royal Commission on Local Government in England: Final Report (Short Version)*. Cmnd. 4039. London: HMSO.

Rees, G. 1984: Rural Regions in National and International Economies. In Bradley, T. and Lowe, P. (ed.), *Rurality and Locality: economy and society in rural regions* (Norwich: GeoBooks), 27–44.

Rees, G. and Lambert, J. 1981: Nationalism as legitimation? towards a political economy of regional development in South Wales. In Harloe, M. (ed.), *New Perspectives in Urban Change and Conflict* (London: Heinemann), 122–37.

Rees, G. and Rees, T. 1983: Migration, industrial restructuring and class relations: an analysis of South Wales. In Williams, G. (ed.), *Crisis of Economy and Ideology: essays on Welsh society 1840–1980*. (Bangor: BSA/SSRC Sociology of Wales Study Group), 103–19.

Regional Studies Association 1983: *Report of an Inquiry into Regional Problems in the United Kingdom*. Norwich: GeoBooks.

Reith Report 1946: *New Towns Committee: Final Report*. Cmnd. 6876. London: HMSO.

Rex, J. 1982: The 1981 urban riots in Britain. *International Journal of Urban and Regional Research* **6**, 99–114.

Rex, J. and Tomlinson, S. 1979: *Colonial Immigrants in a British City*. London: RKP.

Roger Tym and Partners 1981: *Monitoring the Enterprise Zones: Year 1 Report*. London: Roger Tym & Partners.

—— 1982: *Monitoring the Enterprise Zones Year 2 Report*. London: Roger Tym & Partners.

Royal Town Planning Institute 1976: *Planning and the Future*. London: RTPI.

Scarman, Lord 1982: *The Scarman Report: the Brixton disorders 10–12 April 1981*. Harmondsworth: Penguin.

Schaffer, F. 1972: *The New Town Story*. London: Paladin.

Scott, A. 1982: Locational patterns and dynamics of industrial activity in the modern metropolis. *Urban Studies* **19**, 111–42.

Scott Report 1943: *Report of the Committee on Land Utilization in Rural Areas*. London: HMSO.

Seabrook, J. 1984: *The Idea of Neighbourhood: what local politics should be about*. London: Pluto.

Senior, D. 1969: *Memorandum of Dissent to the Report of the Royal Commission on Local Government in England. Volume II*. Cmnd. 4040–1. London: HMSO.

Shanks, M. 1977: *Planning and Politics: the British experience 1960–1976*. London: PEP.

Sharpe, L. 1975: Innovation and change in British land-use planning. In Hayward, J. and Watson, M. (eds.), *Planning, Politics and Public Policy: the British, French and Italian experience* (Cambridge: CUP).

Shelter 1972: *Another Chance for the Cities, SNAP 69/72*. London: Shelter.

Shutt, J. 1984: Tory enterprise zones and the Labour Movement. *Capital and Class* **23**, 19–44.

Skeffington report 1969: *People and Planning: report of the committee on public participation*. London: HMSO.

Smith, D. 1977: *Racial Disadvantage in Britain: the PEP Report*. Harmondsworth: Penguin.

Spiers, M. 1975: *Techniques and Public Administration*. London: Fontana.

Stedman Jones, G. 1971: *Outcast London: a study of the relationships between classes in Victorian society*. Oxford: OUP.

Stewart, J. 1984: Storming the town halls: a rate-cap revolution. *Marxism Today* **28**, 8–13.

Stewart, M. 1983: The inner area planning system. *Policy and Politics* **11**, 203–14.

Stewart, M. and Underwood, J. 1983: New relationships in the inner city. In Young and Mason 1983, 131–54.

Sutcliffe, A. 1981: *Towards the Planned City: Germany, Britain, the United States and France, 1780–1914*. Oxford: Basil Blackwell.

Swenarton, M. 1981: *Homes Fit for Heroes*. London: Heinemann.

Tarling, R. and Wilkinson, F. 1977: The Social Contract: post-war incomes policies and their inflationary impact. *Cambridge Journal of Economics* **1**, 395–414.

Townsend, A. 1980: Unemployment geography and the new government's 'regional' aid. *Area* **12**, 9–18.

Townsend, P. 1979: *Poverty in the United Kingdom: a survey of household resources and standard of living*. Harmondsworth: Penguin.

Thrift, N. 1979: Unemployment in the inner city: urban problem or structural imperative? A review of recent British experience. In Herbert, D. and Johnston, R. (eds.), *Geography and the Urban Environment. Volume Two*. (Chichester: Wiley), 125–226.

Urry, J. 1981a: *The Anatomy of Capitalist Societies: the economy, civil society and the state*. London: Macmillan.

—— 1981b: Localities, regions and social class. *International Journal of Urban and Regional Research* 5, 455–74.

—— 1983: De-industrialisation, classes and politics. In King, R. (ed.), *Capital and Politics* (London: RKP), 28–48.

Uthwatt Report 1942: *Expert Committee on Compensation and Betterment: Final Report*. Cmnd. 6386. London: HMSO.

Wainwright, H. and Elliott, D. 1982: *The Lucas Plan: a new trade unionism in the making*? London: Alison & Busby.

Walker, A. 1984: *Social Planning: a strategy for socialist welfare*. Oxford: Basil Blackwell.

Waller, P. 1981–82: The riots in Toxteth, Liverpool: a survey. *New Community* **IX**, 344–53.

Ward, M. 1983: Labour's capital gains: the GLC experience. *Marxism Today* **27**, 24–31.

Warde, A. 1982: *Consensus and Beyond: the development of Labour Party strategy since the Second World War*. Manchester: Manchester University Press.

Warren, K. 1970: *The British Iron and Steel Industry since 1940*. London: Bell.

Wibberly, G. 1965: *Pressure on Britain's Land Resources*. Loughborough: Nottingham University School of Agriculture.

Williams, R. 1983: *Towards 2000*. London: Chatto & Windus.

Winckler, V. forthcoming 1985: Tertiarisation and feminisation at the periphery: the case of Wales. In Newby, H., Bujra, J., Littlewood, P., Rees, G. and Rees. T. (eds.), *Restructuring Capital: recession and reorganisation in industrial society* (London: Macmillan).

Wohl, A. 1977: *The Eternal Slum*. London: Edward Arnold.

Young, K. and Mason, C. (eds.) 1983: *Urban Economic Development: new roles and relationships*. London: Macmillan.

Young, S. with Lowe, A. 1974: *Intervention in the Mixed Economy*. London: Croom Helm.

Subject index

Author index